T0374294

NUMBER ONE CHICKEN

The strangest, funniest manhunt
on the Equator

G C Soh

PARTRIDGE

A Penguin Random House Company

Also by G C Soh

Slices of Singapore

(a book of essays on life in Singapore)

To order additional copies of this book, contact
Toll Free 800 101 2657 (Singapore)
Toll Free 1 800 81 7340 (Malaysia)
orders.singapore@partridgepublishing.com

www.partridgepublishing.com/singapore

Chapter 1

I hesitated at the door, an old, worn-out piece of wood with paint flaking. What a barrier it was. Should I open it and walk in? It would have needed courage, for memories would have come rushing in and flooding me with unwanted emotions. I stood there for a good length of time. Somehow, I could not walk away either. I was suspended in equilibrium between competing forces pulling in opposite directions. I did not care to decide which way to go, for I knew I could not have come to a decision. Walking away would seem like sweeping the past under a carpet, a denial of what had happened, an admission of defeat, a surrender of my self-worth to darkness, and the giving up of the redemption I had longed for. But walking through the door would have been painful—very painful. Why would I want to subject myself to such pain once again? The events happened so long ago. Why should an old man, who did not have much time in this world, pursue such grievances and not let go? What difference would it have made whether I had hung onto an old score card or had crumpled it and thrown it away? It was because I could remember! I could remember everything!

So I stood there, hoping someone or something would decide for me. Then the door opened and a family came out, chatting and looking happy, unaware that the place held a different sort of memory for the old man obstructing their path. I lifted my gaze over their shoulders, and the moment I peered into the old restaurant, I was pulled in.

The truth must be told—this is the cry of all good men and women from the dawn of humanity to the present. Unfortunately, most of the victims of the madness that ended in the 'unfortunate incident'—the total farce—no longer care. Strange, what is unforgettable to me is forgotten with relief by others. And the chief perpetrator of the outrage is remembered as a hero! The quest to tell the truth depends entirely on me now. By the time I had finished my investigation—interviewing witnesses and gathering materials—I was thoroughly exhausted. But I must carry on with my quest, however tired I may be, for justice must be done. I had written feverishly to complete my draft, all the while apprehensive that I may expire before I had typed the last word.

But, first, I have to get something off my chest; I have been wrestling with this doubt—no, guilt—for a long time. Had I been complicit to the madness? I think not, but maybe I think wrongly. I feel I should have acted differently. Deep in my heart I know I had failed to ask the tough questions needed of me; I had let the situation slide from mere carelessness to madness to total farce—'the unfortunate incident', hah! How did I come to this? I could have retired and led an ordinary life—happy, undisturbed, honorable. But strange things happened and before I knew it, it was all over. And here I am, bitter, heart unsettled—and the path to reclaim justice dim. I never knew doing my best could land me in this sorry state. Yes, I was only doing my best. This pain! I could have done better, much better. Of course, I was not central to this madness—my powers were limited—but there were things I could have done, yet did not do. Instead, I carried on as if I were a robot—unthinking and superficially loyal.

A disaster can germinate from an unremarkable seed, giving no clue of the mayhem that is to come. But the seed of this madness, ending in total farce, was unremarkable only for a brief moment before it showed its true nature. Unfortunately, I was blind to the warning. So I paid the price, and my friends and colleagues paid the price, too. The madness had its beginning when I was at my happiest in months. Some would dispute that that was the beginning (there was no connection, they told me), but to me it was. Anyway, that was, I believe, the best point to start for what I have to say. I was flying south and came exactly—yes, exactly—halfway between the North and South Pole and felt nothing but joy. I looked out the window and saw the coastline below in the distance, the sea dotted with ships of varied sizes, and the land lush green with grey patches of concrete and other colors of human intervention in nature. It was 'my' coastline, which instantly filled me with happiness, for I was home—well, not exactly, but almost. Few things could give rise to happier anticipation than homecoming and seeing our loved ones after a long absence. For me, home was right on the Equator— hot and humid. For most of the day, the sun would behave like a merciless master rather than a friend—boiling anyone not in the shade. As if that was not enough of a daily challenge, the country was small, so that no part of it was far from the sea, which made the air as humid as a fully soaked sponge. The heavily laden air just would not absorb our perspiration and cool us. For visitors from more agreeable latitudes, the hot, humid climate needed getting used to. As the patches and dots that sprawled across the land below took on more distinct shapes to reveal more details of human activity, my family appeared in my mind. The kids were running along the beach, kicking sand, laughing and having a noisy good time the way only kids could. Then I was home, comfortable on my favorite chair, reading to them in the evening; they were so attentive, asking one question after another. I relished the thought of becoming a part of their lives again, which was my dearest role. There was nothing like family and home.

The plane wobbled as it approached the runway in a quick descent, which unsettled me. Suddenly, joy turned into apprehension. What was happening? After the initial gasps of shock from the passengers, a chill seized the cabin and they fell silent. I froze instinctively so that all my senses could gather the faintest disturbance in the air—I was in self-preservation mode. But I could not comprehend whatever was happening as the situation was a new one to me. Sure, I had been in a few landings that were slightly rough, but this felt different. The huge plane landed with a heavy thud, like a goose whose power of flight had failed, and a shockwave invaded the cabin and then my body, as if announcing the start of an unhappy event. The shockwave knocked my bones about as if they were plastic hangers and rattled my teeth the way dice rattled when rolled onto marble floor. Maybe I imagined too much, but that was how I felt. "Hey, what's happening?" I asked my friend anxiously, as if he would know the answer.

A few seats away, a large woman in a tiger-striped suit shook like an earthquake, her eyeballs and cheeks trembling in synchrony with her stomach. Or maybe it was my imagination once more, but it was etched in my mind and would be recalled again and again. The plane hurtled down the runway, sliding like a piece of soap across wet floor. It was so heavy, yet it felt no sturdier than a kite, the cabin fluttering like paper in strong wind. My friend Roger, usually a steady man, gripped the armrests tightly. It was ironic there was nothing he could do about the situation—he was, after all, a security consultant who dealt with danger. But now he was, like everyone else, strapped to his seat like a prisoner under restraint, staring straight ahead to infinity. Something was happening; I scanned the cabin like a frightened cat trying to make sense of the

4

situation, but only seeing people frightened white, heads darting about like a truckload of confused chickens on the way to slaughter. The plane continued hurtling down the runway with a harrowing momentum. The roaring engines, the screeching tires and the rushing wind coalesced into a deafening roar. Was it death calling us? I felt for the seatbelt instinctively.

Then the plane came to a stop—to my tremendous surprise and relief. I held my breath, not knowing what to expect next. Everyone must have had the same thought, for there was a moment of eerie silence; the weak beams of sunlight breaking through the windows looked surreal. A little girl in ponytails turned to her mother and asked what was happening. The mother, looking dazed and confused, turned to her husband and asked the same question, whereupon he looked about and, after a while, replied, "Nothing," before tilting his head onto the headrest and closing his eyes. I was grateful for the answer, even though it was not meant for me. We always cling to hope.

The pilots likely had no great problems controlling the plane, although it had seemed out of control to me and the other passengers. The landing probably felt scarier than it was dangerous. But the passengers were taking no chances, so when it was time to get off, the cabin erupted in a frenzy of jostling bodies and flailing arms, everyone desperately trying to get out as quickly as possible. I was hit with elbows and bags several times as I struggled to the exit. With only the aim of getting out as quickly as possible, I staggered to safety in the airport building, taking a deep breath of life before walking forcefully away from the plane. That was the unusual welcome home I had received, but I was just happy to have come out of it alive and in one piece, and all I wanted was to go home. Of course, I did not realize then that the ordeal would return to haunt me. A runaway plane was quickly brought under control by pilots who knew their business; I only wish I was as sure of myself in life as those pilots were of flying. The only way to regain control of a runaway plane or any situation is to seize the reins deftly. There was no other way. My regret is that I did not learn that lesson even though it was forced upon me. Why do we so often fail to learn a hard lesson?

I reunited with Roger at the arrival hall; he was steadier than I was, but no happier. As we walked out, even the immigration officers seemed kind to us. Past the exit, we were greeted by a man with a placard asking for "Mr. Ken Lock, Mr. Roger Anderson." The company had arranged for transport and we were glad something was going right; I was hoping it was a sign that things would go smoothly from then on. However, the moment we stepped out of the air-conditioned building into the sunlight, Roger felt a blast of heat and humidity, which seized him like a bear hug. He winced and looked at me, as if I could do something about it. He hesitated for a moment, seemingly hoping to turn back into the building, before resuming his stride. That was the equatorial embrace—stifling, oppressive heat and humidity clinging onto the visitor. The Equator, true to form, had let my first-time visitor know who the master was. The combination of stifling, oppressive heat and humidity was overwhelming and pervasive, and this envelope that reminded one of an oven would follow the visitor everywhere outdoors. There was no escape.

"Welcome to the Equator," I said, feeling great to be standing on 0° latitude, right on that imaginary line that went round the Earth's fat waist, except that no imagination was needed at Orderland Airport. Just beyond the arrival hall exit there was a white line on the ground showing visitors exactly where that longest latitude ran. We Orderlanders were proud to live on this imaginary line, and we would remind visitors of our special place on Earth, never mind the stifling, oppressive heat. We had adapted to life on the Equator, and the imaginary line became more real than the actual heat and humidity. People adapt to every condition, don't they? That is how they are lulled into a sense of comfort and safety even when danger is plainly looming ahead.

The next day, not quite recovered from the landing ordeal, I dutifully set off for work, fetching Roger along the way in my car. His clothes were a little crumpled—after a long flight, turning out in well-ironed clothes the next day could hardly have been anyone's priority. I was eager for things to return to normal; routines had a calming effect. I was, shall we say, a routine person—predictable, no surprises. Office was the headquarters of the biggest, most powerful corporation in Orderland, with connections to the highest places in the country. It was, as I had always told everyone, a privilege to work there, and I counted myself lucky to be part of the organization. Who in the country would not feel that way? Other than the rebellious, anarchic types, every Orderlander saw the organization as the employer of choice. In the spacious lobby was the corporation's emblem, prominently displayed on the wall. Although he had seen it in pictures, Roger was quite unprepared for the moment; seeing the real thing startled him—he was not quite sure whether he was being greeted or intimidated. Roger, in mock trepidation and in an awe-struck, trembling voice, read the organization's name, "Croctopus." At the center of the emblem was the creature itself—an animal with a crocodile head and the tentacles of an octopus. Whenever I accompanied first-time visitors to the building, I would invariably feel a little apologetic about the emblem. Do not get me wrong; I am proud of the organization, as almost any Orderlander would, but a crocodile head and octopus tentacles? You know what I mean. I was a low-key person, but the emblem was, well, a little too direct and loud, the message lacking subtlety. I was relieved that it was not the first time Roger came across that thing. Anyway, who was I to comment on or worry about such a matter? Some things were best left to top management and the experts. We should know when to speak up and when to keep quiet. Most Orderlanders would agree with me.

The receptionist smiled and was about to say something when Roger spoke. "Quite an animal; spread like an octopus, snap like a crocodile." That shocked the receptionist, who gave a quizzical look, but she recovered quickly and managed another smile. The receptionists in the organization were well trained and knew their job. We took a lift and entered the big, thickly carpeted boardroom; the quiet order of the place exuded dignity, power and prestige. Visitors would be left in no doubt what kind of organization they were dealing with. The three senior men of the company were at the conference table. To Roger, they must have looked unnecessarily serious and stiff—as stiff as bowling pins waiting for the rolling ball to strike. But I did not notice this stifling atmosphere then, so familiar and comfortable was I on home ground, even after a fairly long absence. However, Kate, in her twenties, surely looked charming without having to say or do anything. Somehow, her presence made the carefully cultivated order look less than perfect. She was, shall I say, non-routine.

"This is Colonel Bobby Boon, first senior executive vice-president," I said.

Although Roger had never met any of the men now facing him in the boardroom, he did know something about them, having been briefed before flying to Orderland. After the initial greetings, he said, "Colonel Boon, I was told you were a no-nonsense guy who had studied engineering and later obtained an MBA. You retired from the army some years ago."

"Very good," said Bobby Boon with a big smile. "Ken told you this?"

"No, the top people in Croctopus are quite well known in my firm."

"Looks like we've engaged the right bunch of guys," said Bobby Boon, looking very pleased.

"This is Colonel Sammy Sam, second senior executive vice-president," I continued.

"Colonel Sam, you're also a no-nonsense man who had studied engineering and later obtained an MBA. You retired from the navy several years ago."

"I guess I'm also well known," said Sammy Sam with a smile. "Looks like you know a good deal about us."

"This is Colonel Sonny Song, our third senior executive vice-president."

"Colonel Song, you too are a no-nonsense man who had studied engineering and later obtained an MBA. You retired from the air force a few years ago."

"Glad I'm also well known," said Sonny Song. "You're a guy who does your homework; very good."

"And this is Kate Tan, manager, like me," I said.

"Ken is a senior manager," said Kate. "Am I well known too?"

"I'm afraid I was never told about you," said Roger, smiling.

"This is very reassuring."

As if to emphasize that he was a no-nonsense man, Bobby Boon wasted no time launching into business, as though he had waited all his life for it. "Mr. Anderson, as you must be aware, we're half-way through the security upgrade of our buildings," he said with all the gravity he could muster. "You know, of course, that when we first decided to upgrade our security it was based on a different, less comprehensive plan. The revised plan is a lot different from the old one."

"Yes, I'm aware of this; I've been the consultant from the very beginning." Roger leaned back on his seat, eyes droopy, the jet lag still taking its toll. I settled into mine, trying to relax as much as possible. At least, I only needed to appear interested in the briefing, that I was listening; I was not expected to take part in the discussion, which was, I believed, deemed beyond my competence. I surveyed the familiar surroundings; nothing seemed to have changed, even the voice droning on had that same predictable

9

monotony. Not that I seriously disliked anything; the briefing was, I thought, necessary, never mind the tedium. After a fairly one time, Bobby Boon was still on the difference between the original and the revised plan. Roger started to drum the table with his fingers unconsciously, but stopped quickly when he realized what he was doing. He stared blankly and appeared to be waiting for something more informative to come from Bobby Boon. I tried to suppress a yawn and pretended to be listening, before shifting my gaze to Kate, as if that would help me stay awake. She seemed to sense our predicament, but beyond looking attentive there was nothing she could do about it, let alone help us get out of Bobby Boon's lecture on a subject Roger already knew. I cleared my throat and pretended to cough every now and then, hoping that the sound of my discomfort would act as a verbal full stop to Bobby Boon's long-winded briefing, but I failed. After a long while, Bobby Boon appeared to have finished and asked Roger whether he had any questions. My consultant friend mentioned something (I cannot tell you what, as I was not paying attention).

"Yes, it's very important," said Bobby Boon. "Let me repeat so that it's absolutely clear." With that, Bobby Boon launched another round of briefing, covering mostly the same thing.

I took a deep breath—slowly, so as not to let my heaving chest and shoulders betray my disappointment. A while later, I scribbled something on my notepad, but it was really nothing; the physical exertion, though slight, helped me stay awake for a few minutes. I tried to daydream about other things but failed, as the voice droning on had too much presence. I thought, how could we get out of this? The briefing was important, I believed, but Roger was an intelligent man and had been the consultant from the beginning, so there was no need for all this long-winded stuff. But Bobby Boon, like all senior men in the organization, was conscientious, disciplined and thorough—what had to be said would be said, never mind if nobody listened.

Bobby Boon finally appeared done and said, "Give us your assessment on the upgrade and your recommendations for improvement."

"Certainly, I'll send it to you as soon as possible; that's what I'm here for." Roger then took a sip of coffee, as if to signal that it was time to end the meeting.

However, Bobby Boon did not take the hint and continued, "Should we need to tighten security even more, we'd be willing to revise the plan further. The thing is to have another look after every phase to see whether there had been any new security developments that would require further revision. Money is not a problem."

"Yes, that's good," said Roger, holding the armrests and leaning slightly forward, as if to get up.

"Right now, our country is not targeted by any terrorist group. Still, we mustn't be complacent; we're the biggest, most important corporation in the country, and therefore a very juicy target for terrorists."

"I understand that; complacency is a poison." Roger must have been surprised that he could utter more than monosyllables by then, the meeting surely must have gotten stifling and oppressive for him. There was a moment of silence as each waited for the other, Roger apparently afraid to say anything that would spark another long clarification from Booby Boon. I gave another cough and cleared my throat. That should have been the final full stop, I thought.

"Any questions?" asked Bobby Boon.

"No," said Roger, as he prepared to rise, apparently ready to flee. Then, as if to prevent Bobby Boon from repeating the same thing, he changed the subject, saying, "It's quite a coincidence that all you three gentlemen have almost identical backgrounds."

That seemed to have lightened the atmosphere, and Bobby Boon became less serious. "You call this coincidence?" said Bobby Boon before breaking into a hearty laugh. "There's more; we all came from the same school!" Bobby Boon laughed even louder. "We pick people carefully, very carefully; we know exactly what to look for. We even take into account whether they had bothered to give themselves a name that was unique—to stand out."

"I see, that's interesting," said Roger, apparently not knowing what else to say.

"We look for solid, dependable people—team players, people who are loyal and disciplined, sticklers for keeping to protocol and proper procedures. I can't overemphasize the need for good people; we want the entire organization to move together in the same direction."

"You always managed to get the people you looked for?" said Roger.

"Well, yes, most of the time, although we do make the occasional mistake," said Bobby Boon, turning to where Kate was without being aware of the signal he was sending.

*

He looked like what Roger had expected—in his sixties, well-built with short, neat hair—only much more impressive than what Roger had seen in photographs. He looked every bit a general.

"This is General Kong," said Kate.

"General . . ."

"No, no, don't call me that; I know you Americans don't go for that kind of formality," said the General in a commanding voice. "Just call me Kong."

Roger was impressed once more; Kate was speechless.

"Back where I came from, you're very well regarded," said Roger.

"Thank you; never thought I'd be that famous."

"Oh yes, you are. I'm told you're a brigadier-general who had retired from the army some years ago. You're a no-nonsense man who had studied engineering and later obtained an MBA."

12

"You sure did your homework before coming here." Kong flashed a smile, looking pleased. He asked about Roger's flight and his accommodation in Orderland, and then proceeded with the briefing. He said there was no terrorist threat to the country; the government was in complete control of the security situation, but Croctopus would not be complacent; it would do its part. It was a huge corporation, the biggest in the country, and therefore a very tempting target for terrorists. He did not go into the details of Roger's work, but gave a broad sweep of Croctopus's needs and strategies concerning security. He said, "Any terrorist attack against us must stand no chance of success. Croctopus must be protected by a skin as thick as a crocodile's; our security apparatus must spread out like an octopus's tentacles. We must break any terrorist attack like a crocodile breaking the neck of its prey."

Kong spoke standing up, so Roger and Kate listened standing up. Kong paced up and down the room, like a cat prowling its territory; Roger and Kate followed Kong with their eyes. Sometimes he was at the windows, apparently looking at something outside, hands behind his back, but continuing to talk; sometimes he was at the whiteboard, but not using it at all during the briefing. Sometimes he stood near Roger and Kate; at times he was at a distance, but all the while in command. Roger and Kate listened without interrupting. Kong spoke as if he was addressing his troops about to go into battle. He punched the air with his fist several times to emphasize his points; he karate-chopped the air, too. What an awesome performance; what a commanding presence. He must have had lots of experience speaking to a rapt audience, made up of troops who had entrusted their lives to him. Then Kong sat down, so Roger and Kate sat down, too. Kong seemed pleased with himself and asked Roger whether he had any questions. Roger figured that he ought to say something, but fearing a repeat of Bobby Boon's long-winded performance he decided it would be prudent not to dwell on something that nobody had anything fresh to say.

"Croctopus is lucky to have a person like you in charge," said Roger. "You're very sure of your assessment; the know the situation very well."

"I always know what I'm talking about; I'm never wrong in my assessments of a situation."

"I can't quarrel with you on that; the organization is in good hands."

"Ha, ha, ha, I'll admit I have good hands," said Kong, looking very pleased. "I'm a volunteer martial arts instructor and, naturally, a martial arts movie fan."

"Very interesting."

"We've another American working for us on security," said Kong, "but his work has to do with communications; how to keep our communication lines secure. We call him Socky, but I don't really know him; in fact, I've never met him. Croctopus is very big." Kong was in a chatty mood. To Roger's relief, the meeting was not as long as he had feared; the General was not long-winded.

"What's on your mind?" Kate asked Roger at the lift lobby after the briefing.

"Well, he's the boss, but he doesn't quite care about rank. Everyone calls him 'General' but he'd rather be addressed as 'Kong'. I was surprised by this, actually. I'd been told repeatedly before coming here that rank mattered in your country, and to keep that in mind so as not to offend anyone. So he's pretty humble I'd say, a request not to refer to his rank coming from a man of his position."

"Well, 'Kong' in our language sounds like 'grandfather'."

Roger was speechless. Did the briefings back in the US miss something? he thought.

Chapter 2

It was a wet, gloomy morning when Kong entered the boardroom hunched and looking disturbed; he sat down slowly, very much an old man. Kong's face was drained of color and pale as a plucked chicken. Kate, Roger, the three senior executive vice-presidents and I were at the large conference table, all apprehensive after being summoned for the meeting at very short notice.

"I've never seen him like this before," I whispered to Kate.

"Something very serious must've happened."

There was a stranger who accompanied Kong into the boardroom. He was tall and expressionless, his face like a mask. He did not look at all like someone from the business world, who would have been warmer, like a real person. So what was a character like that doing in the boardroom? I mean, he did not appear open and friendly, like someone coming to talk business with us. There was something sinister and secretive about him that made me uncomfortable, and my eyes instinctively followed him. Kong introduced him, "This is Colonel Lenny Loon of the OSD, the Orderland Security Department." That caused an immediate stir.

"The OSD?" said Bobby Boon. "Sir, may I ask why is the OSD here?"

"This is a total surprise, sir," said Sammy Sam.

"General, never in my wildest dream did I meet anyone from the OSD," said Sonny Song. "May I ask what's going on, General?"

"Something very serious has happened," said Kong. A chill descended upon us, and the boardroom became quiet and still as a mortuary. Kong composed himself before holding up a note and continued, "Colonel Loon brought this; it has been cleared by the Director of the OSD for us." He paused, unable to go on. Then with some effort, he continued, "I've shocking news for you. Never have I ever imagined that this could happen to us . . . Never." He took a sip of water, but did not continue immediately; he seemed lost. "I'm just shocked, just so shocked." He shook his head and stared into infinity. By then, we were all on the edge of our seats and straining forward; not a word came from us. Kong held up the note again, hand shaking noticeably. "This is from the Director of the OSD; he has grave news for us."

"We're ready, please go ahead," said Roger, as if sensing that Kong needed a nudge to say what he had wanted to say.

There was yet another pause. Then, as if he was mustering all his strength, Kong continued slowly, "My fellow Croctopus people, loyal citizens of Orderland, we . . . we . . . we have a . . . we have a terrorist mole in our midst." Then he stopped, but breathing hard, as if he had just unloaded the heaviest burden he had ever carried in his life.

A collective gasp, from air sucked quickly through narrow windpipes, emanated from us, but the anxious noise was followed by momentary silence as the terrible news sank in. Then the place erupted with frantic noise and undirected activities, as everyone in the room had decided to talk at the same time. Such disorderly

16

behavior was rare in the company, but things were vastly different this time.

"A terrorist mole? How could this be, sir? Never in my wildest dream . . . If I may ask, sir, who is the mole?" said Bobby Boon.

"We've no idea; the only bit of intelligence we have is a strange statement from the OSD source within the terrorist organization." Looking at the note, Kong continued, "It says, 'If you meet him you would know' . . . that's all." Kong looked up and stared blankly ahead, unable to continue. He seemed lost in thought, or maybe lost in every way.

"If you meet him you would know. Colonel Loon, you call this intelligence?" said Bobby Boon. "I don't understand it at all. What's the meaning of this?"

"Let me explain," said Lenny Loon quickly, as if anticipating the question. "Our source is codenamed Chatterbig. He's a rather unusual man, extraordinarily careful, even by the standards of intelligence operatives. He always gives intelligence in bits and pieces and in puzzles. He has never told us why, but we suspect he does it for two reasons. First, by releasing his intelligence to us in little bits, he hopes to receive more payments. Second, if he gives very direct clues, he could be unmasked easily. So he delivers intelligence in puzzles, and we always end up pursuing our prey in a roundabout way, and therefore the intelligence cannot be easily traced to him. He's that careful."

"And you rely on him and pay him for this?" said Bobby Boon, an incredulous expression hanging on his face.

"Yes, of course, because he's all we've got in the terrorist organization, which is not easy to infiltrate, especially at a high level. He's vital to us."

"Colonel, what a rat you've got," said Sammy Sam, looking aggrieved. "A rat that chews up money and gives us crap in return; you're not getting value for your money."

"Only a rat will sell intelligence to us purely for money, without blackmail or ideological motive. Thank goodness for rats, they make our job easier." Lenny Loon leaned back on his seat, satisfied with his reply.

"Which terrorist organization are we talking about?" asked Roger.

"You don't have to know for now; I'll let you know if it becomes necessary."

"I hope you all realize the grave danger we're in," said Kong, slowly coming out of his daze, his face regaining the color of life.

"The important question now is, what should we do next?" said Roger.

"We've to speed up our security upgrading," said Bobby Boon.

"Our security measures are all designed to thwart an attack from the outside," said Roger. "But now a mole is chewing us up from the inside; it's a completely different problem we're facing."

"Then we've to revise our plan," said Bobby Boon.

"Most important of all, we've to find the mole, and find him quickly," said Roger.

"How do we find him?" said Kong. "We don't have a clue, other than the unhelpful puzzle from this so-called insider, Chatterbig."

Compared to the people giving their opinions in the boardroom, I was junior rank, senior only to Kate, so I sat on the sidelines and listened. But after a while I thought the discussion had been bouncing about the room for too long without regard to the note, so I decided to tell them what I thought was the obvious, which ought to be a safe thing for me to do among the senior men. "Well, the clue says, 'If you meet him you would know.' I suppose what we've to do next is to go meet everyone in Croctopus, and eventually we'll know who the mole is."

"How could we ever know who the mole is just by meeting everyone?" sneered Sammy Sam to chuckles from the other two senior executive vice-presidents.

"I know it doesn't sound logical at first, but think about it, that's what the note says," I replied. "So I suppose we should start by following it; there seems to be no other way of using the note."

"It's not that simple; you can't solve a puzzle by taking it literally," said Bobby Boon. "If a puzzle could be solved simply by following it in a straightforward way, then everyone would be able to solve it; it'd be no puzzle."

"I understand what you're saying, but I presume Chatterbig wants us to solve the puzzle, and there seems to be no other way to start," I said. "I mean, all we have is Chatterbig's puzzle, so I think we ought to squeeze whatever we can out of it. I can't figure out how else we could start."

"Just because you're unable to think of a way, it doesn't follow that there's no way other than taking the note literally," said Bobby Boon. There's always a trick somewhere. The way to go about this is to look for the trick."

"I'm not sure how we could look for it," Kate said. "Perhaps you've something in mind?"

"Don't ask a question that no one can answer," said Bobby Boon, visibly annoyed. "We've to work at it, obviously."

"I'm sorry, but I think Ken is right," said Kate. "Really, the only way to solve the puzzle is to begin by following it; we should go where it leads us. There seems to be no other way; we don't have anything else to go on." Kate was pushing my idea more than I would in Croctopus, especially when it was not what the company's top men believed in, but we were faced with a very serious threat, and I supposed she also felt confident that I was right because there simply was no other way to make use of the note.

"I've told you, there's a trick somewhere; don't argue with me about security. I'm the head of security in Croctopus; I know about security, you don't. And Ken doesn't know either."

"That's right," said Sammy Sam. "As the head of security, Colonel Boon knows far more about security than you do. I'd rather listen to him."

Kate looked annoyed at the use of rank to argue; Roger raised his eyebrows.

I knew I had to steer the discussion away from rank and bring it back to the note; Kate had the same idea and she was quicker. She said, "Well, of course, I don't know that much about security; I could have missed something here, but I think we've to start with what's possible, and that's to go where the puzzle takes us. It may not appear to be a very smart thing to do, but it's the only way to make use of the note."

"Don't argue with Colonel Boon about security; he's the security expert here, whereas you know nothing about security," said Sammy Sam. "I respect his views."

"I think, in the final analysis, we've to solve this puzzle in a rational way," replied Kate. "Let me put it this way, what do we do next?"

I knew Kate was trying again to make another detour around rank, which was the smart thing to do. I had been in Croctopus long enough to know that once rank got in the way, which happened often, there would be no real discussion. Still, she was pushing the point a little too hard for my comfort.

"As I've said, and I really dislike repeating it, we look for the trick in the puzzle," insisted Bobby Boon.

"But that's not saying much," said Kate.

I immediately felt that she had crossed the line with the top men of the organization. She had said something I would not have said to those men, however exasperated I may have been. I wished she had stayed on the sidelines and let me fight my battle. I regretted not having intervened earlier; now it was too late.

"What do you mean by that? How could you say such a thing?" said Sonny Song. "Colonel Boon is the security expert in Croctopus; he knows what he's saying, unlike you."

"Well, the point really is what we should do next," said Kate. "We've to be practical and do the possible; it's no use looking for a golden key, there may not be one." The problem with Kate was that sometimes she did not know when to stop, and I always worry for her.

"I thought I've just told you I dislike repeating myself," said Bobby Boon, "but as you still can't see the obvious I'll say it once more; we have to look for the trick in the puzzle." Bobby Boon jabbed his forefinger onto the table top several times for emphasis. "This is the only way to go, and don't make me repeat myself."

"Then we sit here and stare at the note?" said Kate.

"Er . . . ," I said.

"I didn't say that," said Bobby Boon. "Don't put words in my mouth."

"Don't be rude, Kate," said Sammy Sam.

"I'm not . . ."

"Yes, you are," said Sonny Song. "And it's also insubordination."

"What's that?" asked Roger.

"It may be difficult for an American to understand this," said Sonny Song, "but here in Orderland, we expect some respect from a subordinate."

"I still don't get it," said Roger. "What has this got to do with what Kate had just said?"

"I've listened enough," said Kong, bringing up his hand authoritatively, like a policeman stopping traffic. Then, glaring at Kate, he continued, "You should've known better than to act this way toward your superiors; we've rules of behavior here, unwritten they may be, and you know them. Now, I don't want any more of this nonsense from you, Kate. If you still don't know how to behave toward your superiors I'd have someone escort you out of the company." After a pause for the message to sink in, he said, "Colonel Loon, what do we do next? You're from the OSD; you should be able to tell us."

Lenny Loon thought for a moment and then said, "We've to start by following the one lead we have, and that is to meet everyone in Croctopus."

The senior executive vice-presidents looked gravely injured, as if they had been stabbed on their backs. Shock and pain contorted their faces, and no amount of effort could have relaxed their muscles and hidden their anguish. Booby Boon fixed an unfriendly gaze at the man from the OSD and Sammy Sam looked out the window, uninterested, while Sonny Song checked his nails. But the show of both hostility and lack of interest made no difference to the outcome.

Kong thought for a moment and said, "You're right, Colonel Loon, we've to do what is possible in the circumstances and take the only path open to us. There's no other way, at least for now."

Bobby Boon looked as if another dagger had been thrust deep into his heart. Like a badly wounded man fighting for his life and honor, he uttered, "But, sir, this would be a mammoth task; it wouldn't work."

"There's no imminent danger of an attack at present, so you've a bit of time," said Lenny Loon. "It can be done, and in any case there's just no other way for us to get going on the note."

The three senior executive vice-presidents looked grave, as if they were at a funeral, but they had no intention of being defeated by their subordinates and an outsider. Their honor and credibility were at stake; it was that serious—at least to them. They had to regain the upper hand at all costs.

"Still, the question is how to go about this," said Bobby Boon, giving another shot at saving his honor.

"I'll strategize a plan to produce some synergy," said Sonny Song, the head of strategic planning and synergy.

"What's he talking about?" Kate whispered to me, while I tried very hard to keep a straight face.

"I'll work out the procedure," said Sammy Sam, head of procedures.

"How can we produce any synergy or work out any procedure when we don't really know what we're doing?" said Kong. "Now, tell me, and I want good answers, what do we do next?"

"We could hold a fire evacuation exercise," I said. "Sound the fire alarm and evacuate everyone to an assembly area. That would allow us to meet everyone."

"That's a splendid idea," said Kong, pointing a finger at me emphatically, like a teacher to a pupil who had just given the right answer. "We'll start with the HQ staff here. If we don't find the mole here, we'll repeat the same exercise in other branches all over the country until we find him, or maybe her. Colonel Boon, make arrangements for a fire evacuation exercise this afternoon. And remember to announce it first; I don't want a panic."

"Yes, sir," said Bobby Boon, like a prisoner of war soundly defeated but trying his best to look brave.

"One minor detail before we leave this room," said Roger. "We can't go on talking about a terrorist mole. We'll have to give him or her a codename."

"Yes, that's right. Don't you have a codename for the mole, Colonel Loon?" asked Kong.

"Please go ahead with a codename of your own; the OSD has its own codename, but I can't share it with you."

"How about Hidden Mole?" Sonny Song volunteered quickly.

Kate looked at me, while trying to suppress a snigger.

"What kind of codename is that? I don't like it," growled Kong. "There's absolutely no subtlety there. I want something subtle, not a declaration that there's a hidden mole in our midst. I want you all to think harder. C'mon, give me something better; we can do it. Now, let's see . . ." Kong rubbed his chin and continued, "This person is obviously keeping a very low profile and telling us lies about himself."

"How about Low Rat, sir?" said Sammy Sam.

"No! That's not much better than Hidden Mole. Can't you people come up with a better name? You're supposed to be intelligent people, but you're giving me names that only kids would like. Don't tell me I've to spend thousands of dollars for a branding consultant to come up with a name. How about you, Ken? Throw us a name."

"Well, you're a martial arts movie fan; I'm sure you could find something from the movies."

"That's right, Ken; that's the way. Why didn't I think of this? Hmm, let's see . . ." Everyone kept silent, not daring to disturb Kong, who continued rubbing his chin reflexively, deep in thought. Sammy Sam and Sonny Song looked as if they were thinking hard trying to come up with another name, but it was obvious to me they would not risk a second rebuke. Lenny Loon looked like he did not care what name we would come up with. As for Kate and me, once Kong had started thinking we would rather let him be the smart guy who came up with the clever codename. After a short while, Kong exclaimed, "Aha! Yes! I've got it." He smiled and looked pleased with himself, but did not proceed further; he was thinking about something, either about the codename that he had just thought of or how smart he was to have thought of it.

"Sir, may I ask what's the codename?" said Bobby Boon.

"We'll call him Crouching Liar."

"Fantastic!" exclaimed Bobby Boon, manufacturing a broad smile and shifting his body as if he was about to give a standing ovation.

"Spot on!" shouted Sammy Sam, not to be outdone.

"Absolutely great!" said Sonny Song, giving the thumbs up.

Kong was pleased, and kept quiet for a while to enjoy the praises lavished on him. Then, as if rallying his troops for battle, he said forcefully, "Now let's find Crouching Liar and nail him!" I could almost expect Bobby Boon, Sammy Sam and Sonny Song to rise in unison and give a smart salute.

After the meeting, Kate, Roger and I headed for lunch at the Croctopus Café. All three of us were preoccupied with the strange statement from Chatterbig. I told them that after leaving the boardroom, I had been looking closely at everyone crossing our path, but did not see Crouching Liar.

"I've been doing the same thing and I haven't met him or her either," said Kate.

"That makes three of us," said Roger. "The clue seems easy to solve, but it's not."

As we ate, we kept searching the café with our eyes. There were small groups of people here and there in the café, but nobody looked suspicious. They all looked normal, no one looked like a secret agent out of a movie. I took a walk around the place to have a better look at everyone; I even looked closely at the people serving food, though they were familiar to me. There was no one that caused me to take a second look.

"Most of people here are just kids," I said. "We should keep a lookout for someone older; a mole is likely to be someone experienced, who could handle unexpected situations."

"We should pay special attention to loners, as there's only one mole," said Kate.

"What troubles me is this," I said, "someone in Croctopus must have met Crouching Liar. In fact, hundreds might have met him, but none has reported anything unusual, so how would we know it's him when we meet him?"

"Yes, this bothers me too," said Roger. "Notice that Chatterbig's statement is not addressed to anyone in particular. That means anyone who meets Crouching Liar ought to know who he really is or at least suspect that he's up to no good. We should have report after report about this person, but we don't. We don't have a single report of someone suspicious."

"The puzzle sounds so simple: if you meet him you would know," I said. "So, why haven't people rushed to us screaming they had seen a mole?"

"C'mon mole, show yourself; we'd like to meet you," said Roger, looking at the people in the café. "Hey people, come to us about the mole you've met."

*

The fire alarm wailed like it was the end of the world and people streamed out of all buildings at the HQ premises at Croctopus Road. They walked unhurriedly and reluctantly, obviously because they knew it was only an exercise. Some women were armed with umbrellas and newspapers as they headed for the assembly area. Once out in the open, the umbrellas and newspapers went up to protect their owners from the merciless equatorial sun. Those who came without means headed straight for the nearest shade, bunching in small groups. In the Equator, shades were always much sought after. Security guards went from floor to floor to flush out people hiding inside the buildings because they were too lazy to go out. As fire marshals with red armbands conducted roll calls, Kong, Roger and the three senior executive vice-presidents, stationed two stories above, were sweeping the assembly area with their binoculars. They were sweating profusely in the stifling, oppressive heat, even though they were in the shade. Kate and I were also there, but we had no binoculars and had to rely on our naked eyes.

"Anyone seen anything?" asked Kong.

"Nothing suspicious, sir," reported Bobby Boon, delighted.

"No Crouching Liar, General," said Sammy Sam in support.

26

"I've swept the whole area, sir," said Sonny Song, "I've not seen anyone that I should worry about, sir."

After the search had failed to spot anyone who looked like a terrorist mole, the people were asked to return to work and they dispersed quickly, as the heat was oppressive and unbearable. Kong then left in a hurry to attend a meeting, with the rest of us following immediately after.

Booby Boon said loudly, apparently to no one in particular, "I knew this wouldn't work; it was a silly idea; what a complete waste of time. We should've looked for the trick in the puzzle."

Kate was indignant and was about to reply when I stopped her. She was her impulsive self, but it was no use confronting Bobby Boon, as he was senior rank while we were relatively junior. He could get away with a lot of things, but we could not. Rank mattered in Croctopus and we just had to be realistic. Besides, the equatorial heat was stifling and oppressive, and I just wanted to get away quickly. The failure of the exercise naturally left me disappointed and puzzled. It was as if we had gone on a fishing expedition to an area teeming with fish and ended up with nothing. Where did we go wrong? We had followed the puzzle to the letter. Maybe the mole was in some other premises, but surely a mole would want to be in the headquarters?

*

The Croctopus management and staff gathered at Orderland's most famous hotel, the Founder's Hotel, to celebrate Kong's wedding anniversary. It was a glittering affair, attended by the country's elite. There were the rich and famous, ambassadors and even a minister. One by one they arrived; smartly dressed chauffeurs opened the doors of their limousines for them to step out in all their finery and elegance. Some had no chauffer, but that was because they drove very expensive sports cars, each of which came with a very beautiful woman. Kong's wife Mahogany, or Mah as she was often called, ever the socialite and perfect hostess, flitted about the ballroom like a dragonfly. She embraced this person and that, telling them how good they looked or marveling at how much weight they had lost, and receiving similar compliments in return. She smiled, joked and laughed the way people do at parties of important people. The wives of Bobby Boon, Sammy Sam and Sonny Song hovered about Mah like fireflies about a light. Kong was sharing a good joke with the minister. In fact, he had been sharing one good joke after another with the minister since the latter's arrival, as if the world was endlessly funny. The three senior executive vice-presidents were hovering about Kong and the minister, and laughing along loudly, as though it was their duty to laugh. Croctopus's lower ranks kept their distance and enjoyed themselves in their own way.

Roger introduced me to his friend, Jack, who had just arrived from the United States. We waited a while for my wife, Arm, to finish talking on her cellphone before I introduced them.

"Pleased to meet you, Mrs Lock," said Jack.

"Call me Arm, please." My wife was medium in built and height. Except for slightly big arms, she looked like the average woman in the country in every way, or maybe it was just my modesty at her expense.

"I know you're trying to figure out my name; it's spelt A-r-m. Friends called me Arm in school because I beat all the girls in arm-wrestling. That's how I got my name." As usual, she was soft-spoken in social conversation.

"I was hoping to meet a friend of mine," said Jack. "We call him Socky. Like me, he's from the United States. I understand he's working on Croctopus's communications."

"Actually, I'd like to meet him, too. I've been here awhile, but I haven't met him," said Roger.

I told Roger they would certainly meet one day—people working in security and communications would eventually meet, as their paths would inevitably cross. Of course, I could not know at that time, when we were just making small talk, that all our paths would cross and change our lives.

A short distance away, reporters and cameramen were crowding and jostling around a buxom beauty in a black dress that seemed to hang precariously on her assets. Flashlights popped non-stop while she smiled and posed for the cameras in between answering reporters' questions.

"See that woman over there?" whispered Arm after taking me aside. "She's that actress Monica Moon."

"I know."

"She had breast implants not long ago."

"I know."

"Well, at least she's honest enough to admit it when she was interviewed by the press some time ago."

"I know, I've read the interview."

"How come you know everything about her? You even bothered to read about her in the papers."

"There was a big picture of her."

"So that's why you read the interview? Well, like I said, at least she's honest about it."

"Honesty doesn't come in here. Surely, she can't tell the world her breasts sprang up overnight like toadstools, can she?"

"What would you say if I go for breast implants?"

"You're sure you want to do that?"

"Just kidding."

That was all we could talk about Monica Moon, so we rejoined the others.

"Looks like we've quite a number of famous people here this evening," I said. "That's Colonel Hantam. If you want to know anything about the Croctopus legend, you can ask him."

"He's a scholar of some sort?" asked Roger.

"No, he's the top bureaucrat at the Ministry of Culture, which created Croctopus."

"But you said legend."

"It's a legend created by the Ministry of Culture."

"You mean Croctopus is not a mythological creature from time immemorial? I mean, I had assumed it was."

"No, of course not; it was created some decades ago to boost our culture.

"What? Why would . . . I don't understand."

"You see, Orderland plans everything, even our culture. This is how we do things because we don't believe in letting them happen by chance. We take deliberate steps to make things happen—according to plan. Ours is an orderly society; we like orderly developments. You could say this is our strength—the entire country marching in one direction. We're proud of this. I'm afraid we dislike the messy, free-for-all way that you allow things to happen in America."

"Is planning for everything in detail desirable? Every plan, every goal coming only from the top could make things oppressive and stifling."

"Well, it's the efficient way to develop. Unlike haphazard growth, planned developments minimize wastage of resources. And we could put our best people for the task; not just anyone who likes to do something, but the best people, the handpicked people. This way, we get the best and most desired outcome, no nasty surprises."

"You can't manufacture culture, surely. It has to come up from the ground, from the people, over time."

"We like orderly developments, and anything from the ground up is invariably messy and a waste of resources."

At that, Roger could not contain himself anymore and let out a hearty laugh. At that time, I did not know why he found it so funny; I put it down to differences in culture and I did not ask him for an explanation—it would have been pointless to argue over subjective matters. Then someone caught my attention; I waved. "Hey, I want you all to meet a very interesting person," I said. "This is Dr Jade Choice, the discoverer of and the world's foremost expert on Robot Syndrome."

Dr Jade Choice was in her forties and had the bearing and confidence of someone who knew something important that most of the world did not. Just by looking at her, it would be safe to say that her formidable reputation was well deserved.

"What a strange name for a disease," said Roger. "Sounds like something out of this world. I've never heard of it."

"I discovered it only very recently, so it's not well-known. The world's press hasn't learned of it yet. Once they got wind of it, I think my life would be a lot less peaceful. It's a very fascinating disease."

"Well, I'm not surprised to hear this; the name itself is fascinating. I mean, why the 'robot' in the name?" asked Roger.

"When Robot Syndrome strikes, a person acts and speaks like a robot."

"Really?" said Roger. "Unbelievable."

"We know very little about the disease or how it's contracted. But we do know that it could be triggered by sudden, overwhelming stress. The stifling, oppressive heat and humidity here on the Equator could add to the stress. The sufferer often has a deep obsession with certain things, such as an irrational need to be defensive or an obsession with order or obedience. Certain words or action could be the last straw that tips the scale and causes a person to act like a robot."

"Sounds like quite a scary disease, but also a funny one. Does the victim really go about like a robot? Sure hope I don't contract it here," said Roger with a chuckle.

"You don't sound like one who's likely to contract the disease. Where in the US do you come from?"

"I'm from Los Angeles."

"Oh, I did my graduate studies there; I go back every few years to visit old friends. And each time I'm there, I'd head for Pho 87, down at North Broadway; it's my favorite Vietnamese restaurant. I used to eat there almost every Sunday; serves really delicious fare."

That prompted us to get some food. When we were halfway through eating, Bobby Boon came up excitedly and said the General wanted to see us, and so we proceeded to a private room. Kate, Roger and I, as well as the three senior executive vice-presidents and Lenny Loon, were there. Before long, Kong came in, looking excited.

"Colonel Loon, I hear you've important news for us," said Kong.

"Yes, it's about Crouching Liar. Our source Chatterbig just called; he said he had more information on Crouching Liar's identity." There were murmurs of excitement from the people gathered there. "Chatterbig will drop us a note with information on Crouching Liar's identity tomorrow."

"Where will the note be dropped?"

"He will only tell us tomorrow; he'll call me tomorrow morning at 8 o'clock."

"All of you assemble at the boardroom at seven sharp tomorrow morning," ordered Kong.

"Yes, sir!" said Bobby Boon, Sammy Sam and Sonny Song in a chorus.

*

The boardroom was cold in the morning; the air-conditioner was, as usual, out of control. The sandwiches and hot coffee were a nice consolation, but the wait was almost unbearable. At 8 o'clock sharp, Lenny Loon's cellphone came alive, blasting out the theme song from *Mission Impossible*, apparently the favorite with agents at the OSD.

"Hello, this is Colonel Loon." The air was charged with excitement and Lenny Loon's hand was shaking a little. He looked at Kong and nodded, which caused Kong to shift to the edge of his seat. "What?" Lenny Loon said.

Everyone froze; Kong looked as if he had wanted to snatch the cellphone from Lenny Loon and carry on the conversation.

"Retrieve the note from where? It's in Singapore? Oh, my goodness! Can't you give us more time? One hour is too short!" Lenny Loon talked for a while more, then looked at Kong and said, "He hung up."

"So, are we going to get the note?" asked Kong, gripping Lenny Loon's arm.

"We've to retrieve the note in Singapore within the next hour."

"But that's impossible!" screamed Kong. "I knew this character couldn't be trusted. I knew it; I just knew it! My judgment of character is never wrong."

"General, you're right; you're absolutely right," said Bobby Boon, looking grave. "Colonel Loon, what's the meaning of this? Is this some kind of joke?"

"Chatterbig said if he stayed around for more than an hour the others would suspect that he's up to something. He will not give us more than an hour."

"That's just not sufficient time! We're going to lose the note? This is driving me crazy!" bellowed Kong, as he got up from his seat and started to pace about the boardroom. There was an outburst of despair and outrage at the impossibility of the task, and repeated complaints of how unfair the time given was. Sammy Sam covered his face with both hands in a show of deep despair. Sonny Song kept knocking his forehead with the fleshy, thumb-side of his fist.

"Wait a minute," said Kate, "Jimmy's in Singapore right now! He's there on vacation."

"Are you sure?" asked Kong, now sweating in the cold air.

"Absolutely."

There was triumphal cheering all round. Bobby Boon raised his fist to punch the air. Not to be outdone, Sammy Sam shook two fists, while Sonny Song swung a left hook at some imaginary figure in front of him.

"But where exactly will the note be dropped in Singapore?" I asked.

"It'll be at Raffles Place; at the foot of a sculpture . . . a sailing craft."

"I'll call Jimmy; I have his number," I said.

"Be quick, Ken. Well done, Kate; you've saved us," said Kong.

I tapped Jimmy's number on my cellphone, but there was no signal whatsoever. I tried again, but there was still no signal.

"Quick, Ken, we've no time to lose."

"Hey, there's no signal at all," I said after trying a third time.

"What do you mean?" asked Kong.

"There's just no signal on my cellphone," I said.

"Let me try," said Kate as she tapped feverishly on her cellphone. "Nothing!"

"What's Jimmy's number? Everybody, try to get him," said Kong.

Everyone, including Lenny Loon, whipped out their cellphones and started tapping furiously, but none could get any signal at all. I quickly reached for the boardroom telephone.

"Ken, the conference mode has been giving us a bit of a problem," said Kong. "Perhaps only you would be able to hear Jimmy; but we've no choice. Just use the damn phone; we'll depend on you. All the stupid phones have to fail us at the most crucial moment."

"Hi Jimmy, this is Ken." Triumphal cheering and clapping erupted next to me. "How are you? You're having a good time in Singapore? I'm glad I could reach you. We have something very important and very urgent to do, and you're the only one who could help us right now. I want you to please listen carefully; this is very important . . . That's great, I'm glad you're having so much fun in Singapore. You can tell me about it when you're back. Right now, please listen to me carefully; this is very important."

"Jimmy's not the most intelligent dispatcher we have," said Sammy Sam. "He's such a dreamer; he keeps delivering things to the wrong places all the time.

"He's the only person we have at the front line right now," said Kate.

"Jimmy, where are you now?" I asked, while trying hard to focus amid the distractions. "Somewhere in town . . . what building is that? You don't know the name? A very tall building that looked like a calculator? You're there to meet your friend for breakfast . . . Okay, never mind. Tell me, do you know where Raffles Place is? Oh, you're going to Raffles Place for breakfast? That's absolutely great! How far away is Raffles Place?" Every word I spoke electrified the air in the boardroom. "Raffles Place is less than five minutes' walk away?"

Triumphal cheering exploded in the boardroom.

"Never mind about the cheering in the background; Jimmy, please listen carefully. I want you to go to Raffles Place now; this is very important. Please tell your friend you can't have breakfast with him today; tell him you've something very important to do . . . I know this is hard on you . . . Yes, it's going to be difficult to explain to your friend, but it must be done. Could you please tell him now? Don't hang up."

"What's so important about breakfast? It's just breakfast; he takes breakfast every day!" said Bobby Boon, holding a half-eaten sandwich.

"Yes Jimmy . . . Your friend says it's okay? Good! Could you please go to Raffles Place now?"

Suddenly, without the slightest warning, the telephone's conference mode started to work. It crackled with Jimmy's voice announcing to Kong and all, "I can't leave now, seems like there's some problem. I can't use the lift. Here's the announcement again . . ."

A man's deadpan voice announced over the speaker, "Ladies and gentlemen, may I have your attention, please. May I have your attention, please. The fire alarm has been activated. We are investigating the situation; please remain calm. Ladies and gentlemen, may I have your attention, please. May I have your attention, please. The fire alarm has been activated. We are investigating the situation; please remain calm."

A loud collective groan rumbled round the boardroom. "Why? Why?" screamed Kong, eyes looking up at the ceiling and palms upturned, as if complaining to someone unseen and pleading for divine help.

Then the conference mode went dead; everybody froze.

"Don't worry, the line's okay; Jimmy's still with me," I assured everyone. "Jimmy . . . It's a false alarm? You can use the lift now? Great! Please go to Raffles Place immediately. Go now, please."

Then Kate grabbed the telephone from me and shouted, "Go, Jimmy go!"

I waited for Jimmy to reach the ground floor, and then said, "Jimmy, when you arrive at Raffles Place, I want you to please look for a sculpture. It's a sailing craft from long ago; a stylized representation of a sailing craft . . . What's stylized? Well, er . . . it's not like a real sailing craft you see in a picture. It's not a sculpture of a sailing craft with all the details. It's a sailing craft in outline only, an impression of a sailing craft. So, you've got to pay attention. It's somewhere in the middle of the place, so you can't miss it. You understand what I'm saying? Great . . . Now, at the bottom of the sculpture, on the ground, you'll find a note. Take the note and read it to me, then keep it and let me have it when you've returned to Orderland. Do you understand me? Okay, great."

36

Kate grabbed the telephone from me again and said, "Jimmy, you can do it!"

Then the line went dead. I tried desperately to re-connect, but failed. "We've lost him," I told the rest. "His battery could be flat; we'll just have to wait for him to call us later; he should be at Raffles Place in a matter of minutes."

"It's quite simple; any idiot should be able to retrieve the note," said Bobby Boon, looking nervous.

Jimmy arrived at Raffles Place a little short of breath, as he would relate to me years later. There were a number of people there, walking briskly, probably to their offices. There was a plumb woman selling something and shouting, "Please help the disabled! Please help the disabled!"

Jimmy scanned the place for the sculpture of a sailing craft. He scanned left to right, right to left, then left to right again. But where was the sculpture? There was no sailing craft! He searched again: left to right, right to left, and left to right again. There was a sculpture in the middle of the place, sure enough, but it was obvious to him that it was no sailing craft. It looked, to him, like three crows lying on their back reading a newspaper together. He was confused. How could he explain it to me and to the people at Croctopus? Then he panicked. He looked left and right, as if hoping for a sailing craft to cruise into Raffles Place to rescue him from his plight. He could not call me because his battery was flat. He started to sweat in the equatorial heat. So what was he to do? As he rushed about to nowhere in particular, he bumped into a boy selling postcards. As he apologized, he spotted a postcard with a picture of the sculpture of the three crows reading a newspaper. What luck! Now he could explain everything to me and to the rest, especially to Kong. Oh, Kong was the person he feared most! Jimmy bought the postcard quickly and ran back to his friend's office at the building that looked like a calculator. He was sweating profusely and in panic.

The Croctopus people were waiting anxiously in the boardroom; Kong was pacing up and down like a caged tiger. "Where the hell could he be? Why doesn't he call us?" said Kong to no one in particular.

"He must be in dreamland, dreaming his impossible dream," said Sammy Sam. "He's always like that."

All eyes stared at the boardroom telephone. Then it rang. "Hello, Kate?" The voice of Jimmy came out loud and clear through conference speaker.

"Do I sound like Kate?" bellowed Kong, now in charge of the telephone. "Where have you been? Did you get the note?"

"Ken?"

"This is Kong! Now tell me, did you get the note?"

"Well, there was no sculpture of a sailing craft," said Jimmy in a quivering voice.

"You didn't get the note?" screamed Kong.

"I'm sorry, sir, there was no sailing craft . . ."

"How could there be no sailing craft? It's just a sculpture; it couldn't possibly have sailed away!" thundered Kong.

"In the middle of the place, there was a sculpture of three crows lying on their back reading a newspaper together, but no sailing craft."

"What nonsense are you talking about? Three crows having siesta early in the morning, enjoying a newspaper together in the middle of Raffles Place?" said Kong, purple with rage.

"I can fax you a postcard of the sculpture right now."

"The guy's mad! I thought he was only a dreamer, but he's mad, insane!" said Sammy Sam, looking most aggrieved.

Then the fax in the boardroom came alive. The machine sounded like a crow cawing madly. Sonny Song rushed over and retrieved the copy of the postcard. He took a quick look, and appeared puzzled. Then he handed it to Kong, who held the piece of paper with both hands, stared at it for a brief moment, and then

38

turned it right side up. Sonny Song, looking sheepish, faded quickly into the background. By then, Kate was by Kong's side, looking at the picture. She gasped in horror and covered her mouth with her hand.

"Jimmy, that's the sculpture of the sailing craft," said Kate.

"You are the only person in the world who could confuse a sailing craft with three crows lying on their back reading a newspaper together!" screamed Kong.

"I'm sorry, sir, I didn't know it was a sailing craft," said Jimmy in a voice trembling with fear. "It looked like three crows lying on their back reading a newspaper together."

"Jimmy, could you run back to Raffles Place immediately?" I said.

"It's too late," said Lenny Loon, cellphone in hand, "Chatterbig has just informed me that the note had been retrieved by him and destroyed."

"The note's gone? It's gone?" said Kong, his face full of anguish. Then, using all his might, he proceeded to slam the conference table with the palms of his hands several times, after which he stormed out of the boardroom, huffing and puffing. Before anyone could recover, he came storming back. He charged about the boardroom like a bull gone mad, before slamming the fax machine the way he had slammed the table. He seized the telephone with both hands, raised it above his head and smashed it onto the floor. Then he stormed out of the boardroom like a tank.

Chapter 3

We were in a stupor; Roger had trouble keeping his eyes open, while Kate was slumped on her seat, quite unlike her usual self. I tried to move my arms, but they were heavy as a stone. That was how we always felt after a hearty meal at Number One Chicken. I looked at Roger and saw the meaning of satisfaction—a baby after feeding could not have looked more satisfied. How did a security consultant get into such a state? I turned to Kate and realized that that was how she would look if she were drunk. Could anyone be drunk on chicken? I had the answer before me. That woman, intelligent and efficient, could look funny at times. Some people took years of meditation to attain a state of inner peace, but all we took was a hearty meal at Number One Chicken.

With a second effort, I stretched my arm to retrieve a newspaper nearby. "You haven't read the papers? That's a surprise; I thought you don't start the day without reading the papers," said Kate, eyes half-open.

"I told you that? I don't even remember it. Well, I didn't get to read the papers this morning; I had to rush to a meeting." I turned a page and chuckled, "Hey, look at this."

I showed the page to Kate and Roger. It carried an advertisement with Monica Moon flashing a winning smile and thrusting her ample assets out of the page. The blurb from her mouth said, "I enhanced my busts by a full inch in just one week with Moon's Alpine Dream treatment!" There was a picture showing a long queue at the Moon's Beauty Institute, with the following words, "Ten thousand satisfied customers can't be wrong!" At one corner of the advertisement appeared the owner of the Moon's Beauty Institute, Marvey Moon, who happened to be the mother of Monica. Below her was the proclamation "London trained".

"Hey, Monica Moon had breast implants some time ago! It was in the papers. How could they say it was due to whatever treatment?" said Kate.

"Don't truth and honesty matter anymore?" said Roger with a slight grin.

"Of course, they do," said Kate.

"Well, if we ask the question directly, everyone would give the same answer," I said. "But disguise the question a little, and truth and honesty may not matter to a lot of people. Why, ten thousand people didn't care about truth and honesty. They all knew Monica Moon had implants, surely."

"I think many don't read the papers," said Kate. "Still, I'll have to agree that the majority must have known about Moon's implants."

"I've always thought that accepting the truth is a straightforward matter," said Roger. "What's the point of denying the truth to yourself? In my work, depriving yourself of the truth would be a most dangerous thing to do; it could cost you a lot, maybe even your life."

"Well, not everyone's in the security business, where it's so necessary to face the truth and get things absolutely right," I said.

"If you deny the truth, you'd go off in the wrong direction and don't get things right," said Roger. "That's why I've never deprived myself of the truth; it's always the absolute truth that I demand."

"That sounds simple enough. So, why do thousands of people deprive themselves of the truth?" asked Kate. "That's a complete mystery to me."

"It's a matter of preference," I said. "Some people don't seek the truth; they seek happiness, comfort or the validation of their biases. They're moved by instinct rather than reason."

"Profound . . . profound wisdom," said Kate.

"Going for the truth is just a matter of preference and not a matter of principle?" asked Roger.

"Well, ultimately, it's still a question of whether you make it a matter of principle or a matter of preference," I said.

"You've made truth more complicated than I had ever imagined," said Roger with a chuckle.

"Well, it's not complicated at all, really," I said. "But it requires a commitment to the facts."

"Looks like we've gone from breast implants to philosophy," said Kate with a chuckle.

"Not to mention the chicken breast you've just eaten," I said.

"Enough of breast talk; we've got to get back to the office and keep abreast of our work," said Kate.

It was just coffee shop talk about an important subject (I mean, getting to the truth, not breast implants). We did not really exercise our minds very much. As we go through life, we are tested all the time on our commitment to the truth. It was a subject I was very passionate about, so I was hoping we could have remained in the restaurant for a while more to talk, but we had to go. So we made our way past people in a stupor and went out of the place, only to be blasted by the equatorial heat, which made us feel like turning back. The journey to the office was mercifully short, otherwise I would have to pull to the side of the road for a nap. Upon arriving at

Croctopus HQ, we went straight to the boardroom, where the other terrorist hunters were assembled.

"Since the Raffles Place fiasco, we've had no news about Crouching Liar whatsoever," said Kong. "We came so near to nailing him. Chatterbig's clue seems so simple, 'If you meet him, you would know,' but I've met so many people and I still don't know who Crouching Liar is. I hate this roundabout way of getting our man. I'm a straight shooter; I like to aim directly at my target and shoot. This puzzle thing is giving me a headache. It's nonsense; I don't like it. I don't like it at all!" Kong was visibly frustrated.

"That's why I said the other day it was not that simple," said Bobby Boon. "We've got to look for the trick in the puzzle. Somebody's idea of sounding the fire alarm and assembling everyone was plain silly; it was ridiculous and a complete waste of everyone's time."

"No, it wasn't;" said Kate. "Although we didn't find Crouching Liar, I think it was the right thing to do."

"How could something that failed so badly have been the right thing to do? And it wasted everybody's time, too. The entire staff was assembled for nothing. Failure is failure; you can't argue with this."

"Well, there was nothing else we could have done for a start. At least, we took the only avenue opened to us. Ken's suggestion was right."

"You always agree with him," said Bobby Boon, "but that doesn't mean both of you were right."

"I think Ken was right," said Roger. "It was the only thing we could have done to get started, and we would have done ourselves a disfavor if we hadn't assembled everyone to search for Crouching Liar."

"What's the meaning of this?" said Bobby Boon, looking at Kate and me, but leaving Roger out. "Assembling the staff has been proven wrong, so don't argue with me."

"This is insubordination," said Sammy Sam. "Kate doesn't know how to respect her seniors."

"Yes, that's right, insubordination," said Bobby Boon.

Kate was about to reply when I cut her off, saying, "I'm sure Kate intends no disrespect; she just believes my suggestion was correct." Kate had always been a bit impulsive, and I had always tried to prevent her from having a headlong clash with the top men of the company. I believed it was better to be prudent than to win small battles.

Sonny Song leaned forward, as if about to say something, but was cut off by Kong, who said, "I've heard enough. Kate, you should have known that we don't tolerate insubordination here. We've to preserve the integrity of our establishment; if there's no respect for authority, the whole edifice painstakingly built up over the years would collapse overnight. Now, I want the whole team to pull in the same direction; we can't achieve anything if we all do what we liked. We have to put aside our individual preferences and work as a team."

Kate's jaw dropped, and was about to reply when I stopped her with a slight movement of my lips conveying a soundless "No".

Kong continued, "While we're waiting for the next lead from Chatterbig, I've ordered that work on securing our communications be speeded up." He turned to the intercom and asked, "Is he on the way?"

"Yes sir, he'll be at the boardroom any moment now," said a woman at the other end.

"Hi, I'm Socky," said the tall, strapping man walking into the boardroom. He had a prominent, bushy moustache.

Kong introduced himself and said, "We were just wondering when you'd be here." Turning to the rest, he continued," This is the man we've all been waiting to hear from. This is Socky, the American communications expert who is helping us to secure our communications. I'm meeting him for the first time myself. He's an expert in cryptography. Socky, please take a seat."

There was a rumble, which made Kong look up at the air-condition outlet nearest him and said, "This air-conditioner is acting like a cantankerous old man again. Ken, didn't I ask you to get it fixed?"

"The maintenance people came yesterday," I said. "But I think they couldn't really figure out what was wrong. This old man air-conditioner seems to have a life of its own, and nobody could do a thing about it."

"And I always thought I was the boss here," said Kong. Turning to Socky, he said, "Things aren't always what they seem, are they?" It was a profound statement, but at that time we did not know how profound it would be for us.

"Well, I'll take it that you're the boss," said Socky with a smile.

"Thank you, I feel assured."

"I'm surprised to see so many people here," said Socky. "I thought I'd be here to meet only you, General."

"What you're doing is of utmost importance to us, so I've asked the rest to come; I also want them to meet you." Kong paused for a moment, looking grave. He then continued, "You don't know this, but what you're doing has taken on a new urgency." The air-conditioner started to vibrate noticeably, which caused Kong to look up in irritation. "This old man is throwing tantrums; maybe he doesn't like you, Socky."

"I'll have to be careful," said Socky with a wink. "About the new urgency, what's going on?"

"I can't tell you at this moment, but you can take it from me that what you're doing is now very important and must be speeded up."

"Shouldn't I know the reason? I mean, I can respond to this new urgency adequately only if I know what's going on, don't you think so?"

A hissing sound came from the air-conditioner; there was a rush of cold air into the room, which made Kong look up, as if trying to intimidate the air-conditioner.

"You will, eventually," said Kong. "Now, let's just turn to what you're doing. Is everything going smoothly?"

"Well, as you know, I've just started with the communications work here at Croctopus; there's some way to go. There are weaknesses in the system, and I'm helping to plug them and make the communications here more secure. Lots of things have to be sorted out."

"There's some way to go?" asked Kong, sitting up, as if taken by surprise.

"Yes, I'm afraid so; the details are a bit too technical to explain."

"Except for Ken and Kate, we should have no problems understanding the technical details," said Bobby Boon.

Kate's jaw dropped a second time, and was about to reply when Kong said, "Make sure all gaps are plugged immediately."

"As soon as possible," said Socky.

"If you can't explain the technical details, perhaps you could tell us about cryptography then, since you're the expert, and we don't get to meet an expert in this field every day," said Kong. "In fact, I've never met a cryptographer until today."

Socky gave a smile and took a sip of water. "To put it simply, cryptography is the study and practice of writing codes, and the sending and deciphering of such codes. In other words, it's about writing, sending and deciphering secret messages."

"James Bond stuff," said Kong with a wide grin. "This is interesting."

"It's especially important when countries are in conflict. As humans have been at war since time immemorial, cryptography has a long history. To most people, cryptography involves encoding messages. But those messages have to be delivered, so they have to hide them during delivery to reduce the chances of interception.

And, of course, cryptography also involves decoding messages, including cracking your enemy's codes."

"That's for geeks," said Kong, breaking into a smile.

"Codes range from the simple to the very complex that requires computers to crack. Scientists are now working on quantum cryptography, which will, hopefully, make a message impossible to crack without the sender or intended recipient knowing it."

"How could it be?" said Kong. "If a message is intended to be received by someone, then somebody else can intercept it. And if we employ the best minds in large numbers, let them have the most powerful computers, and give them sufficient time, surely any code can be intercepted and cracked without the sender or intended recipient noticing the interception."

"You're absolutely right, sir," said Bobby Boon.

"Well, in quantum cryptography, the idea is to take advantage of the nature of subatomic particles to send messages. Now, subatomic particles are nothing like billiard balls, because they're so tiny. The moment you try to measure the velocity or mass of a subatomic particle or system, you interfere with and change its velocity or mass, the very thing you're trying to measure. Subatomic particles are the absolute in smallness, and you can't create any measuring instrument tiny enough to measure them. In other words, you can't measure a subatomic particle like you measure a billiard ball; the act of measuring a subatomic particle messes things up. The idea in quantum cryptography is to take advantage of this phenomenon. So, when we send a message using quantum cryptography, the key to read the message will be disturbed if the enemy tries to use it. In this way, such a message is, hopefully, impossible to crack without the sender or intended recipient noticing the interception."

That's very interesting. I'm able follow what you were saying, but I'm not sure whether everyone here could," said Bobby Boon, looking at Kate and me.

Kate raised her eyebrows and turned to me; I rolled my eyeballs a little to show support, but did not do anything to encourage her to confront Bobby Boon as I wanted her to calm down. In fact, I shook my head from side to side in tiny movements to tell her not to reply to Bobby Boon. It was always like that when Kate was with the company's top men. She would rather be right than wise. I was the opposite—for me, wisdom comes before showing that I am right.

Bobby Boon continued, "You know, there's something strange in your presentation, Socky; I can't put my finger on it." There came loud hissing from the air-conditioner.

"You don't know what's bothering you?" Kate said.

"Of course I know, don't try to be funny," said Bobby Boon. "I just can't put my finger on it."

"That means you don't know what's bothering you," said Kate.

"Of course I know; I always know what I'm talking about. And how dare you say I don't know what's bothering me?"

"What's so strange about my presentation?" asked Socky. "You said you understood what I had said." I was relieved; Socky just saved Kate from another round of tongue-lashing from the company's top men.

"Actually, it's not what you said. It's how you say it, or rather how you look when you say it," said Bobby Boon.

Socky shrugged his shoulders, indicating it was too vague for him to give a reply.

"What do you mean?" said Kong.

"I mean, sir, he looks like someone I know," said Bobby Boon. "But I can't say who that person is. The thought was nagging me throughout the briefing."

"Yes, you do look very familiar," said Sammy Sam. "It's as if I've seen you a thousand times before. But I, too, can't figure out whom you look like."

48

"That's strange, I feel the same way too," said Sonny Song. "I was looking at you more than I was listening. Have you appeared on television before?"

The air-conditioner gave a loud groan, as if it had a throat and a chunk of meat was stuck in it.

"You mean you were all not listening to me?" said Socky in mock horror. "I look better than I speak? Maybe next time I should just use sign language. And no, I've never appeared on television."

"Yes, now that this has been brought up, you do look very familiar," said Kong. "But I don't believe I've met you before, I'm quite sure."

"Maybe you bumped into me before, but didn't know it was me," said Socky.

"Possible, though I doubt it. Why don't you tell us something about yourself? It'll put an end to all this talk about having seen you before," said Kong with a chuckle.

The air-conditioner became noisy and spewed out unusually cold air. A chill enveloped the boardroom, causing Kate to fold her arms to keep warm.

"What's happening, old man?" I said softly to the air-conditioner, which soon became quiet again.

"I'd like to get to know you guys, too," said Socky. "I'm a private kind of person. Anyway, there's nothing interesting about me. Although I'm spending most of my time working on communications, I've a very wide range of interests; I'm interested in just about anything and everything. And while I'm here, I want to learn everything about your country; it's a very interesting place."

"Yes, Orderland's a very interesting place; there're so many places you could visit," said Sonny Song. "Why do you want to learn everything about us?"

"It's just me," said Socky. "I'm a very curious person; I want to understand everything I come across."

"What's your purpose in learning everything about us?" said Bobby Boon.

"There's no purpose; you don't need a purpose to learn; a baby doesn't need a purpose to explore the world around him," said Socky.

"That's new to us," said Sonny Song.

"He's speaking for himself," whispered Kate to me. I was taken aback by Kate's sudden remark, but managed to act as if I had not heard anything.

"A person who has a big appetite for learning is usually an interesting guy," I said. "Even your name is interesting."

"Everyone calls me Socky."

"How should we address you if we need to introduce you formally to an audience?" I asked.

"Well, Socky would be fine; I'd be quite happy with this."

"No, sometimes this wouldn't do," I said.

"It's okay to introduce me as Socky even to your prime minister, honest."

"It's okay with you, but it may not be okay with the other guy," I said. "We may appear impolite to him, and even impolite to you in his view. And we don't want to appear impolite to someone like the prime minister."

"Well, actually my name is 'Sockem'; 'Socky' is the informal version." The air-conditioner became noisy again, like someone choking. It sent another chill round the boardroom.

"What's wrong with the air-conditioner? It's acting strange," said Kong. "Sounds like it's being strangled . . . Sorry, Socky, I didn't quite get what you said."

"My first name's Sockem, S-o-c-k-e-m."

"That's an unusual name," said Kong. "In fact, this is the first time I've come across such a name."

"Well, I suppose it's a bit unusual. How shall I explain this? You see, it's not the name my parents gave me. To begin at the beginning . . . I hate to say this . . . Well, when I was in school, I was big and aggressive and I liked fighting. I was involved in many fights. But I never started any; I fought only when provoked. I was, in my eyes, always the good guy. Of course, now that I'm older and wiser, I've to admit that, well, it took very little to provoke me when I was young. But I must emphasize that I'm a much better person now.

"Ha ha, that's okay; I wasn't that nice a student myself," said Kong.

"One day, I fought a bully, who was the most hated student in the school, and the crowd cheered me on, shouting 'Sock 'em! Sock 'em!' That's our way of saying, 'Beat him up.' I won the fight; I drove the bully out of the school. He suffered a loss of face and never came back. So, to mark the students' 'liberation' from that bully, they called me 'Sockem'. I became their protector, the good guy."

"That's interesting, but I don't suppose that's the name in your passport," I said.

"Actually, it is. Sometime after I started working, I fell out with my family, so I changed my name and I became 'Sockem' officially."

"I changed my name, too," said Kong with a chuckle. "Didn't like the name my parents gave me. I had no big quarrel with them though, and I changed my name only after my father had passed away. My mother, when she was alive, continued calling me by my old name."

"Sorry to hear about what happened between your family and you, Socky," I said. "I hope you didn't change your family name."

"Yes, I did; I had a completely new name."

"That's really going very far; I'm sorry to hear that. I was just joking when I said I hoped you didn't change your family name." I paused for a while, but nobody continued the conversation,

51

as if everyone was telling me that since I had messed it up I should put things right myself. So I just asked the obvious, "Anyway, what's your family name now?"

There was a continuous rumbling sound from the air-conditioner, as if it was coughing non-stop. "The air-conditioner sounds like it's being beaten to death, all that groaning and choking," said Kong. "And it's throwing out chill air like snow balls, like it's trying to freeze us to death."

"Maybe it's trying to stop this meeting or warning us about something," said Roger.

"Looks like it," said Kate.

"Maybe we should stop the meeting," said Socky.

"Okay, tell us your family name and we'll wrap this up," said Kong. "The cold is getting murderous; I want to get out of here soon."

"Maybe we should just stop now; after all, we're not discussing anything important," said Socky.

"I'd like to wrap things up properly, in an orderly manner," said Kong, the military discipline in him showing. "We're talking about your family name . . ."

"I wouldn't call it a family name; it's a surname," said Socky.

"Well, it doesn't really matter to me. If it makes you feel better, what's your surname?" asked Kong.

"That's another long story." The boardroom became almost unbearably chilly, as if the air-conditioner had gone mad, out of control.

"You see, I was the only one in my family who could sing; the rest were tone deaf. It was well known to everyone in the neighborhood. So, the people there referred to me as 'The one who sings'. I was immensely proud of that, and I kind of enjoyed it when people mentioned my name and then added 'who sings'. So, when I fell out with my family, I changed my surname to 'Whosing', dropping the 's' at the end to simplify things. It's in my passport, too."

52

There was laughter in the boardroom; everyone was amused. The air-conditioner started to sputter, as if its life was going out. The place became cold as a mortuary.

"Actually, we still don't know your original name," said Ken.

"Oh, never mind about that," said Socky.

"It's really funny," said Kong. "So, you're Sockem Whosing."

More laughter from everyone, with Kong laughing loudest, and I thought I saw a tear coming out from a corner of his eye. He and the senior men were still laughing when suddenly Kong's jaws dropped and his face froze, as if he was wearing a mask of ice, his expression changing from hilarity to shock. Cold air from the air-conditioner cascaded onto him without mercy. He looked like an ice carving on display, just a solid mass of coldness, without life.

"Sockem Whosing," repeated Kong, as if he was trying to make sure he got it right. He paused and stared blankly ahead. "You're Sockem Whosing . . . Sockem Who . . ." He paused again, this time longer. "Sockem . . . Sockem . . . Sa . . . Sa . . . Sad . . ." He stopped, as if unable to go on. Then with some effort he continued, as if compelled to do so. "Sad . . . Who . . . Hu . . . ," said Kong, almost choking. Then, as if mustering all his strength, he managed an almost inaudible, "Saddam . . . Hu . . . Saddam . . . ," He turned pale and sat down, mouth open and eyes glassy like a drunk. The air-conditioner continued to rumble loudly, as if coughing uncontrollably. It spewed out cold air with a vengeance, which enveloped the people around the conference table.

Moments later, Kong started to mumble, at first incoherently, then "If you meet him you would know. If you meet him you would know. If you . . ." His lips started to quiver. "Crouch . . . Crouching . . ." His body tensed, as if seized by an unseen power; his hands started to tremble, then his body trembled, too. More cold air cascaded down onto him; for whatever reason, old man air-conditioner seemed to give him no mercy.

"If you meet him you would know," said Bobby Boon gravely. Turning to Socky, he continued, "And you want to know everything about us."

"What's all this? Did I miss something?" asked Socky.

"No, thank you for briefing us. We've finished the meeting; now, if you'll excuse us, we have something to discuss," said Kong, almost in a whisper, as he came out of shock slowly.

After Socky had left the room there was a moment of silence before Kong jumped up from his seat, pointed a hard finger at the door, and screamed, "That's him! Crouching Liar! We've got him! We've got Crouching Liar!"

The air-conditioner started to groan and shake violently, as if warning of an earthquake.

"To think that he's working on securing our communications!" said Bobby Boon. "He's a wolf in our chicken coop!"

"I'll inform Colonel Loon that we've got Crouching Liar; the OSD must know about this immediately!" said Kong, before dashing out of the room like a race horse.

Bobby Boon, Sammy Sam and Sonny Song also ran out, like reporters with the scoop of the year. Kate, Roger and I were left in the room, dumbfounded by the latest event.

"This seems like a very exciting development," said Roger to Kate and me, as we walked along the corridor outside the boardroom.

"So, what should we do next?" I said.

"Maybe the company would send Socky packing," said Roger.

"I don't think Socky would even admit he's Crouching Liar," said Kate. "I mean, we don't really have anything on him. And I don't think we'll even disclose to him the existence of Chatterbig or that strange clue given to us."

According to the staff, who told me later, Kong and the three executive vice presidents were a storm of activities after they returned from the meeting to their desks. Kong talked excitedly on the telephone, raising his volume as his excitement rose, while the other three whipped themselves and their staff into a frenzy of urgent work.

*

"I don't understand this, Colonel Loon," said Kong, his face pained with dejection. The Croctopus terrorist hunters were back at the boardroom facing a new problem.

"As I've explained to you earlier . . . ," said Lenny Loon.

"How could the OSD object to the dismissal of Socky? This is madness!" said Kong. The people in the room stirred; there was uneasy coughing.

"As I've explained earlier, Socky's uncle is a United States senator," said Lenny Loon. "We—that's the OSD, the Foreign Ministry and you—would have a lot to answer if we sent Socky packing with no good reason."

"No good reason? How could there be no good reason?" bellowed Kong. "What are you talking about, Colonel Loon? Isn't the unmasking of Socky as Crouching Liar, as a terrorist mole, good reason? The OSD is the Orderland Security Department, and one of its functions is to pack off dangerous terrorists like Crouching Liar!"

"What evidence are we going to show his senator uncle that he's a terrorist mole?" said Lenny Loon.

"You do agree that Socky is Crouching Liar, don't you?" said Kong, face red with anger.

"Yes, but it'd be different with his uncle. What we have wouldn't be good enough for him," said Lenny Loon.

"What's happening to this world? It's clear as daylight! What more do we need?" said Kong.

"There's another reason for the OSD's objection," said Lenny Loon. "If we sent Socky packing, we'd lose the only lead we have to his network here. We must smash the network even if it means letting Socky stay."

"That's not fair! Smashing the network is your business, not ours," said Kong.

"Smashing the network is everybody's business. It's your duty; it's Croctopus's duty," said Lenny Loon.

At the mention of duty, Kong shut up. If there was one thing he understood, it was duty. Then he turned to Kate and me, "Both of you are now assigned to keep an eye on Crouching Liar. From now on, this is your main job. Let Crouching Liar go where he wants to go, and do what he wants to do. But monitor him, find out what he wants to know about us, about our country. Let him lead you to his network. Catch him before he and his network can cause any damage."

"Isn't the OSD doing anything?" I asked.

"We're conducting our own operations in parallel to yours. We'll have to work closely," said Lenny Loon.

*

Socky met Kate and me at the Croctopus Café. Looking aggrieved and confused, he said dejectedly, "I don't understand this. I've been assigned another job; I'm no more in communications, no more doing security stuff."

"You didn't ask the General for the reason?" I said.

"I did, I went straight to his room and confronted him, but he wouldn't say anything. Well, he did say it had to do with fresh developments, but that's not saying anything. He was keeping something from me; I think it must have something to do with his acting strangely at the boardroom."

"I know how you feel. So, what's your new job?" asked Kate.

"Research . . . general research."

"And what's that?" asked Kate.

"Search me, or research me; I don't know," said Socky, turning up his palms and shrugging his shoulders. "The General said that as I'd like to know everything about Orderland, I could do general research on this country. But I don't understand this at all; what has general research got to do with Croctopus?"

"Looks like you can do anything you want," I said. "Why don't you just go ahead and do what you've always wanted to do, learn about this country and enjoy yourself?"

Socky knitted his eyebrows and thought for a moment. Then he smiled and said, "That's a splendid idea; I think I'll do just that. To hell with all this secrecy."

We left the café; Kate and I headed back to our desks while Socky took a walk along a footpath just outside the building. Through the glass panels, I could see that the equatorial sun was up and merciless; the air outside the building must have been stifling and oppressive, yet Socky seemed to have a spring in his steps, as if he had been unshackled from an invisible chain. He looked free to roam wherever he wanted to.

Chapter 4

The sky was gray when the music started—soulful, but shaky and unsure; the old men played as best they could. And the people cried; Socky and I were solemn.

"What's all that noise?" asked Kong over the cellphone.

"We're at a funeral," I replied.

"A funeral? What are you both doing at a funeral? Who died?"

I tried as best I could to explain to Kong, but it was always difficult when he was excited.

"You don't even know who died? What's the meaning of this?" bellowed Kong.

"We've just arrived and I haven't seen the person's name yet; all I know is that the deceased is a Chinese male."

"I don't understand this. Do you or do you not know who the deceased is?"

"No, I don't."

"Then what the hell are you doing at his funeral?"

I tried to keep calm; there was no point getting excited on the line with Kong. I let him talk, and waited for him to run out of steam, like a typhoon losing energy. But Kong carried on and on. So as soon as I detected a pause in Kong's speech, I cut in quickly to explain.

"What? He wants to know about the undertaking business in Orderland?" Kong was clearly incredulous. "Who but a terrorist would want to know about the undertaking business? That confirms it!"

"Confirms what?"

"It!"

"Er . . . what's it?"

"That he's the mole we're looking for!"

"Oh, okay. As I was saying, he's surprised that Croctopus is in the undertaking business."

"Why shouldn't we be in the undertaking business? It's the best damn business in Orderland! Don't you agree?"

"Well, what I think is not the point; the point is he's surprised. That's why we're here so that he could learn about the undertaking business in Orderland."

"I put him in general research and the first thing he wants to know is the undertaking business! That shows, doesn't it? That's one more proof of whom he is. Now, I want you to watch him closely, very closely; see what he's up to."

Watching Socky very closely was my job, so Kong need not have asked me to. Still, I gave him a short assurance that I would do my duty, more to end the conversation than anything else. Then Socky and I walked around the premises because his curiosity was piqued. I was feeling like a busybody and a little embarrassed, for we had no business snooping around a stranger's funeral, but Socky did not give the slightest hint of unease. There were some stares from people who tried to figure out who we were, but we were left mostly to ourselves as it was a busy time for everyone. Besides, lots

59

of long lost relatives and unknown friends of a deceased always turn up at a funeral, and this one was probably no exception. I tried not to intrude and stayed mostly by the side, away from the flow of human traffic, but Socky went for a closer look. As the band waited patiently, people were scooping big bundles of spirit money from huge plastic bags and throwing them into a bonfire by the side of the driveway. Socky was taking notes.

"This is to ensure that the dead man will live comfortably in the other world," I said as I looked at the fire consuming the currency for the deceased. "It's the practice of Chinese immigrants all over the world."

"Looks like he'll be a billionaire," said Socky with a faint smile. "If you don't make it in this world, there's always a second chance."

Some people brought a meter-high model of a mansion, made of paper, with two paper guards at the gate. Then another person brought a paper luxury car and a paper cellphone set, complete with a battery charger. All were fed to the bonfire.

"Such items were supposed to be burned the night before," I said, "but I overheard that some of the dead man's friends from overseas managed to arrange for them only at a late hour."

"Maybe the dead man could use the cellphone to call his family later, after he had settled down at his new location."

The band came alive again, blasting the place with a marching piece. A short while later, loud wails, like sirens, rolled out of the house in eerie waves. They must have come from some of the dead man's relatives; the women were especially loud and conveyed their overwhelming sorrow like a soprano at the sorrowful ending of an opera. One or two women were saying something while crying at the same time, perhaps reciting the deceased's life story or proclaiming their sadness his departure, but I could not really make out what they were saying. The band stopped the music and remained respectfully silent, conceding the airwaves to the mourners. As the coffin was carried out of the house to the driveway, the people turned bodily to look away, so that the path to the hearse was lined with people with their backs to the coffin.

"What's going on?" asked Socky.

"Staring at a dead man or his coffin could bring you bad luck, so they're looking away."

"If you don't look, then bad luck can't get to you?"

"I guess so."

After the coffin was loaded onto the hearse, the relatives and friends formed a line, three or four abreast, behind it. The band played *When The Saints Go Marching In*. The hearse, with the line of mourners behind, moved slowly out of the driveway onto the road. One woman, probably the widow, was wailing away and thumping her chest.

"Looks like the family wears special clothes for the funeral," said Socky.

"Yes, those are mourning clothes provided by the undertaker. As you can see, they're made from coarse materials."

"I see, they're pretty shabby—ill-fitting, black, white and khaki. The materials look like they came from gunny sacks." Socky scribbled furiously on his notebook.

"Sure, this is to signify that the mourners felt the great loss and could not be bothered to dress up."

"Where are they going? Isn't the crematorium some distance away? Surely, they're not walking all the way there; it'll take hours."

"No, they'll walk a short distance. I guess in the old days the cemetery would not have been that far away; it'd be within walking distance, somewhere just outside the village. So I guess in those days mourners walked from their house to the cemetery with the coffin."

"So they'll walk a short distance now because traditionally there had always been a procession?"

"Very clever of you." I tried not to smile too widely in the midst of a funeral procession.

The band played *Walkin' Back To Happiness*, the old Helen Shapiro hit song. A car with a long white sash running diagonally down the front windscreen led the procession. The only passenger, at the back, was an old man, who sat like a statue, calm and composed, indifferent even.

"Who's that guy seated at the back of the lead car? Why is he not walking behind the hearse?" asked Socky, notebook and pen ready.

"You're very observant; he's what is called a good-life man. He represents the dead man when he was alive. You see, he's seated like a big boss at the back and ferried around in air-conditioned comfort by a chauffeur. The whole act symbolizes the good life of the deceased, that he had lived well."

"I see, that's interesting. What if the dead man didn't have a good life?"

"I guess there'd still be a good-life man. I suppose the family would want to believe that he had a good life, and they'd want to tell the world that he had a good life."

"Is he a relative of the dead man?"

"No, he's a total stranger procured for the occasion by the undertaker."

"Really?" Socky raised his eyebrows. "So, while the whole family and all the other mourners are getting cooked in this stifling, oppressive equatorial heat, a total stranger is leading the way in air-conditioned comfort in a car?"

"Yup, and he gets paid for it."

"Did they have a good-life man in the old days, before the invention of the car and the air-conditioner?"

"I don't know. I think some of the practices don't go back very far. There's no scripture for funerals; it's all customs and tradition passed down from generation to generation. I suspect, from time to time, undertakers invent new practices to add meaning, to make things more colorful or maybe even to earn a few bucks from the extra service; and people would think they're customs and tradition from long ago. I mean, a family goes through only a few funerals each generation; they can't tell new inventions from age-old customs and tradition."

"Very interesting."

"But I'll tell you this, after my retirement, I'll work as a good-life man." I tried to keep a straight face.

That brought a hearty laugh from Socky. But after realizing what he had just done in the midst of mourners, he said, "Sorry, but you shouldn't say crazy things like that." Fortunately, the band had drowned out his laughter.

"I'm not joking; I mean it."

"I'd like to work as a good-life man, too," said Socky through his half-grin. "Maybe we're both mad."

The procession traveled on the main road for a very short distance; it then broke up and the mourners clambered onto two waiting buses. "They're going to the crematorium," I said. "They've to time their arrival with military precision, because crematoria here are heavily booked. If they arrive too early, they'd have to wait because the earlier cremation would not have ended, and it wouldn't be nice to make a dead man wait under the equatorial sun for his turn. But if they arrive late, they'd be pressed to finish their cremation in time for the next one waiting at the doorstep. And it's not nice to rush a dead man either, although for a dead man is eternal."

"That's serious; military precision for a funeral. No wonder they need a marching band. I suppose when you live in a crowded country even the dead must keep to the schedule."

"All right, I think we'll visit the crematorium some other time. I've a report to finish." I looked at my watch. "Let's go. I'm glad I parked the car some distance away; this place's really jammed up. The dead man must have been a very popular guy."

"I've learnt something today," said Socky, kicking stones as he walked. "But I'm still curious about why Croctopus is in the undertaking business."

"Because it's the best business in the country."

"Really? How could this be? I know people must die, but they've been dying since the beginning of the human race, and the undertaking business has never been the best business in any country, at least not during peace time. I mean, no country makes undertaking its main business. I've never heard of the undertaking business driving the economy of any country. Nobody, except the very rich, will want a lavish funeral."

I kept walking, but remained silent for a while as I tried to formulate an answer to the difficult question. I knew the answer, of course, but how was I to explain it to Socky? I kept my gaze straight ahead and steady, so as not to fall into a drain while thinking so hard, but all I could manage at that moment was, "We seem to have done it."

Socky was surprised at such a short answer after the fairly long time I had taken to ponder over his question. So he tried to get a better reply. "But why do it? It's very unusual, strange even. I can't figure out why undertaking is the best business in this country."

"Well, it was not done deliberately; nobody had set out to make it the best business in Orderland. It's like toadstools sprouting up in the garden overnight while you're asleep. You didn't plan or expect to have toadstools in your garden, but they would sneak up on you while you were not paying attention."

"That's nature," said Socky, "but the undertaking business is not part of nature. I mean, dying is part of nature, but undertaking is not. Business is man-made. My question is why did your country make it so?"

"You see, long ago, when we were a poor country, a lot of people were so poor that they couldn't even afford a funeral. But we were a traditional people and a proper funeral was important to us.

So the government devised a clever scheme to ensure that everyone would have a proper funeral; they set up this fund called the Social Welfare Extension Fund or SWEF. It's used to pay for everyone's funeral."

"The government's very generous."

"Well, it's a bit more complicated than that; a dead man actually pays for his own funeral."

"What? I don't understand."

"You see, every working person has an account with SWEF. Before he receives his pay, his employer is by law required to deduct 25% of his pay for his SWEF account. In addition, the employer is also required by law to contribute a sum equal to 25% of the employee's salary to the employee's SWEF account. So, something equal to 50% of a worker's pay ends up in the SWEF, which is really some kind of national funeral fund."

"Wow! Massive forced savings for funerals. With so much money reserved for funerals, I can understand why the undertaking business is the best business in the country.

"Yes, a man may have only one funeral, but he can have a simple or an elaborate one. And if he can't use his money in his SWEF account for anything else, he'd use it for an elaborate, expensive funeral. The undertakers will price funerals higher and higher because there'll always be money for them. In fact, the price would go up even if funerals remain exactly the same. There's this enormous bubble that has been inflating for years; it's a long-term bubble fed by a never-ending stream of forced savings. The price of a commodity or service is proportional to the aggregate saving allocated for it. We think of demand as the number of people desiring particular goods and services. That's not quite correct; it's the quantity of money going for particular goods and services, never mind about the number of people."

"Maybe I should go into the undertaking business, too."

"If you succeed, you'd be rich; if not, you can always work as a good-life man."

"Ha ha! I can't lose, can I?" Suddenly, despite the equatorial heat, Socky was re-vitalized. "How much does a funeral cost here?"

"Before SWEF was set up, a decent funeral used to cost a few thousand dollars; but now it could cost up to a hundred thousand dollars, and several hundred thousand dollars if you desire a really elaborate one."

"Okay, I'm going into the undertaking business," said Socky, smiling and rubbing his hands in an exaggerated way. "I really can't lose, can I? No good-life man job for me; I want the big-time undertaking business."

"And compete with Croctopus? There's no way you can compete; Croctopus is by far the biggest corporation in Orderland. The second largest corporation is so far behind that we don't even know which one it is. Croctopus will crush you like a steamroller; you'd be flat as a pancake."

"Tell me, what's the government doing about the rising cost of funerals?" asked Socky, kicking stones with greater force as he got more interested.

"Make the people save even more. The percentage for compulsory savings in the SWEF has been rising; it was only two percent of a person's wage at the beginning."

"Save some more? Wouldn't that inflate funeral cost further?"

"Of course."

"Why don't you tell the government what you told me?"

"Why would the government listen to me? I'm just a nobody. Besides, they're absolutely sure they're on the right path; they've got battalions of scholars working on it. As far as our government is concerned, if the smart people say it's right, then it's right."

"Sometimes, the ordinary people know better because they're at the receiving end of policies and, unlike the rich, they've to bear the sharp end of any policy; they've little spare cash." Socky rubbed his thumb against two fingers to signify cash.

I didn't know what overcame me. I let go of all my pent-up feelings and told Socky that SWEF took money away from the adventurous, who would otherwise have used it for, say, business. The country did not favor the daring, but favoured the meek instead. The brave were forced to forgo their dreams as they had to save for their funeral. I said the meek would inherit the country, that Orderland was a sheep's paradise. Once the top set the course, nobody would dare to even mention changing it. Hence, mistakes tended to be protected, then perpetuated, and would eventually become sacred cows. As I talked, Socky cleverly kept quiet and let me unload my years of frustration and thinking on the subject. I explained that someone in authority would, say, make an assumption, and although we might feel uncomfortable with the assumption and have our doubts, we would nevertheless go along with it, because it would be easier to go along with what we perceived as established thinking than to go against it. After some time, we would find that we had invested too much in our dubious venture, and would be even more reluctant to stop and turn back. And we would head for disaster.

After I finished talking, I realized that I was sweating profusely in the stifling, oppressive heat, so I was relieved that we had arrived at the car park. The first thing I did after starting my car was to increase the blast of cold air from the air-conditioner. Along the way to Croctopus HQ, we came across people loading a coffin onto a truck by the side of the road. The truck had the words "Better World" on its side.

"What's this?" asked Socky. "Is anyone in the coffin?"

"Yes, there is. Better World is a company that specializes in moving the dead across the border for a funeral. And there are more than one coffin in the truck."

"Why should any family want a funeral outside the country?"

"Because a funeral here is just too expensive."

"But you've SWEF."

"Well, as I've said, a person's savings with the SWEF may not be sufficient for his funeral here; it costs less across the border."

"But what happens if a dead man has more than enough? What happens to his savings in the SWEF if it's not used up?"

"It'd be distributed among his beneficiaries' SWEF accounts. Savings in SWEF cannot be used for any other purposes, so if you don't use it up for your funeral, then your spouse and children can use it for theirs."

We came across a convoy of four Better World trucks rumbling along the road. "Those must be headed for the border," said Socky. "I didn't expect so many families to send their dead across the border for a funeral; before the dead is sent to heaven, they've to be sent to another country first."

"It's a fact of life here."

"This thing about rising funeral cost must have been very troubling for the people, and the government too. After all, you're a traditional society and a proper funeral is important to you. And to think that this scheme to ensure that the dead have a proper funeral started with good intentions."

"Yes, but as I've said, the toadstools sprang up when we were sleeping. The road to hell is paved with good intentions."

We passed another Better World truck by the side of the road. "Hey, that's Robert," I said. "What's he doing here?" I pulled the car to the side of the road, in front of the truck. We got out and walked to the back of the truck, where Robert was.

"Hi Robert, what are you doing here?" asked Socky.

"I'm helping a friend of mine; his father just passed away. I'm helping him to make sure his father is properly loaded onto the truck while he's making other arrangements and heading for the border."

"I'm sorry about this," I said.

"Well, thank goodness for SWEF," said Robert. "Without SWEF, my friend would not be able to afford a funeral across the border."

We ended the conversation and went back to my car quickly; the equatorial heat was stifling and oppressive.

Chapter 5

Kong's room at Croctopus HQ in the morning was, as usual, cold as ice. Whenever he got excited or angry, he would seem to radiate heat, which would warm the place a little or, at least, make it feel that way. Notwithstanding that bit of heat, I was not particularly happy with an interrogation by an excited Kong first thing in the morning. Worse, I had not even taken my usual sip of coffee at the office, which made me feel unprepared for the ordeal.

"What does he mean he wants to test the system?" said Kong. "Look, this is getting dangerous; I want you to stop him before he causes any damage. The full resources of Croctopus are on standby to help you. You hear me? This guy's getting out of hand! First, he snoops around the funeral of a total stranger, pretending to do a scholarly study of the undertaking business here. But, of course, we all know he's gathering intelligence for a terrorist strike! Secondly, he now wants to conduct a test, and he doesn't say what test—it's a secret test that he wants to conduct. A secret test! He wants to test our security and our readiness to meet a strike; that's what he wants. And what gets me boiling is that he's going about as if he owns this country!"

Kong was red in the face from his own heat. I could not understand why he was so excited. After all, it was not as if Socky had unveiled a terrorist plan. But Kong was an excitable person, and everyone in Croctopus had to live with it. As always, I tried to manage Kong as best I could.

"I don't think Socky wants to do anything big or serious," I said. "I mean, he takes you seriously that his job is now general research."

"But he wants to test the system! What can this mean? You tell me!"

"Well, to begin at the beginning, we attended a funeral and he was surprised that Croctopus was in the undertaking business. And . . ."

"I know, you've told me that. And as I've told you, why shouldn't we be in the undertaking business? It's the best damn business in Orderland! Shouldn't we be in the best business in the country? It shows that business was not on his mind at all. He was gathering intelligence for a strike!" Kong heated up the place a bit more.

Oh, stop shouting at me, I thought. Then, literally out of nowhere, Kate appeared in my mind's eye, and I continued mentally, "Kate, could you please tell him to stop it? The whole thing had nothing to do with me. I haven't had my morning coffee in the office, this place is cold as ice, and he's screaming into my face like a drill sergeant. This guy has no sense; he doesn't listen, but screams and shouts. What a start to the day." I stared at an imaginary spot on the wall behind and just above Kong, who was seated behind his desk. It was my substitute for rolling my eyes.

"What are you thinking about?" asked Kong.

"Oh, er . . . nothing."

71

"How could that be? I could tell you're thinking about something."

"Well . . . nothing, really."

"You can't be thinking and not thinking, am I right?"

"Go ahead, tell him what you told me," said the imaginary Kate. "Give it to him; no, blast it to him. That'll teach him not to scream and shout early in the morning."

"Great idea," I said mentally.

"What?" said Kong, confused.

"Er . . . well, as I was saying, Socky was surprised Croctopus was in the undertaking business."

"And as I've said, there's no reason why we shouldn't be; anyone in business would want to be where the money is, and the money's in the undertaking business. It's as straightforward as a fish taking to water."

"Yes, I fully understand that, but he was surprised because he didn't know the undertaking business was the best business here. Now he knows, of course."

"So, is he now happy and satisfied that we're doing the right thing—getting into the right business?" Without waiting for my answer, Kong continued, "Now let me ask you, Ken, you're an intelligent man, have you ever asked yourself why would anyone want to attend the funeral of a total stranger who had been nothing more than an ordinary guy and who had not done anything particularly newsworthy?" Before I could reply, Kong continued, "Have you?"

I have always loathed interrogation by an excited Kong, who had the tendency to become more unreasonable and oppressive than his usual self, which was bad enough. Missing my morning coffee at the office to meet Kong was a terrible mistake; if I could only turn back the clock just a little to take my coffee. I should not have rushed over the moment Kong called; I should have made Kong wait just a few seconds while I take a sip of coffee, just one tiny sip.

"Well, Socky said he wanted to do a study of Oderland society and economy." I tried to put some sense into Kong.

"But why start with a funeral? You tell me."

"I don't think he meant to start with a funeral; it so happened that there was a funeral."

"There are funerals everyday!"

"I know, but someone must've told him about that funeral, and he probably thought it a good idea to attend and learn something."

"Nonsense! Look, I'm never wrong in my assessment of a person's motive. Let me ask you, what does a funeral mean?" Without waiting for my reply, Kong continued, "It means death; he deals in death and he wants to know how we handle it."

"I'm sorry, but how would that be useful to him?"

"Right, good question. Now answer that, you fool," said the imaginary Kate, looking at the real Kong. "How would that be useful to him? Don't try to change the subject; answer me now. And I mean now!"

"He's a terrorist, Ken. Isn't the answer obvious?" said Kong.

"But a terrorist's mission is accomplished once he has caused the destruction he intended. He doesn't care about what comes after, the funeral part."

"You're naïve, Ken. What has happened tells me this: he wants to know whether we would be able to handle a large number of deaths in a terrorist strike." Kong raised a thick forefinger for emphasis.

"Er . . . I don't think terrorists care about whether we can handle a large number of funerals."

"I know what I'm talking about." Kong was visibly annoyed. "It ties in with whether we can handle a big emergency, when there'll be a large number of dead and injured. If we can handle a large number of funerals, then it's likely we can also handle a large number of injured. If we're well prepared in one area, then we're probably also well prepared in a related area. You get me?"

73

"No!" said the imaginary Kate vehemently.

"Yes," I said unconvincingly.

"That's a half-hearted yes," said Kong.

"Tell him no, Ken," pleaded the imaginary Kate. "Let him explain it all over again; let him explain till he's blue in the face."

"Well, er . . . now I understand what you're trying to say," I said.

"Trying to say?" said Kong. "I'm not trying to say anything; I'm actually telling you the facts! Don't you doubt my assessment of the situation."

"You call bullshit facts?" said the imaginary Kate, looking sternly at Kong and pointing an interrogative finger at him.

"Why are you smiling? What's so funny?" said Kong.

"Oh, er . . . nothing. Anyway, Socky was also surprised that we had the Social Welfare Extension Fund."

"Crouching Liar; it's about time we exercised some code discipline and call him by his codename. This is serious."

"Sorry, Crouching Liar. He was surprised we had SWEF."

"Was he impressed? I'm glad he now knows we're prepared for everything, including things that people in other countries overlook."

"He didn't seem too impressed."

"I'm not surprised; you can never impress people like him. He's incapable of being impressed with anything except his own deeds."

"He couldn't understand, first, why we should be compelled by law to save for our funeral and, second, why we should save so much for it."

I would have preferred not to talk about funerals early in the morning, especially when I had not even had my cup of coffee; but I could not avoid the subject; it was not up to me.

"A proper funeral is important because we're a traditional society," said Kong, as if I needed to be told about Orderland society. "Therefore, it's only right that we all save for our funeral. Who can argue with the logic behind this? Our terrorist mole may not know this, but we all know the cost of funerals is rising astronomically here. So, we need a law to make people save a good part of their income for their funeral; otherwise, who would save so much for their funeral? You don't expect a man earning only twenty thousand dollars a year to save a hundred thousand for his funeral, do you? It's simple logic; every child can understand this." Kong rolled his eyes.

"But he didn't understand the SWEF system, so he said he'd test it, although he probably had not figured out how to."

"He wants to test the SWEF system? That's serious! The SWEF is at the very heart of our social security. Hmm . . . everything's falling into place; I sense that he's up to no good. Listen, we've to be vigilant; he might plant a bomb at the SWEF headquarters."

"I don't think he meant that."

"How do you know? Did he say he wouldn't plant a bomb? We must plan for all eventualities, always!"

I always felt oppressed and drained every time I had a long, heated discussion with Kong, partly because only he was allowed to dissipate his heat, whereas I had to suppress mine and, worse, absorb his. My neurons were firing away in frustration and anger, and my imagination became more vivid.

"Oh, come on! Did he say he'd plant a bomb?" said the imaginary Kate, laughing incredulously and shaking her head. "How did you jump from testing to bombing? That's a very big jump. Anyway, he said he wanted to test the system, not test the SWEF building, you fool!"

"What are you thinking?" said Kong. "I seem to see steam rising from your head . . . must be the tears in my eyes playing tricks; I'm so angry."

"You're angry?" said the imaginary Kate. "Hah! We're the ones who should be angry." The imaginary Kate brandished a high-heel shoe at Kong.

"Why are you smiling again?" said Kong. "You're nuts this morning!"

"Well . . . nothing, I'll keep an eye on him," I said sheepishly, and hoping to assure Kong that I would carry out my task and so end the conversation.

"Keep asking him how he'll test the SWEF system; I want some answers from him."

*

"Ken, are you there? Pick up your phone." There was no reply. Kate wondered where could I be so early in the morning. She was lost in thought and nibbling a muffin when Socky came to her desk.

"Kate, the opportunity has come," said Socky, smiling.

"What opportunity? I've been looking for Ken the last hour; he seems to have vanished into thin air."

"Maybe he's with the General; that's why he can't answer your call. Now, as I was saying, the opportunity has come. I'll explain to you as we go, but it's what we've been waiting for."

"I'm not aware I've been waiting for anything, and where are we going?"

"Come, come," said Socky excitedly. "We mustn't miss this one; believe me, it's what we've been waiting for."

"As I've just said, I'm not aware I've been waiting for anything. May I know what are you up to?"

"Remember Mabel, the one who came to us some time ago with her problem?" said Socky, as they both walked out of the office to Kate's car. "We're going to meet her and her father and try to solve her problem . . . well, actually her father's problem."

"Where am I driving us to?"

"Oh, sorry, we're meeting them at the SWEF branch office at Echo Hill."

It wasn't a long journey. When they arrived, there were only a few vehicles in the car park. Echo Hill was a quiet place, and the SWEF branch office occupied an old, one-storey building that looked like it needed a new coat of paint. Mabel and her father, a frail man over seventy, were inside waiting for Kate and Socky. There were a few other people, all waiting their turn and looking bored, despite the Michael Jackson songs played again and again in the background.

"Hi Socky, hi Kate, thank you for coming; I'm so glad to see you. It's so kind of you both to take time off to help us," said Mabel, who then introduced her father to Kate and Socky. "That's our queue number; you arrived just in time."

A woman in her forties was behind the counter hard at work shuffling papers. "Oh, it's you again; I remember you," said the woman to Mabel.

"I'm glad you remember me; it'll save me from having to explain everything all over again. I've brought with me more stuff," said Mabel, taking out a stack of old documents from her briefcase. The stack of slightly dusty old documents seemed to frighten the woman, who recoiled reflexively.

"But I've told you the last time we can't consider your father's application."

"Yes, but now I've more documents; please take a look at these," said Mabel, trying to hand over her stack of old documents, but the woman would not touch it.

"You don't understand; it's not because you had insufficient documents previously. Your father's application simply can't be entertained," said the woman in exasperation, as if she was about to drop everything and flee from her desk.

"Why don't you take a look at these documents?" repeated Mabel, trying to hand over the documents again, but without success.

Before we proceed further, may I record our conversation?" said the woman as she took out her cellphone.

"Is it a practice here to record conversations?" asked Mabel.

"No, but your case is special; it has given me a lot of trouble and I'm doing this on my personal initiative to protect myself."

"In that case I'd like to record our conversation too," said Mabel, as she took out her cellphone. Her recording was a great help in my subsequent investigation and writing.

"Now, I don't have to look at your documents; they won't be helpful to you," said the woman.

"You wouldn't know if you've not seen them," said Mabel, as she thrust the stack forward.

The woman jerked her hands away, as if trying to avoid a hot pan. "I know what I'm saying; they're not relevant," she said.

The stack of documents went back and forth, with Mabel trying repeatedly to hand them over, while the woman kept her hands well away and Mabel having to retract her arms to prevent them from tiring.

"We're getting nowhere," said Kate. "She doesn't have the authority to change anything." Then, turning to the woman, Kate asked, "Could we see the person in charge here?"

"Why do you want to see him? He'd tell you the same thing; the application can't be entertained," said the woman, now starting to sweat, as if the oppressive equatorial heat outside had invaded the air-conditioned interior of the premises.

"I think it'd be easier for you and everybody if we see the person in charge here," said Kate.

"But it wouldn't make any difference in the end," said the woman.

"Let us worry about that; could we see the person in charge?" said Kate.

"If that's what you really want," sighed the woman, who then rose heavily and went into a room behind. After a while, she emerged from the room with a thin man, about fifty years of age, his eyes darting about nervously, as if trying not to walk into a trap.

"How could I help you?" said the thin man, squeezing and playing with his hands.

"My father is applying for exemption from paying his SWEF," said Mabel.

"That's not possible; I understand that my officer has explained to you on a previous occasion, as well as today."

"Well, I've brought with me these documents," said Mabel.

"I'm afraid they won't make any difference. Your father can't apply for exemption. You see, as far as SWEF is concerned, exemptions don't exist; nobody is allowed any exemption."

"But my account with SWEF has over two hundred and fifty thousand dollars," said Mabel's father in a soft, shaky voice.

"That may be so, but you can't apply for exemption; nobody applies for exemption. We don't even have a form for exemption."

"If I may help," said Socky, "the average funeral here costs about a hundred thousand dollars, but this gentleman has over two hundred and fifty thousand dollars in his SWEF account."

"Saving for a funeral is essential; it's good for him."

"I know, thank you for your invaluable advice, but he has over two hundred and fifty thousand dollars in his account with SWEF. That's over a quarter of a million dollars." Socky thought the figure was convincing enough to wrap up the argument, but the thin man was not impressed.

"Yes, the more savings he has, the better it'd be for him. It's the same for everyone."

"But sir," said Mabel's father, "I'm gonna die only once."

"Yes, but the money in your SWEF account will be transferred to the SWEF accounts of your beneficiaries, your wife and children, after you've passed away," said the thin man, playing with his fingers.

"But sir, I'm not saving for their funerals and don't intend to."

"That's not right, you've to plan for everything; you've to be responsible for yourself and your family," said the thin man. "Anyway, SWEF is planning for you, even if you're not planning for yourself."

"I plan not to save for my wife's and children's funerals." Mabel's father was trying to raise his voice, but failed.

"You don't seem to understand," said the thin man, "saving for your funeral is good for you."

"But I'm afraid it's you who don't seem to understand," said Socky. "He has too much money in his SWEF account. Anyway, we're not asking you to make a decision. All we're asking is that you forward the application to your superiors. You don't have to speak on our behalf or say anything good about the application. Please, just forward it to your superiors; that's all we're asking."

"It can't be done."

"I don't understand this; what do you mean it can't be done?"

"It can't be done."

"Why not?" said Socky. "Surely it can be done; I'm sure you send papers to your superiors and meet them every now and then, don't you?"

"No, no, no, it can't be done."

"Excuse me, are you saying you can't send papers to your superiors or see them?" said Socky.

"Haven't I seen you before?" said the thin man.

"I don't think so," said Socky. "And what has this got to do with what we're discussing?"

"You're intimidating me," said the thin man.

"No, I'm not; I'm just trying to explain to you . . ."

"You're intimidating me; I've seen you before."

"What have I done that would amount to intimidating you?"

80

"I've seen you before. You're here to intimidate me; they've brought you here to intimidate me."

"That's not true!" said Mabel, pressing her hands hard on the counter and leaning forward.

"I've not done anything," said Socky. "Why are you talking nonsense?"

"Saving for a funeral is good for you; intimidation will not change anything."

"I'm not intimidating you."

"Yes, you are; they've brought you here to intimidate me."

"That's not true!" said Mabel, raising her voice.

"What have I done to intimidate you?"

"You look dangerous; you *are* dangerous."

"You're going off on a tangent," said Socky. "Now, please don't change the subject; we're talking about applying for an exemption for this gentleman here."

"There's nothing to apply for; there's no exemption, it doesn't exit. Saving for a funeral is good for you." The thin man started to sweat, although there was nothing wrong with the air-conditioning. He took out a handkerchief and dabbed his forehead. "You can't apply for an exemption, and that's final."

"Excuse me, it's not final just because you say so," said Socky.

"Saving for a funeral is good for you."

"I know, but this gentleman has saved for it two and a half times over; he will not need two and a half funerals, I guarantee you this," answered Socky, by then even his bushy moustache seemed to be fuming.

"Saving for a funeral is good for you," repeated the thin man.

"You can't answer me by repeating yourself," said Socky. "We've tried to make you see our point by approaching the problem from different angles, so you've got to meet us at all the different angles and not just repeat yourself. You're not answering us; please answer us."

"Saving for a funeral is good for you. Saving for a funeral is good for you. Saving . . . ." Then, still repeating himself, the thin man turned pale and began to sweat at an alarming rate; his eyes started to spin, and his body stiffened and his face was like a mask, without expression. Then he spoke in another voice. He said the words about saving for a funeral over and over again, but in a different voice, a metallic voice, lifeless. Before anyone could recover from their shock, the thin man started to move about in a mechanical way, like he was doing a break dance, but without any joy or life, although his movements appeared to synchronize with the background music, which suddenly seemed louder.

"My God, what's going on?" said Socky in shock.

The thin man came from behind the counter to the waiting area; everyone moved aside for him, who did not seem conscious of what he was doing. The other people in the office were standing along the walls, as far away from the thin man as possible; one woman fled screaming. Then strange, piercing noise emanated from the thin man; it sounded like machine parts moving without sufficient lubrication.

"How could such noise come from him? He's flesh and blood, not a machine," said Kate, as she whipped out her cellphone to record the strange scene.

"It doesn't sound like his voice, but it's from him," said Socky.

In between repeating the words about saving for a funeral, the thin man was making the strange, piercing noise, which made his movements appear even more mechanical. The thin man turned his head left and right repeatedly in a robotic manner. Then he did what appeared to be a moonwalk, but without the liveliness of a dance; he also moved forward and sideway like a robot. Then to the shock of everyone, the thin man went out of the building into the car park.

"Hey, this is dangerous! I don't think he's aware of what he's doing," said Socky.

"What's going on?" asked Mabel.

"I don't know,' said Socky.

"The Robot Syndrome!" Kate screamed.

"The Robot Syndrome?" said Socky and Mabel at the same time.

"Yes, the Robot Syndrome; it causes people to behave like a robot. We've to call Dr Jade Choice." Kate was fumbling with her cellphone trying to make a call.

The thin man had become a robot-man. While waiting for Dr Choice, the people at the SWEF branch could only watch and follow the robot-man, trying to ensure that he did not go out of the car park onto the road, which would have been most dangerous for him. As the robot-man moved about haphazardly like an automaton, he was pursued by a small crowd trying to shoo him off the gates leading to the road.

"Socky, close the gates!" shouted Kate.

Socky ran to the gates and closed them as fast as he could, just in time to prevent the robot-man from getting out onto the road. The robot-man bumped into a gate and changed direction abruptly, just like a robot.

"Shall we bundle him up and bring him into the building?" said Socky. "Letting him roam about here is risky; he might knock into something and hurt himself."

"Okay, you go first and I'll help you," said Kate.

As Socky and Kate approached the robot-man, the rest followed. Then, as if in self-defense, the robot-man stopped moving forward and started to spin round and round. As he did so, his stiffened, outstretched arms rose slowly over his head. Then they came down, and then up again. As his spinning body gained momentum, so did his arms, until they were flapping.

"I'll tackle him low," said Socky.

"No, Socky, this is hard ground; he could hit his head," said Kate.

The crowd hesitated, not knowing what to do. Then the robot-man stopped spinning his body and flapping his arms, and moved off, saying over and over again in a robotic voice, "Saving for a funeral is good for you. Saving for a funeral is good for you. Saving . . ."

As Socky was scratching his head, wondering what to do with the robot-man, loud wails of siren cascaded down the road. An ambulance and a number of police cars raced to the gates before some policemen appeared and stormed the compound. Some medics also appeared and the crowd pointed out the robot-man to them. They tackled the robot-man and pinned him to the ground. A very confident woman appeared out of nowhere and whipped out a syringe, also seemingly out of nowhere, and deftly jabbed it into the robot-man.

"That should calm him down," said the woman.

"Dr. Choice, am I glad to see you!" said Kate, relief written all over her face.

"You've just seen an attack of the Robot Syndrome," said Dr. Choice.

"It sure is an unforgettable experience," said Kate.

"I've no doubt about that," said Dr. Choice. "I hope it didn't frighten you too much. We're not sure what caused the disease. People who are of a certain mindset are prone to it. They're very inflexible and defensive, and feel oppressed easily; they can't accept certain realities and are easily in denial. When they are unable to cope with a challenge, they feel oppressed and stressed to breaking point. Once that is reached, they act like a robot to escape what they had perceived as unbearable oppression; they hope to remain in their comfort zone and deny reality. Often, the first sign of an attack is when the victim keeps repeating himself to emphasize his stand; it's a defensive act; the person is denying reality. The victim keeps repeating his stand in the hope that by doing so it becomes reality, and the challenge to his stand would hopefully back off and go away."

"This is the first time I've come across this; it's crazy, absolutely crazy," said Socky, scribbling on his notebook.

"Dr. Choice is the discoverer of the Robot Syndrome and its foremost expert," said Kate.

"It's a newly discovered illness, although it must have been with us for some time," said Dr. Choice, watching as the thin man, lying motionless on a stretcher, was wheeled to the ambulance, the robot in him gone.

Chapter 6

There were only the three of us in the room, but Kate was about as comfortable as a sardine in a can, while Kong was glum and in no mood to listen to any explanation, even a reasonable one. I did what I could to help Kate, but I was not at the SWEF branch at Echo Hill when the thin man became the robot-man, so I could only do so much. Kate must have felt exposed, like getting caught in a sniper's sight in an open field, with the nearest cover a hundred meters away.

"What the hell happened? You were supposed to keep an eye on him, not let him run wild," said Kong, face red from a vein-busting combination of anger and frustration. "He turned someone into a robot! That's inexcusable; I can't imagine the mayhem. We're the laughing stock of the world; I don't know where to hide my face!"

"It's not Socky's fault," said Kate. "That SWEF guy was afflicted with Robot Syndrome; Socky didn't give him the disease."

"Don't try to cover up for him. He caused the whole thing; he caused the mayhem. It's fortunate no one was injured or killed."

"I don't know what more can I say; Socky didn't give that guy Robot Syndrome."

"Well, er . . . I think Kate's right; it's not Socky's fault," I said. "I mean . . ."

"Then it's nobody's fault? You stay out of this, Ken, or I'll show you the way out of the company. You think I'm a fool? Don't you two dare gang up on me. Now, I want you to listen carefully; I don't want any more nonsense, you understand? You're supposed to keep an eye on him; not let him run riot. Your job is to nail Crouching Liar, not let him nail us in the eyes of the world. Is that clear?"

Kate was about to argue further when I stopped her by cutting in and managing to say, "Well . . ."

Arguing with the other top men of Croctopus was one thing, but arguing with Kong was a different matter altogether, especially when he was angry. Kate could have gotten into very serious trouble and I felt, as her supervisor, a duty to protect her. I had been in Croctopus long enough to know that it would have been a futile exercise to quarrel with Kong. When an argument got heated, he would never back down and lose face. Anyway, assigning blame for a stranger's disease should not have been discussed at all; it had nothing to do with our task of monitoring Socky. My thoughts must have traveled through the air, because Kate looked at me and seemed to know what I was thinking, and she did not proceed further.

"Now listen, so far we've not caught Crouching Liar with a smoking gun," said Kong. "This investigation is not moving fast enough. We're just fighting fire; that guy lights a fire and we move in to put it out. That's not good enough; I want this investigation to move, to go somewhere. I want something solid, if not a smoking gun, then at least a gun. Right now, we've nothing. We all know he's a terrorist mole, but the rest of the world doesn't. We've to convince people, and we can't convince anyone if we've nothing to show. Also, it's not him alone; we want to uncover his network and smash it. Right now, as far as the rest of the world is concerned, what we've got amounts to a big, fat zero!"

Why is this guy telling me this? I thought.

"You hear me? What are you thinking about?" asked Kong.

"Oh, don't we have anything more from Chatterbig?" I said quickly, trying to take Kong's focus away from us.

"He's an unreliable fellow. There's no steady stream of intelligence from him. As Colonel Loon said, if he needs money, he'd produce something, and probably not everything, just bits and pieces of what he has. I don't know more than you do about Chatterbig. All we've got from him so far is that one bit of intelligence leading to Crouching Liar."

"If we don't have anything from Chatterbig or anyone, we can't do much more than monitor Socky and hope that he'd lead us somewhere," I said.

"Crouching Liar," said Kong, looking irritated.

"Sorry, Crouching Liar." Look, stop playing James Bond, I thought.

"Something came to my mind during breakfast this morning," said Kong.

Something always comes to his mind during breakfast, I thought.

"I was thinking . . . we can set a trap for him."

"A trap? But we're not the OSD or the police," I said. "It's beyond us; we have neither the expertise nor the police powers." He's mad or what? I thought.

"Of course it's well within our capabilities. We're Croctopus, the biggest corporation in Orderland. What's beyond our grasp? We bite like a crocodile and strangle like an octopus. We can do anything we want." Kong's head seemed to have swelled and his chest seemed puffed up; pride was written all over his face. "Even a farmer or fisherman can set a trap, so why can't we?"

Right, madman, you'd get us into big trouble, I thought. "It's different in our case; it'd involve a fair bit of deception against another person," I added. "I'm not sure we should go this far; we're not the OSD."

"The OSD, the OSD! I've just said we're Croctopus, the biggest corporation in the country! Besides, our terrorist mole is right here in our midst; we're on the front lines and the OSD is counting on us to deliver."

Now, don't be funny, I thought. "Why don't we let the OSD set the trap?" I said. "After all, they've the authority; they can to do a lot of things that we can't do."

"Look Ken, I've just said even the OSD is counting on us. Don't argue with me. We'll set a trap for Crouching Liar, and that's it."

"What's the trap you have in mind?" I asked.

"I don't have anything in mind. Don't you ask me silly questions, you understand?"

Great, he doesn't have anything in mind, I thought.

Kate looked at me and seemed to know what I was thinking, as she tried to suppress a smile. "So where do we go from here?" she asked.

"You two go think about it and come back to me in a few days; I want a trap."

That's it? I thought. That simple?

Kate and I left Kong's room and discussed the latest instruction as we walked to our desks. "Set a trap; it's so easy to give an order like that," I said, snapping my fingers. "He thinks we're trappers from the wild. Anyway, trapping a man to expose his secrets is totally different from trapping an animal. To set a trap, you've got to know something about the man—his habits, his routine, his likes and dislikes, his fears and hopes. But we know nothing about Socky. How could the General expect us to set a trap in such circumstances? He's totally unrealistic."

"The whole idea is silly, but it looks like we can't escape this one," said Kate with a sigh. "Anyway, we have a few days before the General breathes down on us again. Let's think about it and discuss later."

As I drove home from work, my mind was full of the day's events, especially Kong's order to set a trap for Socky, so much so I had to make a mental note to drive carefully. No matter which angle I viewed the problem from, I could not get away from the fact that we had very little to go on. The Croctopus people hardly knew Socky. I could not turn to anyone for more information about him; we did not have a handle on the problem. Socky was too elusive; the whole thing was too elusive, but Kong had given his order and he expected an answer in a matter of days, and I knew he would accept no excuses. From my experience working in Croctopus, I knew that a fair answer would always be better than no answer; some kind of trap that could produce some evidence against Socky would be better than no trap. I kept my eyes on the road intently as I knew accidents could happen in a moment's carelessness, but the problem of fashioning a trap kept coming to the forefront of my mind; it kept expanding and threatening to fill my entire consciousness. I tried my best to concentrate on the road and resisted further thoughts about any trap. Yet, the problem would not go away; I felt as if I had become addicted to it within a day. I needed to fashion some kind of trap, I thought; not a perfect trap, maybe not even a good trap, but just some kind of trap. I realized that I was setting a very low standard for myself. How did I come to that? I had always set high standards for myself; now I was thinking of setting what would amount to a shadow of a trap, not a real trap that would snare a meaty prey, but some kind of contraption that I could pass off as a trap to a demanding boss. I felt trapped myself, as if I was entangled in a web, with a giant spider lurking unseen, ready to pounce. And how did I become more concerned with an unnecessary, stupid problem than the real problem of unmasking a terrorist mole? I had no answer.

By the time I was at the doorstep of my house, my mind was reeling from traps, strategies, intelligence gathering and more. I had no answer to my problem; I did not even have a germ of an answer to start with. I took out my key wearily and opened the door.

"Stop! Wait! Don't come in, I've just vacuumed the floor; take off your shoes first," said my wife Arm. Then she continued her conversation on her cellphone.

"Daddy! Daddy!" cried my daughter Mei, ten years old, and son Min, eight. They surrounded me, jumped about and tugged at me for attention. It was the same each time I came home, but I would not have it any other way. I savored the moment, taking it in and letting it fill my whole self. They would grow up quickly and have their own interests and friends, and not be paying me so much attention anymore, so I wanted to enjoy every bit of their company now. Every time I was with them, the office problems would just melt away. But this time there was something nagging at me; this time my office problems were different—they were really national security problems and that had implications for my family. I was lost in thought.

"That box on the floor has been there for two days," said Arm, cellphone still in hand. "Remember to bring it to your office tomorrow."

"I wasn't planning to bring it to the office; they're just small items that I want to donate for a charity auction."

"But the box has been there for two days."

"It's just a small box; it's not much bigger than the microwave oven in the kitchen, as you can see."

"You call that a small box? It's a big box and it's gathering dust."

"It's no dustier than any other item in the house. Anyway, the amount of dust in the house is the same with or without the box."

"But it's gathering dust; it's been gathering dust for two days, and that's a lot of dust."

"Come on, our house is not that dirty. Anyway, I'll bring it to the auction organizers on Monday."

"No, take it away tomorrow."

"The organizers have fixed Monday for collection."

"Then put it in the car boot in the meantime."

"There's no point filling up the car boot. What's the point of the driving the box around in the car for the next few days?"

"At least it won't gather dust in the house."

We carried on arguing until dinner time, when peace returned. After dinner, in the quiet of the night, and after the children had gone to bed and Arm was attending to her own things, the problem of setting a trap for Socky came back to me. It came uninvited and sat in my mind like an enigmatic box gathering dust, refusing to go away. I searched the day's newspapers for an article by some management guru that I had come across in the morning on how to solve problems. I did not think it would solve my trap problem, but I was hoping it would spark off an idea or two.

"Why are you reading the papers?" said Arm. "Haven't you read them in the morning?"

"I'm reading this article on how to solve problems."

"You can't solve problems by reading. Why don't you vacuum the bedroom?"

"I thought you've just vacuumed the floor?"

"That was some time ago."

"But I'll be washing the floor in two days," I said.

"You can still vacuum it today; it's better than sitting around doing nothing."

"I'm not doing nothing."

"You should do something more important."

"Vacuuming a clean floor is more important than reading?"

Arm stormed off to do something important in the storeroom. I finished the newspaper article, but found it too shallow and unhelpful. I reviewed in my mind everything we had known about Socky. Well, what had we known about Socky? Practically nothing. He was an American who used to work on communications and he looked like somebody well-known, but that was about it. We did not know his habits or his likes and dislikes, and we did not know his beliefs. Out of desperation, I took some old self-help books from a shelf to help me work out the trap. I wanted to saturate my mind with the problem and the possible ways to solve it, and then let the mixture come up with a solution while I was asleep. After some time, my eyes got heavy and I went to bed.

I was awakened from my half-sleep by a loud noise and bright lights. It was Arm vacuuming the bedroom floor, holding the suction pipe in one hand and a cellphone in the other, complaining to, I think, her mother.

"Why are you vacuuming the floor?" I stretched for the clock on the table.

"Because it's dirty; how could you sleep in all that dirt?"

"What dirt?" I managed to say in a semi-conscious state.

"You're so unlike my brothers and sisters. Whenever they're home from the office, they'd always find something to do. They'd clean the house, and after that look for more things to do. How could you sleep when I'm working? What's the meaning of this? You don't behave like a husband at all."

"But you don't have to do any work at this time; it's midnight. You're probably the only person in the country vacuuming the floor right now."

"I never knew I'd marry such a lazy man. You should be working when I'm working. I'm now working my head off and you're sleeping; I'm not getting any support from you; there's a whole list of things to do."

"Don't give me any midnight agenda; save midnight for life-and-death tasks or for sleep. I sleep when it's time to sleep." I resumed sleeping in something like factory condition. But I did not sleep well, turning about in bed the whole night. When the

93

clock alarm went off at six o'clock in the morning, I took longer than usual to silence it before resuming my sleep. Then, ten minutes later, the alarm went off from a second clock. I had to get up this time—I had never disobeyed the second alarm. As soon as I got out of bed, Kong or, rather, his trap problem came and clung onto me and refused to let go.

Then, to my surprise, Arm opened her eyes and said, "Remember to take that box away," before closing her eyes and resuming sleep.

I struggled with the trap problem and Arm's reminder in my mind while going to the children's rooms to wake them up for school—it was just the first wake-up call. They had never woken up on the first call, even with all the lights switched on. I washed up before going back to the children's rooms for a second call, which was always a racket. I tickled them, rocked them, pulled their legs and carried them bodily up from their beds. When they were finally up, I had to stand guard over their beds; otherwise, they would dive back in. Eventually, they sleepwalked their way to wash. Arm was also up to prepare breakfast, no doubt eyeing the box on the way to the kitchen. When it was time to leave for school and office, I went into the bedroom and grabbed my briefcase. I looked at the box, but did not want to start the day with a meaningless task, so I left it where it was and went off with the children. After dropping them off, I drove slowly to the office, thinking about the trap problem all the time. I was at my desk no more than five minutes when Kate came to discuss the trap.

"I had saturated my mind with this trap problem, hoping it'd work out a solution while I was asleep, but nothing came of it," I said.

"You always work this way," said Kate with a chuckle. "I'm not sure whether to call it the smart way or the lazy way."

"The smart way, of course; it works, sometimes."

"Oh really? I must try it someday. I'm afraid I've not been able to come up with any trap either; when your brain has too little to work on, it can't come up with a solution."

"The problem, of course, is that it's not reasonable to expect us to come up with a trap when we've nothing to work on. Why can't people be reasonable? Is it so difficult to be reasonable? I was bothered by this the whole of last night; it was a great bother."

We could make no headway with the trap problem and the conversation drifted to something else. A woman, a new secretary, approached us and, after morning greetings, said, "The General wants to see both of you."

"Oh, that's a surprise, whatever for?" I said.

"I don't really know," said the woman, "but he said you were both supposed to give him an answer to his trap problem. He wants to know what you've come up with." Both Kate and I turned cold; the woman's message ruined our morning.

"I thought he said to take a few days before going back to him," I said.

"That's right; a few days, not one day."

"I don't really know; he looked like he was expecting an answer now," said the woman.

"Trouble, trouble, trouble," I said with a sigh.

"Big trouble," said Kate.

Kong did not look happy when Kate and I entered the room, but did not look unhappy either. It was one of those moods that could swing either way, depending on how people handled him. The only consolation for us was that it was early morning, and Kong was not likely to have met anyone or come across anything that would have made him unhappy. Actually, early morning after breakfast was the safest time to meet him. Still, that expressionless face was a bit disconcerting, because the only safe face of Kong was a happy face.

"What a lousy breakfast I had this morning," said Kong.

That's it, we're in big trouble, I told myself in my mind.

"That's worse than no breakfast," said Kong.

Now we're really finished, I thought.

"Maybe you'd like another breakfast, General," said Kate hopefully.

"Why should anyone take two breakfasts? Anyway, I'm in no mood for another breakfast. Actually, I'm in a foul mood."

That's it, man; that's it, I thought.

"What's that you're saying?" said Kong.

"Oh, er . . . nothing," I replied with an unconvincing grin.

"How could it be nothing when your lips were moving and you were saying something?"

"It's just something I was thinking about; I didn't know I was verbalizing my thought."

"You were supposed to come back to me on the trap for our terrorist mole," said Kong.

"But you told us to take a few days," I said.

"Did I? I don't remember giving you a few days."

"Yes, you did," said Kate.

"Yes, you told us to take a few days; I can confirm that," I said.

"It doesn't matter what you can or cannot confirm; I just told you I don't remember giving you a few days. And that means I didn't give you a few days."

"But, General, you did tell us to take a few days," I said desperately.

"Don't argue with me early in the morning, especially when I didn't have a decent breakfast. Now, both of you, tell me about the trap you've come up with."

We're truly finished, I thought. "Well, er . . . the problem is that we had very little to go on. You see . . ."

"Are you telling me you've not done anything? I've just told you I had a lousy breakfast and I'm in a foul mood, so don't make it worse. When I give you an assignment, I expect you to work on it."

"Of course, we've been working on it," I said, "but . . ."

"So, where's the trap?"

"Well, er . . . you see, we thought you gave us . . ." I said.

"Well, what about it?" said Kong, clearly running out of patience.

"You see, it's a little difficult to put in words. Our thoughts are just rudimentary at this stage, having only one day." I thought it necessary to keep hinting at 'one day' as much as possible.

"I know you've been thinking; but what have you got now? Don't explain to me your thought process; just give me the trap."

I knew Kong well enough not to insist that he had actually given us a few days. That would have been like kicking sand onto a man's face. So, I had to argue on his terms; it was not up to me to say what had been his instruction, it was up to him. The truth did not matter; what was deemed as the truth depended on Kong's perception, not ours.

"Yes, the trap . . . We had a very short time; so we couldn't really come up with much. We should start from the beginning," I said as I held my hands at chest height, as if about to outline a cubical trap in the air. "A trap is only as effective as the knowledge we have of the prey."

"Cut out all that reasoning process. Kate, maybe you could explain it better; tell me about the trap that you and Ken have come up with."

"Me? Oh, well . . . er . . . like Ken has just said, a trap is only as effective as the knowledge we have of the prey."

"Not all that laborious stuff! Just give me the trap! Are you two hallucinating or what?"

"Hallucinating? Oh no . . . . We don't hallucinate; ha, ha . . ." I said. My mind was working at double its normal speed, desperate to grab at any straw. "That's it! Hallucinating!" At that moment, I pointed a finger unconsciously at Kong, then quickly withdrawing it when I realized what I was doing. "You see, if we could somehow get Socky . . . I mean, Crouching Liar to hallucinate."

97

"Right! That's right, then he'll spill the beans; he'll tell us everything," said Kate.

"You're quick, Kate" I said.

"You too," said Kate, trying to keep a straight face.

"Why are you two talking with each other as if I don't exist? Talk with me. Don't you . . . Hmm, make him hallucinate; that's interesting."

"Let him hear voices," I said. "That'll disorientate him and lower his guard; you know, voices coming out of the walls, perhaps."

"That's too far-fetched; who hears voices from walls?" said Kong.

"It may not be that far-fetched; it could happen," said Kate.

"I know something's far-fetched when I hear it; don't argue with me. Only mad people hear walls speak." Kong laughed loudly. "I'm in a good mood already. So, how do you both propose to make our terrorist mole hear voices?"

Chapter 7

The battle was ferocious, the shooting non-stop; bullets whizzed left and right, throwing up sand when they hit the ground. People dropped dead faster than one could keep count. The battle raged on for a long time with no end in sight; I could almost smell the gunpowder. I opened two cans of Tiger beer and handed one to Socky, who gulped a mouthful immediately.

"You've a collection of these movies?" asked Socky.

"No, as a matter of fact, this is the only one I have."

The whole train of families trekking west, carrying all their possessions and hopes, was destroyed save for a single family, which had managed to slip away in the midst of battle and escaped the slaughter. Even the horses were not spared; they were either dead or taken away. The tribal chief, whom his enemies derogatorily called 'Come, Me Kill' was mounted on his horse, All See, the pride of his tribe. The chief raised his rifle over his head and yelled, "Come, me kill! Come, me kill!" before tugging the rein and calling out in forced accent, "All See, let's go!" and riding off into the wind.

A man stood on a boulder some distance away and surveyed the scene of carnage; nothing was left standing, everything was destroyed. Smoke billowed from the charred remains on the ground; the smell of death filled the air and attacked the nose mercilessly. Rifle in hand, the man knew it was too late to re-enter the battle to help the other families; it was best to hide where he was until dark, when he and his family could continue their journey west. The sad, forlorn look on the man's face said it all. A woman and three children emerged from behind the boulder to join him. All of them stood there watching, saying nothing. They kept their thoughts to themselves, yet somehow sharing them with one another. They were all alone in the vast plain.

When movie ended, it was only eight o'clock in the evening, so we sat around to enjoy more beer and talked. "Hey, I heard you turned someone into a robot," I said, trying to delve deeper into Socky's mind.

"No, no, rubbish, all rubbish. That guy was already a robot, a closet robot, before I met him. I merely took him out of the closet into the sunlight."

"Sure."

"Of course, that's about all I did. What do I know about robotics? I've never even built a scarecrow, not to mention a moving, talking robot." Socky gulped another mouthful of beer, which left a layer of white foam on his moustache. "Hey, this is good."

"I heard that you had intimidated him so much that he'd rather be a robot than submit himself to further intimidation."

"No, no, no. That's a wild rumor. After it had gone around a few times, everything's distorted."

"Sure."

"It's true, absolutely true." Socky took another gulp of beer from his can.

"Why did you try to test the Social Welfare Extension Fund system?"

100

"I just wanted to help somebody. Well, maybe also to see whether SWEF was responsive; you know, whether it was cruising along on auto-pilot, dishing out the same stuff year in, year out with nobody questioning anything."

"So, what did you find?"

"Well, I found a robot; that's what I found. Actually, two robots, because other than the robot-man, I also found SWEF to be a robot, lumbering along unstoppable, with a life of its own."

*

The usual Croctopus terrorist hunters were at the boardroom with the OSD's Colonel Lenny Loon.

"Colonel Loon, thank you very much for arranging this," said Kong, who appeared relaxed and in a good mood.

"It's my duty to help," said Lenny Loon. "This is the first time we're using the services of Professor Spinner; the hypnotist whose services we usually use is on vacation. Spinner is not really a professor; it's just a title he gives himself for his show. You might have seen it; he's quite a showman. I don't really know how good he is, but I suppose he should be good enough for the task ahead."

I had read something about Spinner sometime ago; I did not have a good impression of him from the article, although I could not remember why. What I could remember was that he was a little hard of hearing. "Spinner's able to get something out of Crouching Liar?" I asked.

"He should; I've briefed him and given him a list of questions to ask. He knows what we want," said Lenny Loon. "Also, during the hypnotism session, we could pass to him notes with further questions that we want our terrorist mole to answer."

"So Spinner knows who Crouching Liar really is and what we're doing?" said Roger.

"Well, to a limited extent, otherwise he wouldn't be able to question our mole effectively," said Lenny Loon. "But he knows just enough and we've sworn him to secrecy; he's aware he shouldn't cross the OSD, so there's nothing to worry."

"If we're all there, wouldn't Socky . . . I mean, Crouching Liar become suspicious?" I asked.

"No, only Professor Spinner will be with him; the rest of us will be at the back of the room, behind curtains. When he has been hypnotized, we'll come out and join the session."

"We're being pretty nasty," said Kate.

"But you and Ken came up with this idea," said Kong.

"Yes, but we're regretting it already," said Kate.

"The security of the country is at stake; what's a little hypnotism?" said Bobby Boon. "Country first. Why are you worried for a terrorist?"

"That's right, country first. It's not the time to be nice," said Sammy Sam.

"Or to doubt or waver," said Sonny Song. "We've a job to do, the country to save."

"Kate, lay to rest your fear that we may be doing something unlawful; the OSD does have the power to attempt such an extraction of information from Crouching Liar," said Kong. "Nobody should doubt this."

"That's a relief," said Kate.

"I was just thinking, aside from this planned hypnotism session, the OSD doesn't seem to be very much involved in the investigation," I said. "It doesn't seem to be taking the lead."

"I can assure you we're very much involved, but we're doing our investigation in parallel to yours," said Lenny Loon. "For our own security reasons, we can't conduct an investigation jointly with you, but we'll render all the help you need."

"Ken, did you manage to get anything out of our terrorist mole when you invited him home for dinner?" asked Kong.

"I'm afraid not, nothing happened; we had dinner, drank beer and watched a movie. I wouldn't say anything out of the ordinary happened. Nothing he said made me sit up and take note."

"Why didn't you prod him more, try to squeeze something out of him?"

"He's a very private guy, not the talkative sort; couldn't get anything out of him. Maybe we'd be luckier at the hypnotism session."

"Roger, you can't attend the hypnotism session?" asked Kong.

"No, I've got a meeting with the minister; I can't cancel this appointment."

"We can handle it," said Kong.

Lenny Loon took out his cellphone and placed it on the table and watched it as though he was waiting for a call. This resulted in the rest watching him watching his cellphone.

"You're expecting something?" asked Kong.

"I'm expecting a message from Chatterbig, but it may not materialize; that's why I didn't inform you earlier."

"You're expecting a message from Chatterbig," said Kong, raising his eyebrows. "It's about time." The atmosphere in the room changed immediately. It was no longer a dreary morning; it was now so charged with excitement and expectation that should Lenny Loon's cellphone come alive, someone could burst into flames.

"This is terribly exciting news," said Roger. "Wow, Chatterbig's sending messages again."

"Or needs money again," said Kate.

"Colonel, you should've informed us of the good news, even if you were not sure whether Chatterbig was really going to call," said Kong in a forgiving tone.

Then Lenny Loon's cellphone came alive, like a little baby kicking vigorously, which caused everyone around the table to lean forward and watch with unblinking eyes Lenny Loon taking his cellphone to read the message. He took a while; he must have re-read it several times.

"What does it say?" asked Kong.

"Someone please take this down," said Lenny Loon. "It says, 'Long box on wheels.' I repeat, 'Long box on wheels.' Have you got it?"

"I've got it," said Kate. She was always the quick one.

"Oh no, not another puzzle!" said Bobby Boon. "What kind of intelligence is this?" Intelligence in the form of a puzzle can be infuriating, especially to people used to having their way immediately.

"Why can't he be more forthcoming? He's getting paid for it, but he's not giving what he's paid for; he's short-changing us," said Sammy Sam.

"I can't make anything out of it; he's not telling us anything," said Sonny Song.

I sat quietly, sometimes staring at the ceiling, avoiding the whiners, trying to figure out the meaning of the message. Kate was scribbling on her notepad, apparently trying to work out something too. Kong creased his eyebrows and rubbed his chin, thinking hard.

Lenny Loon's cellphone came alive again. He snatched it and read, "Death."

"Death?" said Kong unhappily.

"Yes, that's all. 'Death'," said Lenny Loon.

The room exploded with activity and noise; everyone was talking.

"This is maddening. 'Death', what can it mean?" said Bobby Boon.

"Stop all this noise; I'm trying to think," said Kong. "The first message may be enigmatic, but the second message says 'Death' and I don't like it. 'Death' means death; it can't mean anything else."

"This is serious," said Sammy Sam.

104

"Of course, it's serious; that's obvious," said Kong.

"Yes, sir, I'm reminding everyone that death is serious," said Sammy Sam.

Lenny Loon's cellphone came alive once again.

"My goodness, another message!" said Kong.

"It can't be anything good," said Sonny Song. "Why does he keep sending messages like this, in bits and pieces? Now I dread to receive his messages."

Lenny Loon grabbed his cellphone in a lightning movement of his arm and read the message. Then his jaw dropped.

"What does it say?" said Kong.

Lenny Loon was speechless; he stared ahead blankly.

"Colonel Loon, what's the message? Do you hear me?" said Kong.

Lenny Loon moved his lips, but nothing came out.

"Tell us the message," said Kong.

After taking a deep breath, Lenny Loon managed, "W . . . W . . ." Then he stopped.

"Colonel Loon, may I see the message?" I said. But the colonel was gripping his cellphone very tightly. He did not respond to me; he just sat there, face drained white.

"Colonel Loon, tell us the message; you must tell us the message," said Kong.

Lenny Loon moved his lips again. Then, making a great effort, he said, "W . . . W . . ."

"What's that?" said Kong.

"W . . . WM . . ."

"Go on, Colonel Loon, go on," pleaded Kong, face tight with excitement.

"WM . . . WM . . . WMD."

"WMD?" said Kong.

"WMD—weapons of mass destruction?" I said.

A chill raced round the conference room several times. Kong's jaws dropped and he stared blankly at Lenny Loon, who returned the attention with his own blank stare. I sat motionless, not exactly thinking hard, for it was impossible in the circumstances, but trying to connect things in my mind.

After a while, I said, "And 'Long box on wheels' means a mobile container? WMD on a mobile container?"

"God!" screamed Kong, snapping out of his trance-like state.

"I'm going back to OSD headquarters straightaway," said Colonel Loon, jumping up from his seat before dashing out of the room.

"We must get something out of Crouching Liar at the hypnotism session tomorrow. This is serious," said Kong, who also dashed out of the room.

The mood at Croctopus HQ was sombre. None of the Croctopus terrorist hunters could do any fruitful work for the rest of the day. Kate and I spent the whole day discussing Chatterbig's messages.

"Is there really some weapons of mass destruction in our midst? It's hard to believe this," said Kate. "I mean, any time now, we could be blown to bits or die of poison gas or get infected with some dreadful disease and die a slow death. Is this for real? I can't believe this is happening. And save for a few people like us, the whole country doesn't even know about this. This is so unreal."

"How else can you interpret Chatterbig's messages?" I said. "I sure wish there could be some other interpretations, but I can't think of any. It can't mean anything else. 'WMD' can mean only one thing when it comes to terrorism."

"Are we coming to the end of the world, at least our part of the world?" said Kate.

When I arrived home, my mind was in overdrive; I felt that one half of my brain was occupied by thoughts of WMD in a mobile container, and the other half by thoughts of Socky under hypnotism.

The two halves did not seem to mix or communicate; they seemed to be in two separate, sealed compartments. One half of the brain was trying to grapple with the enormity of the situation—WMD in a mobile container under the control of terrorists. The other half had a picture of a man, eyes closed, under hypnotism. There should be a link, but I could not link death and mass destruction with someone who appeared to be sleeping. If only I could shake my head and cause the two separate ingredients to mix, like mixing drinks. As soon as I opened the door and entered the house, Mei and Min dashed out from nowhere and swarmed me. How could two little kids behave like a swarm? It was good to feel swarmed that way. Then I looked at them, lost in thought. How safe are they? Is there really a WMD in the country?

"Daddy, what are you thinking?" asked Mei.

"Oh, just my work."

Then Arm came, waving a little handwritten note. She was talking on her cellphone, so she merely handed me the note. I tried to make sense of what's written as Arm's handwriting was, as usual, illegible—tiny, agitated scribbles and what looked like bean sprouts strewn on a piece of paper. I gave up reading and continued playing with the kids.

After about fifteen minutes, Arm finished talking on her cellphone and turned to me and said, "Hey, I took a long time drawing this up; shouldn't you read it?"

"I tried to, but couldn't make anything of it."

"This is the program for this weekend," said Arm, taking the note and pointing out the items. "On Saturday morning, we'll go marketing with the kids at Mountain Hypermarket. Then, we'll have lunch at Number One Chicken. After lunch we'll go shopping at Orchestra; I heard they're having a sale and things are really cheap; I could spend hours there. After that, we'll visit my mother; maybe you could ask my sisters how to use the latest Big Mouth vacuum cleaner; it's really powerful. I'll ask them to show you how to vacuum; I think you don't vacuum very well; there's always residual dirt after you've finished with the floor. You could also ask my father and brothers how to paint the fence; they always use a cloth instead of a brush, and the method is really fast. We'll have dinner at my mother's place. Then, we'll drop by at Flat Out Pancakes; I've a coupon for a free pancake."

I wondered how much time we would have to find the WMD; it was now a desperate, life-and-death crisis.

"Then on Sunday . . . Hey, you're not listening," said Arm. "I took the trouble to draw up this program; the least you could do is to pay attention to what I'm saying."

"I was just thinking . . . ," I said, staring at the note.

"As I was saying, on Sunday, we'll have dumplings for breakfast at Dumplings House. Then, we'll drop by at Mr. Farmer; I absolutely need to get some flowers for the house."

I wondered how we should start searching for the container with the WMD; we did not have a clue. If the container with the WMD were to be parked right in front of me, I would not know it.

"Hey, you're not paying attention; don't you think the program I've drawn up is good?"

"But today's just the middle of the week," I said. "I was just thinking . . ."

"Where did I stop? You've distracted me; you always disrupt my train of thought. Yes, Mr. Farmer . . . As I was saying, I absolutely need to get some flowers for the house. You can wait in the car while I hop in for the flowers; it won't take me more than half an hour."

"Half an . . ."

"Then we'll come back home because I don't want to leave the flowers in the car while we go from place to place the whole day."

I thought the OSD should at least have given the Croctopus people some guidance on the search for the mobile container with the WMD.

"Hey, you're not paying attention . . . I said you're not paying attention. I'm planning for the family; the least you could do is to pay attention. Don't you like the program so far?"

"So far?"

"Well, I'm half-way through. Don't you like it?"

"Well, so far, it's just your agenda."

"My agenda? My goodness! How could you say this? I'm doing it for the family! It's our agenda, the family's agenda! While you're having a good time at the office, I cracked my head the whole afternoon to come up with this; the least you could do is to appreciate what I've done. It seems that I'm the only one caring for the family; you've got to play your part. I never knew I'd marry a man who wouldn't care for his family. You don't care about the family! You just can't leave everything to me; it's a shared responsibility. I'm the one thinking of the family all the time; I've no support from you at all. My agenda indeed!"

Arm continued the tirade for an hour or so, then stormed off to the bedroom to answer her cellphone in peace.

After the kids had done their homework and gone to bed, I spent the rest of the evening trying to work out some questions for Socky's hypnotism session. It was difficult, with the WMD worry looming large like dark, threatening clouds. But I had to try my best to get some lead out of Socky; there was a fair chance something would come out of it if the right questions were asked. I wanted to give the session a good shot even though I knew next to nothing about hypnotism. But with the WMD threat, I had to seize every opportunity to squeeze something out of nothing. I had not seen Lenny Loon's list of questions for Professor Spinner to ask Socky, but I thought I should produce my own list. I had only one night to do so. However difficult it might be, I had to focus and come up with a list. We no longer had the luxury of time; the terrorists might set off the WMD any time. The right questions drawing the right responses from Socky could mean the difference between life and death for a lot of people, maybe tens of thousands of people. I worked feverishly late into the night and into the early hours of the morning, the only bit of relief was knowing that the OSD was probably working much harder and far ahead of us.

I was unusually early for work at Croctopus HQ. To my surprise, Kate was already there.

"I couldn't sleep the whole night; I was tossing and turning," said Kate. "I was just too worried; I couldn't wait for daybreak; coming to the office was a relief. I'd like to discuss the hypnotism session before Socky comes in."

We sat down to discuss as Kate munched a chocolate muffin; I showed her the list of questions I had prepared. "It's not a good list; I couldn't work well yesterday," I said.

"I do agree with your little note right at the top here that we must ensure that we get precise answers from Socky," said Kate.

About half an hour later, Socky arrived at the office. After greeting everybody, he said, "I don't think I want to go for that hypnotism session."

"What? Oh no, surely you want to go," said Kate. "You've to go; you can't skip it."

"No, I don't think I want to go."

"But I'm told Professor Spinner is good," said Kate.

"It's not that; it has nothing to do with him. I just don't think I need any hypnotherapy."

Kate, starting to panic, said, "But . . . but you have to go; it's all arranged."

"Socky, it may be a life and death thing," I said, trying to disguise and transfer my worry for the WMD threat to him.

"Nah, surely not, you must be joking." Socky sank comfortably into a chair and put his hands behind his head. "Hey, why are you two looking so anxious? Don't worry about me, I'm fine."

"But you said you've got this feeling you're being followed," I said. "Surely, you ought to do something about it; you just can't let this thing go on."

"Well, I don't know; it's just a nagging feeling that I'm being followed, but it's not eating into my bones; it's not giving me any trouble, really."

"But you're bothered by it, surely," I said.

"Well, yes and no; it's just a bit of a bother, but I'm not disabled by it. I still function pretty well; I'm in full control of my faculties." Socky put his foot on the edge of the table and pushed to tilt his chair back.

"You'll never know what would happen if you let this continue," I said. "I mean, I don't want to scare you, but you may have a serious illness."

"Socky, I've arranged everything; I've informed the General and he even insisted that you to take the day off," said Kate.

Socky gave a broad grin and said, "Okay, don't want to put you in a spot; what time is the appointment with Spinner?"

"Great! You don't know how relieved I am; we can go now," said Kate.

"Now? I thought it was later in the morning."

"It has been brought forward; we're all rather anxious that you see Spinner," said Kate.

"Okay, let's go. I don't know what I'm in for, but it better be good."

"Ken, I'll go with Socky in my car. Could you inform the General that we're off?" said Kate, trying to sound as casual as possible.

Kate took a leisurely drive because, she told Socky, she was not sure of the way. But, of course, she was giving the rest of us time to get into position on site. When they arrived at Professor Spinner's premises, he was waiting for them. A short man with intense eyes, he welcomed them warmly.

"I've set aside the whole morning for you," said Spinner, "although the session will probably not take that long."

They entered a spacious room, carpeted and big enough to hold a function for a small gathering. Spinner sat Socky on a chair at the front of the room. Behind the chair hung heavy curtains, which partitioned off part of the room. After satisfying herself that Socky was seated as planned, Kate left the room.

"Let us begin," said Spinner.

Unknown to Socky, the Croctopus terrorist hunters and Lenny Loon were already assembled behind the heavy curtains. Kate joined us there after leaving Spinner and Socky; the only one absent was Roger, who had an appointment with the minister that he could not cancel. The group sat facing the curtains, like an audience waiting for a show to begin. They could hear Spinner and Socky quite well.

Spinner got Socky to relax and focus on something to become less aware of the surroundings. But however hard he tried, Spinner could not hypnotize Socky. After some time, Spinner looked a bit desperate and pressed a button for his assistant to come in and take a note that he had scribbled. The assistant went behind the curtains with the note and wrote Spinner's message on a whiteboard, 'This man is a problem, a big problem.' The Croctopus people expressed their anguish in various ways, like covering their face or holding their head with their hands, but they could not make a sound. Kong stood up, clasped his hands and looked up, as if looking to heaven, although he could only see the ceiling, and mumbled something.

After some more hard work, Spinner looked even more desperate and he scribbled another note before sending his assistant behind the curtains again. The assistant read the note and wrote on the whiteboard, 'This man has a big ego. Big problem.' This caused more anguish to the terrorist hunters, and they displayed their anguish freely but silently. Kong held his head with both hands and looked left and right desperately, as if trying to flee to some refuge, but he had nowhere to go. All the anguish was displayed in total silence, of course.

There was more desperate work by Spinner, but by then he looked like a man owing a mountain of debt and unable to deliver a cent when creditors were tearing down his front door. It was a sorry sight, quite different from the confident hypnotist when Kate and Socky arrived. Again, he sent for the assistant, who then went behind the curtains again with a third note, this time threading hesitantly, as if fearing for his life. He wrote on the whiteboard, 'This man is trying to intimidate me.' Kong stood up, his face filled with rage and looking as if he wanted to charge through the curtains. He was held back desperately by Bobby Boon, Sammy Sam and Sonny Song. The struggle looked like a scene straight from a silent movie—furious action without sound. Seeing that, the assistant dashed off to safety.

Socky remained calm in his chair. In front of him was a desperate hypnotist, who knew he must not fail because the stakes were high; the security of the country was on his shoulders. Behind Socky, a titanic, but silent, struggle was taking place behind heavy curtains. From Spinner's position, the only sign of the wrestling going on was the vague, shifting outlines of bodies and elbows formed on the curtains. Except for Spinner's voice, the place was silent.

"Good, you're now at a place you feel totally safe; you're now among your colleagues, your real colleagues, your brothers, people who share a common cause with you. There are no outsiders," said Spinner, in a voice now full of relief.

Spinner's assistant rushed behind the curtains and, with his hands gesturing in downward motions, pleaded silently for the struggling heap to calm down. When order was restored, he gave a thumbs up sign. Everyone was by then standing up. Then he parted the curtains to let the terrorist hunters into Spinner's section of the room. They stood behind Socky so that he was unaware of their presence.

"You now feel totally free to speak," said Spinner. "Tell me, where are you?"

"I see a vast plain . . . rocks, boulders," mumbled Socky.

Spinner had his ear to Socky's mouth so that he would not miss a word of what Socky was mumbling. Unfortunately, this effectively blocked off Socky's words for the rest of us; we had to rely on Spinner repeating after Socky.

"Where is this place?"

"Home, so beautiful . . . so very beautiful."

"It's your home?"

"Yes . . . it's also everyone's home . . . But I'm on my way to a new home; we're all going to a new home."

No matter what he had asked, Spinner could only get vague answers from Socky: a vast plain which he called home, and which everyone also called home. Everyone was clearly concerned that he was spouting such vague, almost useless, answers. So, Spinner decided to leave the question of place and moved on, probably hoping to return to it later.

"What are you doing there?" asked Spinner.

"I am drinking . . . beer, Tiger . . . from a can."

"You're drinking beer . . . lager, from a can. Who are you with?"

"There's this guy drinking with me, a friend."

"Only the two of you?"

"Yes . . . actually, I feel my family is nearby, but I don't see them."

"You are having a nice time?"

"Yes."

"What is this other guy's name?"

Socky did not answer.

"His name? Do you remember his name? Any name?"

"Come, Me Kill . . . ," mumbled Socky in a strange voice.

"Chemical?" said Spinner.

"All See," mumbled Socky in a voice almost inaudible.

"Ali?" said Spinner.

"Come, Me Kill . . . All See," mumbled Socky again.

"Chemical Ali?" said Spinner in shock.

All of us gathered behind were stunned; we looked at one another and then at Socky again. Tension filled the air, like a balloon stretched to almost bursting.

"Are you discussing anything with this guy?" said Spinner.

"We're talking . . . beer is good, very good."

It was unfortunate, tragic even, that we could not hear Socky, and had to rely on Spinner repeating what was said.

"What are you both talking about?"

"Just talking."

"Yes, but what are you talking about?"

"About the battle."

"The battle? What battle?"

"The big battle . . . long train of wagons."

"Wagons? What wagons?"

"Long train of wagons . . . then, all dead. Mass destruction! Mass destruction!"

Kong could barely contain himself; he wanted to charge forward and question Socky himself, but was held back by Bobby Boon, Sammy Sam and Sonny Song. They wrestled in silence behind Socky.

"What mass destruction?" asked Spinner.

"Come, Me Kill . . . All See . . . weapon over head, screaming."

"A long train of wagons, Chemical Ali, then weapons overhead and people screaming, and then mass destruction," said Spinner excitedly.

"Smoke . . . choking smoke of death all over."

"They're all gassed to death?" asked Spinner.

"Yes, they all died."

"Go on, tell us; you must tell us everything."

"A wagon . . . behind a boulder, a hidden wagon."

"A hidden wagon?"

"Yes, a hidden wagon."

"Where's the hidden wagon?"

"Right here, right here."

"The hidden wagon is here?"

"Yes, here . . . but hidden."

We were all stunned, as though a truck moving at high speed had crashed into our midst.

"What's in the wagon?" said Spinner, his voice quivering.

Socky could not answer.

"What do you see?"

"A weapon."

"A weapon in the hidden wagon?"

"Yes, a weapon . . . I see a weapon . . . finger on trigger, ready to fire."

"A weapon in a hidden wagon ready to fire!" said Spinner.

I went up to Kong with a list and whispered, "We need to be precise about all that he has said. I've a list of questions here to make things more precise; Spinner does not have to use all the questions; just use the ones I've marked."

Kong pushed me away and said, "Don't disrupt the flow of things; it's going very well; we won't have another chance."

"But it's not clear . . ." I said.

"It's clear as daylight to me. We've a WMD in a mobile container in our midst." Kong was furious.

"But . . ."

"You stay out of this." Kong was like a man convinced that his number would win the top prize in a lottery and could not be restrained from placing more bets.

"What's happening?" asked Socky, looking like he had snapped out of his hypnotic trance.

"Just relax; sit here and don't move," said Spinner quickly, at the same time staring intently into Socky's eyes and laying his hands on Socky's shoulders to restrain him from standing up or turning around.

Spinner's assistant immediately ushered us across the carpeted floor to the rear half of the room, and drew the curtains.

Chapter 8

The atmosphere at Croctopus HQ was charged as never before as we and the Orderland Security Department's Lenny Loon gathered in the boardroom. Roger was out meeting the minister and the shadowy director of the OSD to discuss the latest threat. The country had never faced such danger before—a WMD in a mobile container hidden somewhere in the country.

"We could be blown to bits in forty-five minutes," said Lenny Loon. "Orderland could be history in that short a time."

"This is scary; I've never felt so scared and so helpless in my life," said Kong.

"What's the OSD doing about this latest development?" I asked. "Right now, we've no lead; we don't even know what the container with the WMD looks like. I mean, Croctopus can't do the hunting alone. It's like looking for a needle in a haystack. This is a big thing, and we don't even have police powers to search. The full resources of the state have to be mobilized to hunt for the container."

"Why don't you use the codename? Have some code discipline," said Bobby Boon. "We've just given it a codename, so use it."

"That's right, you don't seem to like using codes, do you?" said Sammy Sam. "You keep referring to Crouching Liar by his name, and now you're not using the code name for the mobile container. We don't give code names for nothing."

"I'm very sorry, I didn't mean to disregard something that has been established. I'm just not used to this cloak and dagger stuff," I said. "It'll take a bit of time, but I'll get used to it, not to worry."

"You've got to stick to procedures," said Sammy Sam. "Don't just do your own thing. The General took so much trouble to come up with a good code name, so we ought to use it. We've got to appreciate the General's effort."

"I think we're going off on a tangent," said Kate. "Can we get back to the real issue?"

"Why do you always defend each other?" said Sonny Song. "The failure to stick to procedures and codenames is becoming an issue, and an important issue. There's got to be discipline in this."

"See the unhappiness and disruption we get when you fail to follow established procedures and use codenames?" said Kong. "Stick to proper procedures, Ken; procedures are important; they're made for a reason. You should know this by now; you've been here for years. Besides, I don't want to crack my head to come up with a codename that nobody wants to use." Turning to the man from the OSD, Kong continued, "Now, tell us Colonel Loon, what's the OSD doing in the hunt for Hidden Wagon?"

"All available agents and resources have been mobilized to hunt for Hidden Wagon. I understand that the police and other security branches have also been mobilized."

"So the police and the other security branches are now aware of Hidden Wagon?" asked Kong.

"The Commissioner of Police and the heads of the other security branches, as well as their high-level officers and those directly involved in the case, have been aware of Crouching Liar, Hidden Wagon as soon as we got the intelligence. But the people in the field don't know the true nature of what they're hunting. We don't want a panic, and so this case is still a big secret."

"Colonel Loon, you really have to lean on Chatterbig this time," said Kong. "He must give us some lead to find Hidden Wagon. I think you've got to give him an ultimatum—if he doesn't give us immediate help, you should stop sending him any money. I mean, if we don't find Hidden Wagon, and find it fast, we don't need Chatterbig anymore; we'd be blown to bits."

"I know, we're pressing Chatterbig like never before, and he has promised to send us some intelligence on Hidden Wagon as soon as possible. I've impressed upon him the enormity of the threat and the urgency of the situation, and I believe he understands our concerns."

Lenny Loon's cellphone on the table came alive, shaking vigorously, like a baby crying for milk and not getting it fast enough. And Lenny Loon, like a boxer throwing a lightning right jab, grabbed the tiny thing and answered the call, his head dipping down to focus on the caller's message. There was silence in the room; nothing else mattered except the message, for we had learnt by then that Lenny Loon's calls were often important. If the room could breath, it would have stopped breathing, so high was the suspense. The sound of air seeping out of the air-condition outlets turned into an impatient hum. All were looking at Lenny Loon intently, as if waiting for the message to be transported from his mind to ours through the air.

Then Lenny Loon looked up and moved his lips silently, but in an exaggerated way so that the others could read his lips.

"Chatterbig," said Kong, reading lips.

"Yes, Chatterbig," said Bobby Boon.

Excitement buzzed about in the room. Kong quickly put his hand up to tell everyone to be quiet; all waited anxiously for Lenny Loon to finish with the call.

"Chatterbig has a lead for Hidden Wagon," said Lenny Loon, putting his cellphone on the table.

The news caused an immediate stir; the air-conditioner coughed and groaned.

"His agent, who is with a business delegation here, will deliver us a note at Croctopus City," said Lenny Loon slowly. "The agent will excuse himself from the delegation to go to the washroom on the highest floor of the East wing. I understand it's very quiet there because that side of the floor is quite vacant, with only a relatively few shops. The agent will be in the gents for only a very short while, perhaps a minute or two. He's a very nervous man; he'll not drop the note for us if there's any other person in the washroom."

"When will this take place?" asked Kong with evident excitement.

"In about half an hour; Chatterbig will send me a message when his agent is going to the washroom."

"We've so little time!" said Kong, hand on his forehead and voice full of despair.

"That's when the delegation will be at Croctopus City, I suppose, and the agent is probably unable to change the schedule of the delegation," said Lenny Loon. "There's no time for me to arrange for an OSD agent to take the note, so I'll have to depend on you; I'm sure you've trusted people at Croctopus City.

"I'll get Salleh," suggested Kate.

"Good, he's the right person," said Kong. "Colonel Loon, Salleh is the property manager of Croctopus City; he's also a rugby player and a mixed martial arts exponent. Kate, get Salleh now; tell him it's an industrial espionage case."

"How will Chatterbig's agent know our guy?" I asked.

"Use the blinking hand code," said Lenny Loon.

"The blinking hand code? What's this?" asked Kong.

"Well, I'm sure you'd recognize it when you see it. It's what Chatterbig calls Orderlanders' habit of 'blinking' with our five fingers to indicate 'five' every time we mention the number. You know, opening and closing the hand a few times to make the hand 'blink' like a star. Foreigners are often fascinated by our way of saying five or ten; they tell me Orderlanders can't say five or ten without using one or both hands to 'blink'. That's what your guy has to do to identify himself to the agent."

"Are you sure this blinking hand code will work?" I asked.

"We've no choice; there's very little time to suggest to Chatterbig another code," said Lenny Loon. "Changing code would only cause confusion; better stick to what Chatterbig has decided."

"General," I called out, "Roger's on the line; he has just finished his meeting with the minister and he's at Croctopus City to brief Salleh on security. Why don't we ask him to go with Salleh to take the note?"

"This is great, absolutely great," said Kong, excitement written on his face. "Luck is on our side this time; at least we now have somebody on the ground who knows what's going on. Go ahead, Ken, ask Roger to meet Salleh immediately."

"I'll inform Chatterbig that there'll be two guys from our side to take the note," said Lenny Loon, his fingers tapping on his cellphone.

"Ken, brief Roger on this and tell him to be quick, and remember to tell him to use a blinking hand to identify himself," said Kong. "Kate, are you briefing Salleh?"

"Yes, I'm with him now."

There was a frenzy of briefings: myself briefing Roger, Kate briefing Salleh, Kong briefing Kate and me, Kate and I briefing Kong, Lenny Loon briefing Kong, and Kong briefing Lenny Loon in return. As for Bobby Boon, Sammy Sam and Sonny Song, they briefed one another with what they could gather from the conversations of the rest of us in the room.

Roger and Salleh wasted no time; it was fortunate that the two of them had met before. On the way to the washroom, Salleh demonstrated to Roger how to indicate 'five' the Orderlander way. Salleh opened his hand with his fingers spread wide and straight, like a starburst. Then he closed his hand, which was not closed into a tight fist, but rather with the fingers stretched, the tips of all five fingers meeting at a point, forming something like the beak of a bird. Salleh opened and closed his hand a few times to demonstrate the 'blink'. Roger was fascinated; he told himself silently that the 'blink' could be deployed for dancing, and tried it out a few times with both hands at the same time, as if he was in a disco. They took the lift to the highest floor and headed quickly for the washroom at the East wing.

Salleh stopped at the entrance for a brief moment and muttered, "This is it; here we come." Then he barged straight in, full of anticipation, with Roger close behind. There was a small man, slightly balding and in his late forties or early fifties, looking into the very wide mirror on the wall. He turned to look at Roger and Salleh without saying anything to identify himself, but his eyes gave him away. They were so nervous they looked as if they were about to crack like glass. Roger and Salleh hesitated for a moment, not knowing whether to start blinking with their hands; Roger was especially hesitant for he had never hand-blinked at anyone before. The small man looked at them nervously, as if waiting for something to happen. Roger and Salleh blinked their hands and the small man replied with his own blink. There was total silence all the while. Then the small man put his hand into his shirt pocket.

At that moment, a man in his twenties walked into the washroom, whistling a tune casually. The small man froze, then took his hand out of his pocket—it was empty. He must have decided to leave the note in his pocket for the moment. Then he turned to the mirror and pretended that there was something in his eye. Roger and Salleh were left staring open-mouthed, like kids not given their ice-cream as promised. Salleh once again hand-blinked to the small man, who pretended not to notice it. What a cautious man he was. The whistler went straight to the urinals and took the one in the middle of the row. He must have been a very confident guy, who was used to being in the middle of everything. He eased himself and whistled at the same time, and appeared to enjoy what he was doing; he was apparently good at multi-tasking. And he must have kept his urine for a long time, for it gushed out noisily, like water from a fire hose, almost drowning the tune he was whistling. The other three could only wait. Finally, the whistler finished his business and stopped whistling halfway through a tune, as if defeated by the flushing sound from the urinal. After zipping up his pants with a flourish, like a conductor of an orchestra, he walked to the middle sink and washed his hands. He stood between Roger and Salleh to his left and the small man to his right, the three men about two arms' length away on either side of him.

"Just a matter of seconds more," Salleh muttered to Roger. The sudden speech seemed to surprise the whistler a little; he turned his head slightly to look at the two men. Then he went over to the tissue dispenser and took a tissue to dry his hands, after which he inspected his hands, flipping them this way and that. He curled his fingers to inspect his nails and started to whistle again. Then he stopped whistling and walked toward the exit, but after two steps he appeared to feel that he had not done a good job of drying his hands, for he returned to the dispenser and took another tissue to dry his hands again. Salleh looked impatient; Roger resisted the temptation to look at the whistler and instead looked into the mirror. The small man was looking into the mirror too, still pretending to be troubled by something in his eye, but the pretence was wearing a bit thin as it was taking too long. Finally, whistler threw the ball of tissue into the bin like a basketball player. He opened the door; the collective sigh of relief from the other three men sounded almost like a wave coming from the sea. Then the whistler hesitated, turned around and went back to the middle sink, where he turned the tap for water to rinse his mouth a few times. For the finale, he took in a big gulp of water and gurgled noisily, after which he peered into the mirror to check his teeth. The small man was getting visibly nervous and looked ready to bolt. Salleh must have felt there was no time to lose, so he hand-blinked to the small man again. The whistler, noticing something strange going on, stole a glance at Salleh and Roger. He seemed to notice that Salleh was trying to communicate with the small man, so he turned slowly to look at the small man, who was so nervous that his eyes started to blink involuntarily. The whistler turned to look at Salleh quizzically, and this time he was not glancing; he seemed to feel entitled to take a good look at the three characters acting strangely. This caused Salleh to stop in mid-blink with his hand, but instead of bringing his hand down he raised it naturally to brush his hair. Calm returned to the washroom. The whistler then took out his comb, although there was not a hair out of place. He treated his hair to a leisurely, almost loving, comb. Then he looked into the mirror, turning his head slightly to the left and dipping it a little to inspect the result of his work. After he appeared to be satisfied with the result, he turned his head to the right and repeated the same thing. He patted his hair a few times to shape it. By now, Salleh was cracking his fingers as though getting ready for a fight. The small man turned, as if ready to make a dash for the door. Roger moved his lips as if saying, "No, no," silently to the small man. Fortunately, the whistler turned and headed for the door. The three characters breathed a collective sigh of relief once more.

However, after taking two steps, the whistler stopped for a moment and then walked backward before turning his head to look in the mirror. Then he went back to the mirror and took out his comb and touched up his hair here and there. That was the last straw for the small man, who made a dash for the door. Roger and Salleh tried to stop him, but the whistler must have thought the small man was being attacked, so he jumped on Roger and Salleh. That allowed the small man to escape. Salleh was furious and wanted to beat up the whistler, but Roger stopped him.

"Let's go," said Roger, and the two men chased after the small man, who by then seemed to have disappeared into the air.

Kong took the telephone call and heard the bad news from Roger, whereupon he flew into an uncontrollable rage. He smashed the telephone onto the floor, kicked the door and stormed out like a raging bull, leaving the rest of us open-mouthed.

Having lost the small man, Roger figured that the best thing to do was to return to the washroom, hoping against hope that the small man might have dropped the note. So he and Salleh rushed back to the gents, but nobody was there.

"Let's search this place," said Roger. They did not have to search long; Roger quickly found a piece of paper on the floor near the door. He picked it up, unfolded it and read, "When the circle is closed, boom!"

Kong entered the boardroom, talking on his cellphone; his mood strangely good. Then he announced triumphantly, "I've very good news; we may have got the note from Chattebig's agent after all."

"May have?" I asked.

"Well, Roger got the note, but it was not handed to him by the agent; he found it on the floor. Unfortunately, there's nothing on the note to indicate that it was from the agent."

"So, we can't be sure the note was from Chatterbig," I said.

"Yes, I'm afraid so, but it sounded like the intelligence we've been waiting for," said Kong.

"What does the note say?" I asked.

"When the circle is closed, boom!"

We were stunned into silence; only the air-conditioner was humming leisurely.

"That sounds frightening," said Kate.

"What does that mean?" said Bobby Boon.

"Sounds like when the terrorists have collected all the intelligence they needed, and all gaps are closed, like an electrical circuit is closed, they'll set off the WMD in Hidden Wagon," I said.

"You're too quick with your conclusion," said Bobby Boon.

"That's right, don't be so quick; it may not be that simple," said Sammy Sam.

"You're always too quick with your guesses," said Sonny Song, "and they're only guesses."

"I tend to agree with Ken; I can't think of any other interpretation," said Kong. "Our terrorist mole and his gang want to set off Hidden Wagon to cause the worst possible damage. To do that, they must have a sufficient understanding of Orderland; that's why Crouching Liar is making such an extensive study of our country."

"You're absolutely right, General," said Bobby Boon.

"Right on target with your assessment, General," said Sammy Sam.

"You're always spot on, Sir," said Sonny Song. "We're so fortunate to have you leading the way."

"I've just spoken to Chatterbig on the phone," said Lenny Loon. "I asked him about the note and he confirmed that it was from him."

"That's fantastic!" exclaimed Kong. "Absolutely fantastic!"

"But was it really his note or did he say it was his so as to collect payment from you?" I said.

"You've a point," said Lenny Loon. "I shouldn't have told him the statement in the note; I should've let him mention it first."

"What a pity we can't be completely sure," said Kong. "But, we can't cry over spilt milk. We'll just have to assume the note's from Chatterbig and carry on from there."

"Actually, the note is not very helpful; it seems obvious to me that the terrorists would gather sufficient intelligence before setting off Hidden Wagon," I said.

"There's nothing obvious or easy about the General's interpretation of the note," said Bobby Boon.

"Even if I had spent the whole day looking at the note, I'd not be able to decipher it," said Sammy Sam.

"The General's interpretation is a master stroke; don't trivialize it," said Sonny Song.

"Actually, at the start of the meeting, Colonel Loon told us Chatterbig would give us a lead for Hidden Wagon, didn't you Colonel?" I said.

"Yes, that's right," said Lenny Loon. "So what does that mean?"

"The note has no intelligence on Hidden Wagon's location," I said. "Is that really Chatterbig's note?"

"Of course it is," said Bobby Boon. "It has to be."

"It may not be," said Kong. "But we'll proceed as if it's from Chatterbig until we've reason to believe otherwise. We have no choice."

Chapter 9

Roger looked at the submachine gun—beautiful, yet mean and dangerous. The finger was resting on the trigger guard, and the barrel pointed at an angle toward the sky. That was reassuring, for the Heckler & Koch could fire eight hundred rounds a minute. The whole of Croctopus was on heightened alert these days—for industrial espionage and sabotage, they were told; only the few terrorist hunters there knew the real reason. The company had always prided itself on being alert, and the extraordinary situation unfolding called for extraordinary measures.

As the security consultant, it was Roger's responsibility to advise on security for all Crotopus's premises, especially the one where the headquarters was situated. That day Roger had arrived early for work, so he decided not to take his usual shortcut across the grounds to his office. As he walked along a narrow path and took in the morning air, he observed that the old driveway had been closed, replaced by a new one with sharp bends to thwart anyone from racing in a vehicle filled with explosive to the HQ building.

A steel beam hung low overhead, allowing cars, but not trucks, to pass; guards would have to shift the beam for trucks. Spikes were embedded across the driveway at two points, and they could be raised instantaneously at the touch of a button to puncture the tires of a vehicle. Halfway to the HQ building, just before a sharp bend, was a high hump. Any vehicle racing at high speed would fly off the road and crash-land into a pond. Outside the HQ building's main entrance was a line of flowerbeds—excellent for guards to take cover and fire at hostile persons or vehicles coming up the driveway. The windows were narrow slits—not easy to lob a grenade through. The windowsills all sloped downward. A grenade failing to go through a window would not land and remain on a sill; it would roll off into a moat below and the water would absorb the force of any explosion as well as the shrapnel. Roger was pleased that the upgrade was proceeding according to his recommendations.

He went into the HQ building intending to do some paperwork at his desk. Much work still needed to be done to boost the security of Croctopus's installations all over Orderland. With the intelligence that Hidden Wagon had been slipped into the country, the security situation had changed greatly for the worse; there was no room for complacency, and the installation of all security facilities had to be speeded up. At the ground floor lobby Roger felt a chill as the air-conditioning was rather strong, or maybe it was because things were getting scary. The receptionist greeted Roger and gave him a sunny smile, which warmed things up a bit. In late morning, Roger was out again inspecting the grounds and buildings. Outside the Croctopus grounds, there were other, less impressive, buildings to the left and right. Behind the grounds was a big, empty land with patches of shrub and grass. But it was not exactly empty that day; a huge circus tent had been erected on it and workmen were putting the final touches, decorating the place with flags and setting up ticket booths. A few men were looking at the tent, discussing something. A young girl was fussing over a pony. A short distance away, a young boy was practicing juggling under the watchful eyes of an adult, probably his father. Further away from the tent, six Indian elephants were munching stalks of sugarcane contentedly. They were a bit too near Croctopus's back fence for Roger's comfort, but there was nothing he could do about it.

*

Unpleasant noises came from Bobby Boon's room—actually angry, accusative shouting, although it was difficult to make out what he was screaming. The door was closed, and unfortunately I was the only other person in there with the screamer. I was told later, in my investigation, that the people outside looked tense, concerned and unhappy. But they were also curious, their ears behaving like those giant radio dishes used to gather the faintest signals from outer space. The people listened intently, trying to make out what was being said behind the closed door. Some looked in the direction of the door, whispering to one another. Others faced their monitors, fingers on keyboard but definitely not typing. Movements, and even breathing, were kept to a minimum so as not to interfere with the sound waves from the room. There was full concentration, not on work but on what was happening in the room. Despite the tightly closed door, it was apparent to all outside that Bobby Boon was enraged, while I was speaking loudly, but calmly, trying to explain something.

"You call this a plan? What kind of plan is this? It's crap! The biggest crap I've ever seen in my life!"

"If you . . ."

"Don't say anything more! I've heard enough! Get out of here!"

What could have driven the head of security to such rage? The door opened and I came out, looking thoroughly disgusted. The people outside turned away at lightning speed. They stared at their monitors and pretended to type furiously, but ears wide open for the weakest vibrations. Then files and papers went flying out of the room, almost striking me. They fell onto the floor, unwanted and forlorn, like abandoned kittens.

As I walked away, Sammy Sam and Sonny Song came into view, both turning at the same time to look at me, catching a glimpse of my back before I turned a corner. They walked into the room expectantly, only to see Bobby Boon purple with rage. He lost no time, complaining immediately and loudly, like a man done a grave injustice. They did not bother to close the door, and the people outside could see them and hear their conversation, as some of them told me later.

"I've been busy and I've waited a long time to give him a piece of my mind!"

"What happened?" asked Sammy Sam.

"I told him to come up with a plan to defend this place in case of a terrorist attack," said Bobby Boon, his voice now hoarse. "And you know what? Tell me, if it were you, what would you have done?"

"Isn't there a standing order for the defense of our installations?" said Sammy Sam.

"Yes, I wanted to see how we could improve on the existing plan," said Bobby Boon.

"Sound the alarm and all the guards scramble out of the guardhouse and take up their designated positions along the perimeter fence surrounding the entire grounds," said Sonny Song. "That's the standing order; just reduce the time for the guards to get to their positions."

"Precisely!" said Bobby Boon, pointing to Sonny Song like a quizmaster hearing the correct answer. "It's that simple; all he needed to do was to give me a plan with the reduced time frame, but he got it wrong!"

Sammy Sam and Sonny Song made a show of astonishment at my apparent stupidity, both putting on anguished faces and shaking their heads to give Bobby Boon their assurance that they felt his pain.

"How did he go wrong? What was his plan?" asked Sammy Sam. "I mean, I don't think it's worth knowing, but I'm just curious. You know, how he could get something so simple wrong."

"His plan called for all the guards to pull back to the HQ building! It's a plan to defend the HQ building and nothing more. There was no perimeter defense at all! Can you believe it? He wanted to abandon all the areas beyond the vicinity of the HQ building to terrorists without a fight! It was complete nonsense!" said Bobby Boon.

"Are you sure he drew up such a plan?" asked Sammy Sam, looking incredulous, but actually just acting to heighten their collective outrage.

"It's all in his plan; you can see it for yourselves," said Bobby Boon.

Sonny Song stepped out of the room to retrieve the files and papers from the floor. Bobby Boon took the papers and shuffled them to get the pages in order.

"There, see . . . ," said Bobby Boon, jabbing his finger at a certain page.

"I can't believe it," said Sammy Sam, shaking his head in an exaggerated manner.

Sonny Song shook his head too and said, "He always does things in the simplest way imaginable. His plans always require minimal effort and resources. That's a lazy man's way of doing things. He can't see that this place is huge and requires an elaborate defense; it should be as elaborate as possible."

"You're in big trouble because the General will be inspecting the defense set-up soon, and he'll want a demonstration," said Sammy Sam, looking grave.

"Don't worry," said Bobby Boon. "I've drawn up a plan myself and personally shown each guard his position along the fence. We've had several practices, and things are under control; I'm ready. I've a perimeter defense now; I don't depend on that guy at all."

*

Roger walked hurriedly back to the HQ building and took a lift to the highest floor, where Kate was waiting for him at the lift lobby. As they entered the room, Roger realized that Kong looked more like a general than ever before. Hidden Wagon must have heightened his security concerns to the highest pitch; his posture was erect and he looked as if he was about to go into battle. Roger briefed Kong on his meeting with the minister, who had wanted an update on the progress in the Crouching Liar, Hidden Wagon case. Kong was anxious to know what the minister had felt about the contributions Croctopus had made. The briefing with Kong lasted for about an hour.

"The General is having security fever," said Roger to Kate at the corridor outside Kong's room. "He's thinking about nothing but Crouching Liar, Hidden Wagon and the security of Croctopus's premises and installations."

"He seems less cheerful these days," said Kate. "Dark clouds are gathering."

"He's getting very impatient; he wants to test Croctopus's security systems as soon as possible. I expect a major exercise any time soon."

"Actually, that would be interesting; in all my years here I've never seen a major test."

"The big one is coming." Roger seemed aware of some confidential information. They took a lift to their floor, and Roger went to his desk to finish some paperwork, while Kate met me. I told her about what had happened at Bobby Boon's room.

"It was like talking to a dinosaur," I said. "He's not thinking at all; his brain is ossified. Life is so easy for him—just do what has always been done, with a tweak here and a tweak there. If scientists think dinosaurs are extinct, they're wrong."

"Maybe he just didn't want to admit that the standard defense was wrong, that they didn't address the reality on the ground at all. Not only did he refuse to admit it to you, I think he also refused to admit it to himself. After all, the existing standard defense was drawn up by him."

"I've always found it strange that people would refuse to admit reality, and would actually fight with all their strength to preserve a falsehood, even if the falsehood could get them into serious trouble or kill them."

"Change is often difficult, especially if it'd involve overturning a longstanding way of doing things that has been accepted by people generally."

"Somehow, it's easier to live with an existing, comfortable condition than to make a change."

"Maybe we should invite Dr Jade Choice to come here and fix their heads. The way I see it, they—the whole lot—are prime candidates for Robot Syndrome."

"Yes, I wouldn't be surprised if one day they all behave like robots; in fact, they're already behaving like robots. I really feel like handing in my resignation."

"Don't do that, Ken. It's not easy to get another job in this economic condition; don't go just because of him; we've all taken his nonsense before. You're right to try to change things, but if you don't succeed, don't blame yourself . . . Hey, why am I telling you this? I'm the impatient one, and you're the one who usually tells me to be patient."

"The standard defense for all Croctopus facilities is wrong; there should be a complete overhaul, but all he wants to do is to increase the speed of deployment of the guards. He calls it improving system efficiency, but he doesn't care whether the system is right or wrong in the first place."

"You're right, the whole unquestioning way of doing things is wrong. How long must we put up with this?" said Kate. "Hey, you're not defending the system? Good for you. The system in Croctopus is rotten, and I hate the stifling conformism everywhere in Orderland. We've erected this artificial conformist structure to add to the natural stifling, oppressive heat here. 'Don't rock the boat' seems to be our motto. Where's that eagerness to examine and re-examine things continually? We're a complacent people; we don't ask questions."

"Well, there's nothing really wrong with the organization or the country; it's just that some parts needed fixing every now and then."

"I think a bit of fixing here and there won't be enough to change the system or stop the rot; institutional inertia makes things very difficult to change. But we shouldn't abandon the battlefield to the complacent non-visionary. I'm prepared to march into the General's office with you to sort this out, but promise me you won't resign."

I thought for a while and said, "Thanks for that, you're really kind, but I don't want you to go through all that trouble; I'll stay."

*

I had hoped to forget about the argument with Bobby Boon as soon as I left the office, but it was not to be. The bad experience followed me home and stayed for dinner. I lost my appetite and Arm was furious I did not seem to enjoy the food she had cooked. My time with the kids, playing with them and helping in their homework, did bring me some cheer. But as soon as they had gone to bed, the scene of Bobby Boon's rage came back and kept swirling in my head and refused to leave me in peace. I went to the living room and tried to read the newspapers, but it did not help. Realizing that Arm had sensed that something was troubling me, I told her what had happened in the office.

"You should've given Bobby Boon the standard defense, but cut the time for the guards to run to their positions," said Arm.

"There's no way to cut the time for the guards to get into their positions; they're running as fast as they possibly can; we've timed them before."

"It doesn't matter; it'd look good on paper," said Arm, rolling her eyes. "I'm sure Bobby Boon knew it couldn't be done, but did he care? What he needed was a plan that looked good. You should've given him what he needed. If the guards fail to reach their positions within the time stipulated, it's their fault, not yours."

"Look, I don't want a plan that only looks good on paper; I want one that will actually work."

"Don't give me this crap; you should've given your bosses the plan they had wanted. You knew what the standard defense was and what was expected of you, but you had to break with accepted thinking." By now, Arm was pacing up and down, too worked up to sit. I regretted telling her what had happened, but it was too late to change anything.

"It's not that I wanted to break with accepted thinking, the standard defense is no good and now there's an opportunity to set things right."

"You always had to be the one to be stupidly conscientious; you don't understand what's required of you at all. You've got to toe the line, play along, keep your bosses happy. What's the point of playing hero and getting hanged? Would anyone thank you or give you a medal for being a hero?"

"I wasn't playing hero; I was just doing the right thing."

"The right thing! The right thing! It's never the right thing to play hero the wrong way, to break with accepted thinking and offend your bosses. Don't you know that, you fool? You're in the office to deliver what's expected of you, secure your position, and make sure you get promoted."

"And ignore what's blatantly wrong and carry on as if everything's right?"

"You just don't get it. You don't think of me; you don't think of the family. I look after the family all the time, so you've got to play your part; you've done nothing for the family. Instead of giving a good account of yourself at work, you get into trouble—unnecessary, avoidable trouble. Why didn't you think of me and the family when you were asked to revise the standard defense? Shouldn't the family be uppermost on your mind—always? Instead of safeguarding the family, you had to play hero. What did playing hero get you? A scolding from your supervisor. And, more than that, I'm sure your future in the organization is now doubtful. Even if they don't sack you immediately, you don't have much of a future there anymore. Is this what you look for at work; what you should look for at work? Didn't you realize that getting into trouble at work would cost your family dearly? Why should the family suffer for your stupidity? Why should I, the innocent one, suffer for your stupidity? If you had half a brain all that would not have happened. I want you to go back to your bosses tomorrow and apologize to them for your mistake, your stupidity. Tell them you were not yourself when you drew up your stupid recommendation. You understand me? You understand that I have to suffer each time you make a stupid mistake at work? You understand that I'm the one holding the family together all these years while you fumble along? You've done nothing for the family at all!"

Arm did not appear she would to stop in the next hour and I did not want to hear any more, so went off to the bedroom.

Arm followed me there and continued, "Look at Andy, see how successful he is. He was your classmate at school, but he's way ahead of you now."

"He's not way ahead; he's just one or two rungs higher."

"He's way ahead of everyone in your class; give him a few more years and he'll be many rungs higher."

"Well, you know that a scholarship student gets a fast-track career everywhere in Orderland."

"Then why didn't you go get yourself a scholarship?"

"It was not whether I wanted to have a scholarship. Scholarships were given only for a very narrow band of courses, and certainly not for the course I was taking; you know that, surely."

"I also know that successful people do what's right and failures do what's wrong. And you do what's wrong—always." I went off to the kitchen, but Arm followed me there. "Look at Andy's wife. I met her at the tea party the other day; she was wearing a very expensive gold watch. Now, that's success; there's no denying it."

"That's not the only way to measure success."

"What have you given me? Why don't you give me an expensive gold watch? I'm your wife; I'm the one keeping the family sane while you keep getting into trouble. How I've suffered all these years! Do you know the pain I've had to bear? Don't I deserve something from you?" I went out of the kitchen into the living room; Arm followed me there. "Answer me, what have you given me all these years?"

"Surely you know what I've given you?"

"Tell me, what have you given me? Do I have an expensive gold watch? I work for the family while you have a good time at the office everyday; you don't appreciate my sacrifice at all. Andy's wife has such a nice gold watch without having to work at all, whereas I've to slave away. And what do I get? Nothing, nothing at all! When are you buying me a gold watch?"

"You talk as if my parents brought me into this world to get you a gold watch. I've given you and the kids all I have—my time, my life, everything. That's a lot more than a lousy gold watch."

"You've given me nothing; you've done nothing for the family at all. Nothing!"

"That's not true. I've done my best; I've made a difference to the family."

"You have not! You have made no contribution at all. A man must do what is right. Always!"

Chapter 10

"Sound the alarm," said Bobby Boon to the guard commander at the guardhouse. It was no small alarm; it was an air raid siren, with a blare that was frighteningly loud and urgent. All the guards except the commander scrambled out of the guardhouse with their submachine guns and disappeared in seconds to take up their positions along the perimeter fence. Pedestrians outside the Croctopus grounds stopped to watch the spectacle; cars stopped at the side of the road, too. Soon, a large crowd formed outside the grounds—the show was too good to miss. With the siren wailing unbearably, some people covered their ears with their hands, others jammed their ear holes with their forefingers.

The guardhouse was next to the main gate. Bobby Boon was in full view of the crowd that had gathered; it was his show. He strutted about, barking orders to the guard commander. Then he took hold of the guardhouse telephone and barked more orders into it; he pointed his forefinger here and there, bossing about the only other person left in the guardhouse. With his arms akimbo, he struck a pose that reminded the crowd of General Douglas McArthur, only the pipe was missing. He strutted along the fence, shoulders swaying in a confident rhythm, and the crowd followed him with their eyes. He turned around and strutted back, and the crowd followed him back with their eyes. He exuded importance and authority; the air was thick with his presence.

A small group of about ten people from Croctopus, including Kate and I, were there as observers to learn from the exercise. We were standing in a group just outside the guardhouse, but did not speak because the siren was too loud. Sammy Sam and Sonny Song were also there, but they stood apart from the group.

Bobby Boon asked the guard commander, already sweating from the stress and the equatorial heat, to switch off the siren and follow him to inspect the guards along the perimeter fence. The silence brought grateful relief to everyone. From the guardhouse facing the HQ building, they turned and walked to the left. Sammy Sam and Sonny Song followed behind; further back were the rest of us. The crowd followed Bobby Boon by walking along the fence on the outside. As the Croctopus grounds stood by itself, not adjacent to other premises, it was possible for the crowd to follow Bobby Boon and walk around the entire perimeter on the outside, which was what they appeared determined to do, so exciting was the spectacle.

After a fairly short distance, Bobby Boon came across the first guard, who was kneeling on the grass, looking through the fence at the road outside, his submachine gun pointing in that direction. The guard looked tense. Before Bobby Boon could say or do anything to show off his rank, the crowd came right in front of the guard, with only the fence separating them. Pressed against the fence, the spectators in front were close enough to touch the guard on the head if they could put their hands through the fence. It was a serious exercise to Croctopus, but a carnival to the crowd. The encounter was like the meeting of hot and cold air—with lots of hot air from Croctopus. There knelt the guard, submachine gun ready and looking deadly serious; but just outside, an arm's length away, was the crowd in carnival mood. A few young men (and one or two older folks, who should have known better) were making faces at the guard, trying to make him laugh, but succeeded only in making him look even more grimfaced. Bobby Boon, exuding authority, spoke to the guard, who turned his head slightly and nodded.

Suddenly, the guard commander called out to Bobby Boon, "Sir, there's a call from the General!"

All of Bobby Boon's muscles tensed immediately, squeezing out a bead of sweat, which trickled down from his temple. He took the cellphone from the guard commander and spoke for a very brief moment and became even more tense. Now, sweat glided down his face like big raindrops gliding down a glass pane. Then he turned and addressed the observer party, "I've just got a call from the General; he wants to inspect the defense. We're on show!" Suddenly, the sun seemed to get hotter.

Bobby Boon stood rooted to the ground and stared with great apprehension at the point in the distance where he had expected Kong to appear. The observer party also faced the same direction. The crowd sensed that something big was brewing, and they did not have to wait long before they were rewarded. Kong, with sunglasses and a cigarette sticking out of a black holder that protruded from the side of his mouth, came out of the HQ building, followed by his own entourage of about twenty people. When Kong arrived, Bobby Boon looked like he was ready to burst like a balloon, so tense was he. But the guard commander looked calmer than before, appearing to have loosened up. Somehow, he seemed to have sensed that Bobby Boon was the one taking the heat this time, the head of security now acting like a shield between Kong and himself. Bobby Boon was hot as an iron, whereas the guard commander was cool as a cucumber. Standing next to each other, the pair looked comical.

Kong surveyed the crowd; it was his show and he was ready to enjoy himself; he had just hijacked Bobby Boon's show.

Kong started to walk along the fence, the crowd following to his left, showman and spectators separated by the thin, silver fence. Bobby Boon followed quickly, careful to walk on Kong's right so as not to come between Kong and the crowd. Also, now that he had been reduced to a trembling supplicant, Bobby Boon looked like he preferred to use Kong to hide from the crowd. As he walked, Kong looked like he had one eye looking ahead and the other eye to the crowd. He was certainly not looking at Bobby Boon, who was briefing him as they walked. Unlike Kong, Bobby Boon was not looking at the crowd; I think he would rather they disappear—those good-for-nothing busybodies who apparently had nothing better to do during the day. The guard commander walked just behind the two leading actors; he was followed by the rest of the Croctopus people.

"What happened, boss?" a spectator shouted. The crowd roared, obviously amused at Bobby Boon's downgrade from star of the show to sidekick in so short a time. Kong looked every bit the person in charge now. Sometimes, he asked a short question, giving the impression that he understood the situation well enough to ask questions, but mostly to show he was the boss. Sometimes, he nodded his head a little as Bobby Boon briefed him, each nod so slight that Bobby Boon had to pay careful attention, lest he missed it. Once in a while, Kong placed his hands behind his back, showing he was at ease. Bobby Boon followed Kong's actions, as though he was playing *Follow the leader*. Where Kong looked at something, he looked at that thing; when Kong laughed, he laughed. When Kong cracked a lousy joke, he laughed loudly and heartily. "No terrorist could get through this bunch of clowns following us," said Kong. Bobby Boon laughed till his whole body shook, as though he had just heard the best joke in twenty years.

"What's so funny?" someone in the crowd shouted.

Kong looked annoyed; Bobby Boon pretended not to have heard anything, as there was nothing he could do about the spectators. All the guards that the inspection party came across looked very tense. One spectator tried to push a stalk of flower into the barrel of a submachine gun. The guard kept moving his weapon left and right to avoid the stalk, Kong and Bobby Boon pretending not to notice the quiet struggle. It would have been unseemly for the big boss to get into a quarrel with a mere bystander. After a short while, but long enough to show that he had an eye for details, Kong walked on, maintaining his proud bearing.

The guards were positioned at intervals of about a hundred to a hundred and fifty meters. After a long walk, the inspection party arrived near the back of the grounds and found a guard kneeling like the rest, but breathing very lightly, almost holding his breath in the stifling, oppressive heat. They had arrived at the garbage dump. Bobby Boon, clearly uncomfortable, spoke to the guard as if acting out a ritual.

"Everything's okay?" asked Bobby Boon.

"You bet!" a spectator shouted. The crowd roared; the guard appeared too distressed to pay attention to the question.

Bobby Boon was annoyed and spoke again, this time in a louder and sterner voice, which made what he said sound like a rebuke rather than a question, "I said is everything okay?"

"Yes, sir!" shouted the guard.

"Yes, sir!" roared the crowd.

Most people in the crowd were either covering or pinching their nose. But they were very amused to see the guard looking very serious next to a garbage dump. Bobby Boon turned to Kong and, pointing to the garbage bins, said, "This gives very good cover against enemy fire."

"You bet!" shouted a spectator, "Where's the gas mask?" The crowd roared.

"That's enough! Let's go!" another spectator shouted impatiently. The crowd roared again. That was too much for Kong and Bobby Boon, but there was nothing they could do about it.

Some spectators went ahead of the inspection party in an attempt to escape the suffocating stench. Bobby Boon, looking annoyed as ever, waited for Kong to give the cue to move on, while Kong, looking like he had just surfaced from a deep dive without oxygen tank, tried to pretend that the stench was not there. Kong did not cover his nose—he had to set a good example and appear dignified. The rest of the inspection party behind Kong, Bobby Boon and the guard commander did not feel the same sense of duty; they all covered their nose in various ways. After enough of pretense, Kong walked on, and the crowd clapped and cheered.

At the back of the Croctopus grounds, the inspection party came across a guard who was the only one looking happy and relaxed. The strong aroma of fried chickens from the canteen may have something to do with it. The crowd was visibly happier too. One chap in the crowd compared loudly the misfortune of the guard at the garbage dump with the fortune of this one at the canteen. "Same work, different rewards!" shouted the spectator.

The crowd became more boisterous, but Bobby Boon looked as serious as ever. He spent more time talking to the guard there than any other, but nobody apparently could understand why that sector needed so much of Bobby Boon's time.

"You staying for lunch?" a spectator shouted.

"I'm hungry!" another screamed.

The crowd roared, but Bobby Boon was not amused; it was a serious security exercise but the crowd was turning it into a circus. What would Kong think of him? Someone who had lost control of the situation? In Orderland, especially in Croctopus, losing control was almost a crime for a person in charge of anything. The crowd ought to show him more respect as head of security and the man running the show, but the crowd was determined to have a good time. The wisecracks kept coming. When Bobby Boon looked at what was going on in the Croctopus grounds, it was all seriousness; but when he shifted his gaze a little to the scene outside the grounds, all he saw was a bunch of grinning faces, as if the people were waiting in anticipation for the entry of clowns into a circus ring. Since when did a bunch of grinning faces become so unbearable? Bobby Boon could not run away from the crowd or wish them away; he also could not cut short the inspection, for it was not up to him as Kong was dictating the pace. He must have felt like being cooked to death slowly in a giant pot.

Mercifully, Kong walked on. That stopped the wisecracks from the crowd for a while. After some time, Kong stopped and gazed ahead; the next guard appeared more than fifty meters away. He turned and looked back; the previous guard was about the same distance behind. They were about half way between two guards along the fence. Then he noticed the circus tent.

Kong used his nose to point to the crowd and whispered to Bobby Boon, "These clowns ought to be in that tent." Bobby Boon laughed so hard that his body almost went limp. Kong was pleased with himself.

By that time, the size of the crowd had swelled considerably. Those behind could not see what was going on, so they started to entertain themselves by throwing stones at the six circus elephants munching grass nearby. It was a very foolish thing to do.

Indian elephants were known to have better temper than African ones, and that must have been the reason they were trained for circuses. But no elephant would take nonsense from a weakling like man. And no elephant would tolerate being disturbed when having a nice meal.

It did not take long for the elephants to react; a few stones were all that was needed. The bull elephant moved first; it stiffened and stared at the crowd with a steady, intimidating gaze, before raising its trunk and trumpeting loudly. At the same time, it flared its ears to present a bigger front and aimed its tusks at the crowd, with the other five elephants following suit. Everyone was stunned into silence; the stoning stopped abruptly. Then, like a bad dream turned real, the elephants charged, with the bull elephant out in front and looking very angry and aggressive, and trumpeting repeatedly. The herd headed straight for the crowd. Not having faced a charging herd of elephants before, everyone stood rooted to the ground for a moment. Then the crowd parted like the Red Sea. They were now the spectacle, not the spectators. A number of them fell onto the ground. The Croctopus people stood for a second or two longer, but they soon realized that only a flimsy fence stood between them and the charging herd. They dispersed like an explosive cloudburst, scattering in panic in every direction. Kong abandoned his proud bearing and ran as though only half his age; he was pale as a ghost. Bobby Boon abandoned Kong and ran off in his own direction, like a monkey with its fur on fire. The guard commander galloped away like a racehorse.

The elephants crashed through the fence without breaking stride, then turned and rumbled angrily along the road, trumpeting as they went and heading straight for the canteen. Some distance behind, the mahouts and the rest of the circus people were frantically giving chase. The path of the herd was strewn with debris. When the elephants reached the canteen they thrashed everything; tables and chairs broke like matchsticks. Then frozen chickens flew about like oversized hand grenades. The circus people used their hands to ward off the chicken grenades hurtling in their direction at high speed. By now, they were joined by the Croctopus people, who were all frantic, but without a clue as to what to do. Bobby Boon was trying to direct operations from behind a solid wall, but no one was listening. Kong, standing alone, was screaming orders at the elephants, which had not the slightest intention of obeying him. The guards were rushing left and right, but not forward. Some of the spectators had entered the grounds to watch the chaos, but this time they were not laughing. The elephants left the canteen in devastation and headed for the garbage dump. Soon garbage bins and rotting food were propelled into the air and rained down on the pursuers without mercy. To be pelted with frozen chickens was one thing, but to be pelted with rotting food was quite another.

By some incredible good luck, the elephants crashed through the fence out of the Croctopus grounds and back onto the field. Reinforcements from the circus arrived with stems of sugar cane. They threw the stems at the marauding herd, like ancient tribesmen trying to appease a volcanic god. That seemed to work; the anger subsided. After some time, the raging herd turned into a peaceful one, and munched the sugar cane like an innocent herd of cattle minding its own business. The circus people stood and stared open-mouthed with relief; the Croctopus people, just as relieved, stood farther back, not knowing what to do next. The spectators were silent and kept their distance, happy that the show had ended.

*

Kong whacked the newspaper onto the table as though he was trying to smash the wood. Bobby Boon stood trembling like a child who had done a mischief. They were just outside Kong's room, in full view of the staff, some of whom later told me what had happened.

"Look at this!" screamed Kong.

"I've read the papers, sir" stuttered Bobby Boon.

The Orderland Times carried the headline, "Croctopus fails elephant test."

Kong seized the newspaper that he had slammed onto the table seconds ago and said, "Let me read this to you."

"I have . . ."

"I know you've read the papers, but let me read it to you so that the event will be replayed in your mind again. I don't want you ever to forget your stupid mistake." Kong held the newspaper up to his chest with one hand and smacked it backhanded with the other. Then he read, "Gaps in Croctopus's perimeter defense were exposed yesterday. The gaps were so huge a herd of elephants managed to pass through one of them."

Kong brought down the newspaper with the speed of an executioner bringing down his blade, and stared at Bobby Boon with the eyes of a hungry tiger.

"It was the crowd's stoning that caused the elephants to stampede," offered Bobby Boon in a shaky voice.

"Don't try to wriggle your way out of this, you worm! I know what I'm talking about. I always know what I'm talking about, you understand?"

Bobby Boon swallowed the biggest lump of saliva in his life, then opened his mouth but failed to say anything.

"I'm not blaming you for the stampede, but I'm definitely, absolutely blaming you for having a perimeter defense with gaps so huge that a herd of elephants could charge through. We're the laughing stock of the country and it's all your fault!" Kong, still staring at Bobby Boon, threw the newspaper up into the air with both hands. The sheets parted and floated down slowly like parachutes.

"What's the point of having a perimeter defense of the entire grounds? We just don't have enough guards! You should've pulled back all the guards to the vicinity of the HQ building—it's the only place we needed to defend, you fool!"

"Yes sir!"

"What's the point of guarding frozen chickens? That's stupid!"

"Yes sir!"

"What's the point of guarding rotting food? That's stupidity running riot!"

"Yes sir!" said Bobby Boon again, as if by repeating those two words often enough Kong would be appeased and he would be forgiven.

"Gaps big enough for a herd of elephants to charge through! That's . . . that's a completely nonsensical defense! And I repeat, it's your fault! The stupid defense was drawn up by you! But I'm the one having to face the bloody public! Is this fair? You tell me! Is this fair to me? Why don't I deliver your butt to the public so that it could be kicked about like a football? Instead, my butt is the one getting kicked!" Kong then let loose a hot stream of obscenities, which must have burned up Bobby Boon's ears.

"I'm sorry, sir! It's all my fault, sir."

"Get out of here!" bellowed Kong, pointing to the door.

"Yes sir!"

That day, the whole of Croctopus was abuzz with the newspaper report. Kate, Roger and I were discussing the bad publicity as well as Croctopus's perimeter defense. The whole department was busy—not with work but with the 'elephant test' news report.

"Ken, you've been vindicated," said Kate. "I'm so happy for you." She took an uncharacteristic big bite of her chocolate muffin, as if in celebration of my vindication.

"I'm happy for you, too," said Roger. "We really didn't need an elephant test to know that yours was the much better plan."

"Even the elephants were on your side," said Kate, looking elated.

On another side of the office, two women were talking about the news report. "What an embarrassment," said one woman in a hushed tone.

"I've been getting calls from friends the whole morning; I didn't know what to say to them," said the other.

"I thought we've been upgrading our security," said the first woman. "How could this have happened?"

An administrative assistant came in and pinned onto the bulletin board Croctopus's press release, which also served as the company bulletin. As soon as Kate, Roger and I went to the board, the staff surged forward and crowded around us. I read aloud for those behind, "Colonel Bobby Boon has relinquished his post as Head of Security. He has been transferred out of Security to head the important Annual Ball Committee, where he will contribute his talent and extensive experience to achieve the best year-end corporate event in Orderland. He is replaced as Head of Security by Colonel Vento Voon. Colonel Voon is a no nonsense man who had studied engineering and later obtained an MBA. He retired from the Army several years ago."

Chapter 11

Kate was happy as a schoolgirl out for recess, almost skipping as she headed for Croctopus Café, clutching three long paper cones as if they were treasures. It did not take long for her to find Roger and me.

"Here you are," said Kate triumphantly as she handed Roger and me a cone each. "Try it."

"Hmm . . . it's delicious," said Roger, as he munched the white, sugar-coated peanuts.

"It's called *kachang putih* in Malay," said Kate, as Roger wrote it down on a piece of paper on which he was writing something else earlier. "It literally means white nuts, although it's also used to refer to all the other assorted nuts sold by itinerary vendors who traditionally wore all white. I got them from the Indian gentleman outside the main gate; he's called the *kacang putih* man. Customers get the nuts in long cones folded from recycled paper like the ones we're holding now; it's environmentally friendly."

"*Kacang putih* brings back memories of school days, especially recess," I said. "Recess is one of the happiest and most treasured periods of the school day. No teacher should ever deprive pupils of recess, not even for five minutes. Try it more than once and the teacher's standing among the pupils will plunge."

We had finished lunch and were, as usual, talking about anything that comes to mind.

"Hey, have you read today's papers?" I asked. "There's something about a guy behaving strangely."

"In what way?" asked Roger.

"The report's a bit sketchy at the beginning, but what caught my attention and made me read the entire report was that Dr Jade Choice was called to the scene. Witnesses reported that the guy was behaving like a robot."

"So it must be . . . ," said Kate.

"The report didn't mention Robot Syndrome, but I guess what you're thinking is right. I mean, Dr Jade Choice had to rush to the scene, and that could mean only one thing."

"This is serious, I'd thought Robot Syndrome was a rather rare disease," said Kate.

"Well, it's beginning to look like it's not that rare," I said.

"I wonder whether I'd have the opportunity to witness the disease at work, like you had, Kate," said Roger.

"You wouldn't like to be in that situation; it's scary."

"What fascinates me is that the truth could be so unpalatable to some people that they'd rather turn themselves into a robot than face it," said Roger.

"Well, the truth can be very uncomfortable, and behaving unthinkingly, like a robot, is one way of keeping yourself happy," said Kate.

"Strange that anyone should do that," said Roger.

"People would rather remain in their comfort zone; getting out of it could be unbearable to some," I said.

"But holding on to one's comfort zone to this extent?" said Roger.

"You'd be surprised the extent people would go so as not to face the truth," I said.

Don't remind me of the disease again; let's change subject," said Kate.

"Wow, I didn't know it had such a big impact on you," said Roger. "Must have been really terrifying to see a robot man."

"Let's talk about Socky. I'm not too happy with how things are going with the case," said Kate.

"As far as the General is concerned, we've got him," I said. "Well, not under arrest, but at least we know who he really is. I mean, the General believes we've a good case to arrest him, but are prevented from doing so because his uncle is a US senator and also because we need to smash his network."

"Actually, we've not got anything solid against Socky at all, and it's not getting better," said Kate. "I'm not happy with Spinner's session; the answers we got from Socky were all too vague and elusive. It was like grabbing a fistful of sand, and before you knew it, the sand spills out from all the gaps that your clenched fist fails to close, leaving you with very little. There are too many unanswered questions."

"The General and the rest seemed very sure of themselves after Spinner's session," said Roger, "although, having listened to the record, I tend to agree with you."

"This thing is like a train racing out of control down the track," said Kate. "We've lost control, lost the initiative. This case is moving on its own momentum, as if it has a life of its own. And now we've Hidden Wagon. We're lumping bits and pieces together and coming to conclusion without much thought. I think we need to get a lot more evidence and also review carefully what we already have."

"There seems to be a gulf between the General and you," I said. As far as the General is concerned, we could arrest him or send him packing, but are prevented from doing so by practical considerations. While I fully understand your dissatisfaction in not finding a smoking gun, I think the General expects loyalty and unity in our mission to nail Socky and find his network and Hidden Wagon."

"Oh boy, blind loyalty and enforced unity as a substitute for doing the right thing. That's what those people are good at; it's a terrible addiction," said Kate. "It's quite clear to me the case against Socky is still not good enough, but the General refuses to see the gaping holes; he sees only what he wants to see—an air-tight case—and doesn't tolerate any doubts. Is he dumb or is he afraid of the truth?"

"Well, we ought to have been more rigorous in our work and probe deeper and ask tougher questions," said Roger, popping more *kacang putih* into his mouth. "We've been rather careless and amateurish. I know Croctopus is not the OSD, but we could have done a better job."

"You two don't believe we've a good case?" I asked.

"C'mon Ken, I don't think you really believe we've a good case either," said Kate.

"Well, I know there's no smoking gun, but the General thinks there's persuasive evidence against Socky, and that's good enough for him to act. I mean, we may have our doubts, but we can't just march up to him and tell him to stop everything. There are limits to what we can do." Loyalty and doubt sparred in my mind until my attention was attracted to a report in the newspaper I was holding.

"Take a look at this," I said. "This guy is convicted of abusing, beating and starving his foreign maid for months. And she eventually died from all the abuse, beatings and starvation."

"That's terrible; how could anyone do such a thing?" said Kate shaking her head. "A life lost, just like that. And it says here, she was only eighteen years old. This is terrible, just terrible."

I continued, "In his remorse, the guy told the court, 'I am a monster.' I wonder what took him so long to realize that he was a monster. I mean, it took months and a death for him to realize it."

"Some people need a disaster before they know that what they've been doing was wrong," said Roger.

"It's absurd; the girl wasted away for months and he couldn't see anything wrong with what he had been doing," I said. "The girl was dying before his very eyes, but he didn't see it. How could it be? It's beyond my comprehension."

Except for the *kacang putih* treat and perhaps the newspaper report, it was an uneventful day for me. I left the office a little earlier than usual, looking forward to having a quiet evening at home. I thought I would spend the evening reading a good book; no office papers, just a good book. The kids would be back from school soon; they were my treat every evening when I came home. *Kacang putih* treat in the afternoon, Mei and Min treat in the evening. These were small things; peanuts, some would say, but I lived for small things. Arm was having a night out with her friends.

Mei and Min came home soon enough. After dinner, washing up and homework, they refused to go to bed because, they said, it was early. They wanted me to tell them a story, but after a few years of telling stories I had used up my stock of stories. Fortunately, a quiet day at the office and the quiet evening at home made my mind relax and ready for any minor challenge. With the kids seated facing me, looking at me attentively, I began the story.

"Once upon a time, there lived a man called Retsnom. He was mean and treated others badly; he cared only for himself and he was cruel. Once, he had a heart attack and the doctors operated on him. They opened up his chest, but had trouble finding his heart. He had no feelings for others. Even when someone was in pain or suffered in his presence, he could feel nothing. But he didn't know he was such a bad man; he actually believed he was a good man. That was because he saw only what he wanted to see."

"He's like the big bad wolf!" said Min.

"Yes, but maybe worse," I said.

"Shh . . . Min, don't interrupt; Daddy, continue with the story, please," said Mei.

"One day, Retsnom looked into the mirror as he was combing his hair. But his image didn't appear in the mirror; instead something else appeared. In the mirror, there was a green monster, oozing sticky green liquid from every pore. The monster was also combing his hair. But Retsnom didn't see the monster in the mirror; he saw only himself."

Mei and Min looked at me and listened attentively; not a word came from them this time.

"The next day, the same thing happened; when Retsnom looked into the mirror to comb his hair, the green monster appeared, but still Retsnom didn't notice anything unusual. He saw only himself in the mirror. On the third day, the same thing happened. But this time, the green monster was combing his hair with a comb in one hand while his other hand was holding what looked like a big piece of chicken drumstick. On the fourth day, the same thing happened, but the piece of meat the green monster was eating now looked too big for a chicken drumstick. Anyone standing next to Retsnom would have been able to tell that the piece of meat looked like a human arm, but not Retsnom. Day after day, the same thing happened; the green monster appeared in the mirror eating human flesh, but Retsnom didn't notice anything wrong. Every day was just a normal day to him. He didn't see the green monster eating parts of people; he only saw himself combing his hair. It went on for months."

"That's scary, Daddy," said Min.

"Stop interrupting, Min," said Mei. "Daddy, go on, please. What happened next?"

"One day, the green monster appeared as usual. There was a human foot sticking out of his mouth. He swallowed the foot in one gulp and moments later gave a loud belch. The monster then took a human bone fragment to pick his teeth, and gave out another satisfied belch. Retsnom whistled a tune as he continued combing his hair, oblivious to the terrible events taking place on the other side of the mirror.

"Then one day, Retsnom heard loud, frightful banging on the front door, and the apparent tranquility of the house was shattered. Retsnom was shocked, but before he could investigate the police crashed through the door and charged into the bedroom and handcuffed him. They said they were arresting him for abusing, beating and starving a young girl to death. Retsnom was confused and said he didn't do anything wrong. As he was being led out of the bedroom, something in the mirror caught his attention. He stopped and looked into the mirror closely, and there for the first time saw the green monster, who smiled slyly and asked Retsnom why he looked so surprised. Retsnom asked the green monster why he didn't tell him what had been happening over the past months, but the green monster merely shrugged his shoulders and replied that Retsnom could have seen everything for himself in the mirror every day. Retsnom protested that he didn't see anything unusual; he didn't see the monster at all. Then suddenly everything became clear to him and he said, 'I'm the monster.' The green monster said it was Retsnom's fault that he didn't see anything for so many months, as any normal person would have seen a monster. The green monster gave a broad, evil grin and waved Retsnom goodbye before turning away contemptuously."

"Daddy, can a person turn into a monster?" asked Mei.

"That can happen; a person won't turn into a monster physically, but he can in thought and action."

"Why didn't Retsnom see the green monster in the mirror?" asked Min.

"Because he didn't want to."

"If you don't want to see something, then you wouldn't see it?" asked Min.

"Yes, that's right, if you try hard enough."

"What if a person wants to see something that's not there?" asked Mei.

"If he insists on seeing something that's not there, then he'd see it."

"Daddy, you mean we can see something even if that something is not there?" replied Mei.

"If you're not honest with yourself, you'd see it."

"So, honesty stops you from seeing things that are not there?" asked Min.

"That's right, it stops you from seeing things that are not there. It also lets you see things that are really there, even if you would rather not see it."

"So, Retsnom was not honest?" asked Mei.

"Yes, he wasn't honest, not even to himself."

"Honesty is very important," said Min.

"Yes, very important."

We talked for a while more before I packed them off to bed. Of course, I should have paid closer attention to my story. How could I have been so dumb at that time?

*

Roger was looking around Croctopus City, the largest shopping mall in Orderland. The loud cheering attracted his attention and, as he had time to spare, went to the large atrium to investigate. There was a big crowd and a big stage. It was the Monica Moon Road Show. The star was working the crowd like a magician; she smiled her Monica Moon smile, waved at her screaming fans, spun around to show off her figure, and took deep breaths repeatedly to feign breathless excitement, but actually to inflate and show off her ample top. The crowd loved it; it went wild with every minor bit of Monica Moon's showmanship.

"I love you!" declared Monica Moon to the crowd, and the people responded with a loud cheer. Then turning to another segment of the crowd, she repeated, "I love you!" There came another, even louder cheer. She cupped her ear with her hand expectantly and the crowd roared, "We love you!" She cracked a few jokes and sang two songs.

Roger was fascinated; she was just a young woman, but already an expert at working a crowd. How could a person become so famous and successful at such a young age?

After the songs and some more jokes, Monica Moon announced, "Ladies and gentlemen, please welcome my special guest, Ms Marvey "Marvellous" Moon of the famous Moon Beauty Institute," whereupon Marvey Moon came onto the stage to much fanfare. She was the well-known mother of Monica and was there to promote her Moon's Alpine Dream, a treatment that promised to enhance a woman's chest by up to three centimeters in a week. She was also an expert at working the crowd, smiling and getting the people's attention with such ease that Roger felt he was receiving an education for free. Marvey Moon told the crowd that to increase her chest measurement by up to three centimeters in a week, all a woman needed to do was to apply Moon's Alpine Dream cream before going to bed every night. Then Marvey Moon proceeded with a demonstration. A young, beautiful girl came on stage, wearing shorts and a matching bikini top. She then went behind a large, white screen with backlighting, which cast her shadow onto the screen. She removed her bikini top and an assistant used a tape to measure the girl's chest. This was done before the crowd so that, looking at the shadows, the people would be satisfied that there was no cheating. The girl, with bikini top back on, and the assistant came out from behind the screen and Marvey Moon, reading from a piece of paper handed to her by the assistant, announced the girl's chest measurement. An assistant then appeared carrying a tray covered with a white silk cloth and with a small jar on it. Marvey Moon took the jar and raised it to face level and showed it confidently to the crowd on all sides of the stage. She then opened the jar of Moon's Alpine Dream cream and proceeded to apply it onto the girl's chest. It was done with the care and attention of a true professional, as everyone in the crowd could see. The girl was then led behind the screen once more, where she took off her bikini top again and Marvey Moon, like a magician conjuring an illusion, applied more cream. Then Marvey Moon came out from behind the screen with the girl, now with a towel wrapped around her. The girl was led to a chair and she sat down, flashing a smile. At all times, either she or her shadow was in full view of the crowd, so the spectators should be satisfied that there was no cheating.

Roger looked around and wondered why there were so many men in the crowd. He asked a man standing next to him why he was interested in Moon's Alpine Dream. The man replied, "Why are *you* interested?" and walked to another part of the crowd.

Monica Moon interviewed Marvey Moon, who went on to give more details of the wonders of Moon's Alpine Dream. Monica Moon then sang two more songs, after which it was time for Marvey Moon to resume her demonstration. The girl came back to center stage and, after smiling and confirming that she felt great, was led behind the screen, where she removed her towel for a second measurement. Then the girl, with towel back on, and the assistant came out. Marvey Moon took a piece of paper from the assistant and, with the measured pace of a true professional building up tension in the audience, announced the startling result.

"There's an increase in size of half a centimeter!" announced Marvey Moon with the flair of a host announcing the latest movie award. The crowd was in awe, and they clapped and cheered loudly. The young girl looked overwhelmed with joy and covered her mouth with both hands, almost in tears. The assistant smiled and stretched out her arm to direct attention to the girl, like a magician's assistant would do at the end of a performance. Marvey Moon continued, "Half a centimeter may not sound like much, but we've only had a few minutes. Imagine what Moon's Alpine Dream can do in a week."

After the Monica Moon Road Show, Roger did some shopping, but did not buy anything. On the way out of Croctopus City, he came across the Moon Beauty Institute. There was a long queue of about a hundred excited people, many with an application form in hand. Later, at the office, Roger related what took place at Croctopus City to me.

"That must be a triumph of hope over the truth," I said. "I wonder what Dr Jade Choice would think of them."

*

Kate, nibbling a chocolate muffin, came to my desk, where I was sipping a cup of coffee. We discussed Socky's case.

"Remember our discussion the other day over *kacang putih*?" said Kate.

"Yes, of course. What about it?"

"I can't get over it; I don't think we've sufficient evidence against Socky. And it's not just me, Roger thought so too, and, I dare say, you too, although you wouldn't admit it."

"But the General is absolutely sure that we've solid proof of whom Socky really is. Is the General seeing things that you and Roger can't see, or is he seeing things that are not there?"

"I think we should tell him what's on our mind."

"But you've tried that already, and it didn't work; it only made him angry, and things carried on as usual."

"But things shouldn't carry on as usual." Kate started to pace about, thinking hard. "Ken, I really feel we should do something about this."

"And go to war with the General? Is this a reasonable path to take? You know how he is; he expects us to be united and not cast doubts and weaken our resolve."

"So, we let this case go where we don't want it to go?"

I thought for a while and replied, "Is it up to us?"

Chapter 12

Kong called an early morning conference of Croctopus terrorist hunters; it surprised everyone as there had been no warning that something was brewing and that an urgent meeting was needed. As usual, the environment in the boardroom in early morning was hostile to all creatures alive, as the air-conditioner was pumping air as cold as arctic winds. The machine had a life of its own and it was acting like a mythic god who could not be appeased or controlled.

"Good morning," said Kong. "I called this meeting because things are going nowhere and, therefore, I'm in a bad mood, made worse by the lousy breakfast I had. The piece of oily sausage I had is still stuck somewhere in my chest, refusing to go down to my stomach like a good sausage should. Actually, I had thought of calling the meeting later in the morning when you'd be more settled, but I changed my mind. I thought the arctic condition here in early morning would put the chill into you and convey to you my mood more accurately."

I had felt fine earlier that morning and thought that I could have a good day in the office, and was disappointed by such an early turn of events. Kate had left her half-eaten chocolate muffin sitting at her desk before rushing to the boardroom, only to be devastated by Kong's bad mood. The sweetness of the muffin was still in her mouth, but fading quickly; her tongue was getting numb from the cold and her mind was even more numb from Kong's bad mood, all very bad for sensing the last traces of the muffin. Roger was not in the room as he was having a meeting with government officials to discuss security matters. Sammy Sam and Sonny Song looked cowed and sheepish and unready for any mental exertion. Vento Voon, the replacement for Bobby Boon, had much more spirit as he was new to the job.

I wondered which was more tolerable: arctic winds or thunder and lightning. Kong was capable of both. Anyway, it was not Kong's character to give anyone a choice; it was arctic winds that morning. I looked at Kate, who seemed to sense what I was thinking. She shrugged her shoulders slightly and took a deep breath, which camouflaged her shoulder movement. We all waited in apprehension for Kong's morning breakfast show to start.

"There's a terrorist mole right here in our midst. We know who he is, but can't do a damn thing to him. We can't kick him out or have him arrested. We want him to lead us to his network, but he's leading us nowhere. And, most frightening of all, there's Hidden Wagon somewhere in Orderland, but we have no idea where. Some terrorist finger is on the button, yet we can't do anything about it. Our country is in great danger; we could be wiped out from the face of the earth in forty-five minutes, I was told."

"And he's complaining about a bad breakfast," Kate whispered to me, while keeping a straight face and pretending to show me a document. I froze at her audacity. Not getting a response, she gave me a kick to defrost me.

"Kate, you're looking rather strange," said Kong.

166

"Oh, I'm alright . . . I didn't have a good breakfast either."

"Why are so many young women not having proper breakfasts?" asked Kong.

"Well, we do try to have proper breakfasts, it's just that some of us can't eat so early in the morning. We're like animals that had just awoken from hibernation and needed to warm up before eating," said Kate.

"You should be like me—I don't need to warm up before I eat; I can eat soon after waking up," said Kong proudly. "As I was saying, we're in great danger; our country is in great danger. We have to get to the bottom of this fast. If this thing doesn't move faster, you'd all be answerable, especially you, Ken."

"Me?" I wondered what nonsense Kong was talking about, but I was too dumbfounded to say anything more. Also, my mind was not working at normal speed so early in the morning.

"Yes, you. As the point man monitoring Crouching Liar, everything depends on you," said Kong. "If nothing comes from you, we'd have nothing to work on."

"But this is a team effort," I protested without raising my voice.

"And the whole team is relying on you to come up with something."

"But I'm not from the Orderland Security Department; I can't just barge into people's private lives or threaten anybody. I've no power of investigation whatsoever." I was getting agitated, but had to pretend to be calm as there was no way anyone could have a head-on clash with Kong.

"You know I'm right, Ken; there's no way I could be wrong here. So, I don't want excuses; just bring me results."

"But Ken has a point," said Kate.

"I said just bring me results."

Why don't you bring us results? I thought.

"I propose we re-examine all the evidence before proceeding further," said Kate. "As I see it . . ."

"What on Earth are you trying to do? No back-tracking; go forward and get me results," said Kong.

"We're making a lot of assumptions," said Kate. "We ought to re-examine what we've got so that we don't go off in the wrong direction."

"You're mad this morning, Kate? No more talk; I want action and results," said Kong. "Do you hear me? I believe in action; I don't sit around debating academic points of interest."

"The General has made himself quite clear," said Vento Voon. "Let's not waste time debating; we need to get moving faster, as the General has very rightly pointed out."

"Yes, that's true, but it's still of utmost importance that we go in the right direction," said Kate.

"Are you suggesting we're a bunch of idiots who didn't know what we had been doing and had gone off on a tangent?" said Sammy Sam.

The discussion got heated up and the atmosphere became stifling and oppressive, with the three executive vice-presidents backing Kong like eunuchs standing firmly on the emperor's side. Kate thought the opportunity had arrived for her to press for a review of the case and, therefore, argued with some force.

"Kate, that's insubordination!" said Vento Voon, his face red with anger. "You've made the General very angry."

I thought Vento Voon should stop yelling and listen to reason; any fool can yell, but not all can reason. I did not want Kate to take the heat because she was trying to help me. "Why don't we get back to the discussion?" I suggested.

"I want no more nonsense from you, Kate; you should know what's permissible and what's not in our organization," said Kong. "Now, whilst this is a team effort, I hold Ken primarily responsible for the progress in the hunt for Crouching Liar, Hidden Wagon, as well as the terrorist network. My orders are clear, and everyone knows I'm right. I don't sit around arguing endlessly. That's not my style; you know that. No more arguments. This meeting is adjourned."

That spoiled the day for me. We were hunting for terrorists with a WMD and the country could be destroyed in forty-five minutes, and I was the one primarily responsible for the progress of the hunt? Why, I wasn't even a private in the police force! Not only did I feel unfairly treated, I also felt that I was dealing with a boss who refused to admit the possibility that he might be wrong, and who knew only how to assign responsibilities and expect results to appear from thin air. It was a bad day for me, so I did whatever I could in the office and went home as early as possible.

As soon as I stepped into the house, my two kids came bouncing to me. Even a bad day could end beautifully.

"Sorry, I've to end here, my husband's back," said Arm on her cellphone. Then she turned to me and said, "Could you please take this box and keep it in the car boot?"

"What's this?"

"Some old books," said Arm.

"Why am I keeping old books in the car?"

"Because there's no space in the house."

"That's not possible; the house is much bigger than this box."

"There's no space in the house. They're your books, anyway; you should be keeping them."

"But I have kept them; all my books are on the shelves."

"I needed some shelf space, so I removed these books. They're old books and I'm sure you've read them."

"That's not the point . . ."

"That's the point, your books are occupying too much space in the house."

"We've the same number of shelves since we moved into the house; I've not expanded my shelf space at all. If you need a shelf, we can get one."

"There's no space for another shelf."

"Yes, there is."

"Your books are gathering dust. Look, I'm trying to keep the house clean; I'm doing this for the family. You've a nice time at the office everyday, but I'm the one who has to take care of everything at home. It's about time you got rid of your books!"

"I'm not putting the books in the car; I'll find some space for them."

"If you're not reading them again, I suggest you throw them away. And don't forget to mop the floor after dinner."

"Oh, I've got two places to go today," I said. "I'm going to the Sunshine Old Folks' Home to deliver some crates of oranges. All the other guys will be there. On the way, I'll go to Mother's place to give her some oranges."

"Why are you wasting your time doing delivery work?"

"I'm not wasting time; all the other guys will bring their stuff to the old folks' home, too."

"But you've to mop the floor today."

"That's not a problem, I'll go off for just a while, and I'll mop the floor after I'm back."

"You're supposed to mop the floor after dinner; you know that. You're now telling me you're not mopping the floor after dinner. How could you? This home is a shared responsibility; you've got to do your part. You can't expect me to do everything." Arm looked really aggrieved and about to burst into tears.

"I've told you I'll mop the floor after I'm back."

"You're not playing your part; what kind of a husband are you? You're a married man with a wife and kids, but you seem to be spending more time taking care of others than your family. Where are your priorities? Don't you think of your family? And that's us, if you don't already know. I think of our family all the time, but do you? Seems like you don't. This is sad, isn't it? You have a family, but you act as if you don't. How did you get to this? Must I tell you how to behave like a man with a family? Think about it."

"Look, all this is unnecessary. Why are you . . ."

"Unnecessary? My goodness, I've never thought I'd hear such words from you. Are you saying your family's well-being is unnecessary? Am I unnecessary? Are your kids unnecessary? Then who in your life is necessary? Unnecessary, indeed! I'm disappointed with you! This is sad, isn't it? Sad! And why are you running to your mother? You can't be running to your mother all the time. You're still attached to your mother's apron strings! You're not a man at all; real men don't go running to their mother like you do."

"You're talking nonsense; I'll drop off the oranges and then come back and mop the floor."

"Shame on you! You really don't care about the family, do you? You don't care about me, do you? If you don't like this family, you should get out of here. This home's not for you . . ."

"Don't be abusive," I said before walking off.

"Ken, you listen to me . . ."

After dinner, I went off as planned, but made it a point to return home as soon as possible. When I arrived home, Arm and the children were nowhere to be found. I tried to call Arm on her cellphone, but she did not answer. I mopped the floor quickly, after which I tried to reach Arm again, but she still did not answer my call. A few minutes later, my cellphone rang.

"Don't bother to call me again," said Arm.

"What's happening?"

"The kids are with me and we're not coming back." Arm sounded like she was in tears. "You and I are finished; we're divorced. You can go ahead and file the court papers tomorrow to make it official."

"Where are you now?"

"You don't have to know. I'm very disappointed with you. I've done so much for the family, but you can't even mop the floor, and you've promised to do it. What kind of a husband are you? Don't call me again." Then Arm hung up before I could say more.

As it was not the first time Arm had left home in anger or asked me to proceed with divorce, I did not panic. However, that night I went to bed knowing that I would not get to sleep well. My heart was heavy and my mind was swirling with unresolved issues. I tossed and turned in bed, but dozed off eventually. Then the dream started.

It was an uncomfortable flight, made worse by Kong sitting next to me. Kong, who looked unhappy, was talking to me and emphasizing a point with his finger, but I could not hear what he was saying, although the low humming sound of the plane engines in the background was not a problem. There was movement in Kong's lips, but no sound emanated from him. Suddenly, the plane shook violently as it approached the runway in a frighteningly quick descent, and it landed with a heavy thud, like a goose whose power of flight had failed. Everyone was scared white. The plane hurtled down the runway with a harrowing momentum; the pilots had lost control! As the wheels screeched and friction burned up the tires, leaving long lines of track on the ground, a frightening roar rushed into the cabin. The passengers asked themselves whether the plane would become their collective coffin. The roaring engines, the screeching tires and the rushing wind coalesced into a deafening, terrifying call of death. I felt for the seatbelt instinctively. It seemed that my time was up; there was no appeal; I felt the cruelty of fate. Then I noticed that Kong was wearing a tiger-striped suit. Strange, I thought, how come I did not notice it earlier? I took another look. Stranger still, Kong was not there anymore; instead, a tiger was on Kong's seat! It glared at me and gave a menacing growl; I broke out in cold sweat. The tiger extended a paw and made a swipe at me, but missed. The other passengers did not seem to notice the tiger; they were bracing themselves in anticipation of a frightful crash. The tiger seemed unsettled by the momentum of the runaway plane and seemed to feel that I was responsible for its discomfort. It kept clawing at me, but, strangely, I managed to escape injury. The plane was about to crash anytime and we were all going to die, but all the tiger wanted to do was to claw at me. It could not comprehend the reality of the situation; it could not relate to the dire situation beyond me. To the tiger, I was the troublemaker who caused the discomfort, and must be attacked. The absurdity of the tiger's behavior angered me. I was angry and frightened at the same time, but there was nothing I could do to the tiger.

Then the plane crashed with a terrifying force. Pandemonium erupted in the plane; people were screaming and pushing, as if the animals in a zoo had escaped all at once. Everyone was trying to escape from the cabin, which had become a trap. An air stewardess was trying to open the door while a man was pounding on it, making her task more difficult. Strangely, I could not hear anything; people were screaming, but there was no sound. The stewards and stewardesses were trying to guide passengers to the exits, but no one listened, no one cared; the passengers surged toward the exits like there would be no tomorrow. I was trapped in my seat, my path blocked by the tiger. With courage borne out of desperation, I screamed at the tiger to get out of the way. Then, just as the cabin was almost empty, the tiger leapt from its seat and ran to an exit and jumped out. Wasting no time, I followed it. Standing at the exit, I surveyed the scene below. People were running frantically, trying to get as far away from the plane as possible, and the tiger was running after them. Then, a strange thing happened. The tiger turned into a goose. At that moment, the people stopped running away; instead, they turned back and started chasing the goose, which ran about wildly in all directions, dodging pursuers left and right, and flapping its wings frantically. I stood at the exit watching entranced the silent scene below. The people did not seem to know what they were doing; they chased the goose just because it was running away. But nobody was able to catch it. Sometimes they came very close to catching it, but it always managed to elude them. It darted in and out of pockets of people with outstretched arms.

Then I woke up. I was wet all over, and it took me a few moments to realize that the strange scene was only a dream. I sat up, trying to reassure myself that I was all right. Although the dream had disappeared like a puff of smoke, the absurdity of the tiger's and the people's behavior did not leave me. The plane in the dream was hurtling out of control and was about to crash, but the tiger only wanted to attack me, unable to comprehend the real danger. The people chased the goose for no apparent reason, not asking why and forgetting that the plane could explode any time. The scene from the strange dream swirled round and round in my head and kept me awake. I seldom could recall my dreams, but this one felt different. Then I remembered that Arm was not with me and the kids were not at home either. Mine was not a happy situation, whether in or out of my dream. I fell back into bed with eyes open and remained awake. The next morning I set off for the office as usual, but something in me was not the same; something inside had changed. I could feel that the dream was inside me; not just in my head, but all over me. I felt disturbed.

Chapter 13

Sammy Sam hurried up and down Croctopus Center, almost knocking into shoppers several times. He looked left and right, up and down, but to no avail; his quarry had eluded him. Beads of sweat rained down his forehead and temple, as his eyes darted about in the hope of catching his quarry again. But the more he searched, the more he looked like he was about to explode from the tension; his shirt was stained with large blotches of sweat. In panic his first resort was his cellphone; he tapped the keys quickly to report the unfortunate situation. The reply from Kong was so loud and ferocious that Sammy Sam jerked the cellphone away from his ear and grimaced like a schoolboy being scolded by the headmaster. A few shoppers noticed Sammy Sam's predicament, as some of them would tell me later in my investigation, but they did not do anything as the culprit inflicting the pain appeared to be only the cellphone.

"Yes, sir . . . yes, sir," said Sammy Sam. "I'll find him, one way or another, sir." The shoppers noticed that he went off frantically in one direction and then another, apparently with no clue as to where he should head to. As he passed by the Croctopus Center Management office, the idea apparently struck him that he should go in and get reinforcement for the hunt. He dashed in to look for the manager, but had the shock of his life. His quarry was there, seated and looking at him.

"Hello Sammy, why are you tailing me?" asked Socky with a half-smile.

"Tailing you? I'm not tailing you. What are you talking about? I'm just shopping, and I'm surprised to see you here."

"Shopping for management services?" asked Socky.

"Well, er . . . just looking for a friend. What are you doing here?"

"I'm doing research."

"On Croctopus Center?"

"No, on shopping mall management."

"I never knew you were interested in shopping mall management."

"There's a lot you don't know about me."

"Actually, I may know more than you realize. Anyway, enjoy your research; I've got to make a call, excuse me." Sammy Sam hurried to a corner to make a call on his cellphone.

"He's doing research on shopping mall management?" said Kong excitedly. As Kate was with him, he was using the conference mode of his telephone. "Why would he be interested in this sort of thing? Is Croctopus Center his target?"

"Holy smoke! That's right, why didn't I think of it?" said Sammy Sam, looking in Socky's direction. "You're very sharp, General; I couldn't have guessed. Why, that sly fox; he's really dangerous, isn't he?"

"He's definitely on to something. Things are getting dangerous for us; if a bomb goes off at Croctopus Center and the building collapses, there'd be thousands of casualties. We must never let it happen. Keep an eye on him; find out what he wants to know about Croctopus Center. He's picking a target; I'm sure of it."

"Yes sir, you can depend on me, sir. There's no way I'll let him get away; no way, sir; no quarry ever gets away from me, sir."

"I'm not sure about that; keep me updated."

"Yes, sir!" Sammy Sam breathed a sigh of relief.

"And where's Ken? He's supposed to monitor Crouching Liar until he hands over the task to you at Croctopus Center."

"Well, er . . . I don't know where Ken is, sir. It's his fault for disappearing . . . Wait a minute, sir, he's actually here talking to some people."

"Okay, now take over from Ken and do your job."

Sammy Sam came over to Socky and me as we were talking to an old couple, and he said, "Ken, where have you been the whole day? I was looking for you."

"The whole day?" I said. "It's still morning. Socky and I had arranged to meet here." Noticing that Sammy Sam was looking at the old couple, I continued, "They need help; they're trying to call Croctopus Travel."

"But this is not Croctopus Travel," said Sammy Sam, "The Travel office is at Croctopus City, not here; this is Croctopus Center."

"Yes, we know," said the old man, "but we were shopping and then we tried calling Croctopus Travel on the phone but couldn't get through, so we dropped in here hoping that somebody could help."

"But there's no connection between Croctopus Center Management and Croctopus Travel; they're two different offices doing different things," said Sammy Sam.

"Well, there's the Croctopus name in both," said the old woman.

"Yes, but they're really two different entities providing different services."

"It doesn't really matter," I said. "I'll call Croctopus Travel for you." Socky and I led the old couple to a telephone at a corner; Sammy Sam followed close behind.

"It's okay, we can manage," said Socky, looking a bit puzzled that Sammy Sam seemed to have attached himself to us. As soon as we sat down Sammy Sam used the office telephone to call Croctopus Travel. Socky was surprised that Sammy Sam seemed to have abandoned the idea of looking for his friend.

"I'll help them; I know about Croctopus Travel," said Sammy Sam. The old woman told him they wanted to know more about Singapore. "Sure," said Sammy Sam, as he tapped some keys on the telephone and activated the conference mode as well.

"Welcome to the world of Croctopus Travel, we hope to be of service to you," said a voice from the telephone. It was a woman's voice, very melodious, velvety and friendly. "For travel information please press 1, for travel reservations please press 2, for hotel reservations please press 3, for insurance services please press 4, for local travel please press 5, for office services please press 6, for credit card services please press 7, for airport information please press 8, for airfares please press 9, for weather information please press 10, for time at major cities please press 11, for translation services please press 12, for restaurants please press 13, for taxi services please press 14, for bus information please press 15, for train services please press 16, for laundry services please press 17, for gym information please press 18, for pet grooming and amusement services please press 19, for medical services please press 20, and if you wish to speak to our travel consultant please press 21."

The old couple kept their eyes on the telephone as if trying hard to remember the mass of information given. Sammy Sam pressed a key, but did not tell the couple what number he had selected or explain to them why he had chosen that number.

"We thank you for your interest in our travel services," said the voice. We have the best and widest range of travel options here in Orderland. Our travel consultant will attend to you shortly. Your call is important to us. In the meantime, please let us take you round the world . . ." The voice took them on a talking tour round the world, dispensing information on various countries and promoting Croctopus Travel tour packages. Nice background music accompanied them to every country. After the tour, the voice said, "Thank you for waiting. Our travel consultant will attend to you shortly. Your call is important to us. In the meantime, if you wish to access other information, please feel free to do so."

"The travel consultant will attend to us in a little while," said Sammy Sam to the old couple. "In the meantime, please don't hesitate to let me know what information you need from Croctopus Travel."

"Thank you very much, we just need some information on Singapore," said the old man. Could we go straight to the information on Singapore?"

Then the voice returned and said, "For travel information please press 1, for travel reservations please press 2, for hotel reservations please press 3, for insurance services please press 4, for local travel please press 5, for office services please press 6, for credit card services please press 7, for airport information please press 8, for airfares please press 9, for weather information please press 10, for time at major cities please press 11, for translation services please press 12, for restaurants please press 13, for taxi services please press 14, for bus information please press 15, for train services please press 16, for laundry services please press 17, for gym information please press 18, for pet grooming and amusement services please press 19, for medical services please press 20. Thank you for waiting. Our travel consultant will attend to you shortly. Your call is important to us. In the meantime, please let us take you round the world . . ."

"Actually, we need only a bit of information on Singapore," pleaded the old woman to Sammy Sam. "We'll be happy just to go straight to the information on Singapore."

"Sure, the information on Singapore will come shortly," assured Sammy Sam, smiling. "A little patience will get us there."

"Time is not on our side, as you can see," said the old man before breaking into a hearty laugh.

The voice came back and said, "Thank you for waiting. Our travel consultant will attend to you shortly. Your call is important to us. In the meantime, if you wish to access other information please feel free to do so."

"The travel consultant must be very busy," said Sammy Sam, trying hard to force a smile.

"Why don't we just give them some brochures?" I said.

"That's right, good idea," said Socky.

"No, no," said Sammy Sam, "we've excellent telephone access; we've spent a fortune on it."

"We'll be happy with a couple of brochures," said the old man.

Then the voice said, "For travel information please press 1, for travel reservations please press 2, for hotel reservations please press 3, for insurance services please press 4, for local travel please press 5, for office services please press 6, for credit card services please press 7, for airport information please press 8, for airfares please press 9, for weather information please press 10, for time at major cities please press 11, for translation services please press 12, for restaurants please press 13, for taxi services please press 14, for bus information please press 15, for train services please press 16, for laundry services please press 17, for gym information please press 18, for pet grooming and amusement services please press 19, for medical services please press 20."

"Thank you, we know all that already," said the old woman to the voice.

The voice continued, "Thank you for waiting. Our travel consultant will attend to you shortly. Your call is important to us. In the meantime, please let us take you round the world . . ."

"Here we go again," said the old woman. The voice took them for another talking tour round the world.

"Well, I've got to get going; the office just called for me," I said before going off, leaving Sammy Sam to monitor Socky.

"It was a wonderful tour round the world, don't you agree?" said Sammy Sam after the world tour. "The company spent a small fortune to produce it."

When the tour ended, the old couple stood up, the old man turned to Sammy Sam and said, "Well, thank you very much for all your help; we really appreciate it, but we don't think we should take up any more of your time."

"But it has been a wonderful tour round the world; I'm sure you'll agree."

"Oh yes, it was just wonderful; but we've been round the world three times today and we've still not got to Singapore," said the old man. "We'll just go get ourselves some printed stuff. Thank you very much for all your help; we appreciate that, really."

"Please wait a minute," said Sammy Sam, turning to the telephone for one more attempt. But it was too late; the old couple had walked off, probably in search of some brochures. Then Sammy Sam realized that Socky was gone too. According to the Travel office people who told me later, he stood up immediately and rushed about in the office, but could not find his prey. He then dashed outside to look for Socky, but to no avail. Some of the office people ran after him, thinking that he was in trouble and needed help, but Sammy Sam was so frantic that he did not notice them.

"I need reinforcement," said Sammy Sam on his cellphone, "Crouching Liar has disappeared."

"Disappeared? Disappeared into thin air? What nonsense are you talking about?" bellowed Kong. "Nobody can disappear into thin air! You find him now! And I mean now!"

Sammy Sam sweated so profusely that, according to the office people following him, his face seemed to be melting. The verbal onslaught by Kong reduced Sammy Sam to a quivering mass, much to his embarrassment. Some shoppers actually stared at him.

"Yes sir . . . certainly, sir. Not to worry, sir, I'll get him; he won't get away, sir . . . yes sir; you can depend on me, sir."

Meanwhile, in a small restaurant in Croctopus Center, Socky was alone having a cup of coffee. The place was cozy, the lighting low. He could see Sammy Sam at the other side of the mall. Realizing that Sammy Sam was in some trouble, he smiled slyly. A while later, a small, bespectacled man, his face obscured by the low lighting, joined Socky at the table. They talked in hushed tones, laughing every now and then. The small man turned to look at Sammy Sam and grinned mischievously.

"Let's have some fun," said Socky, before leaving the restaurant with the small man. They walked into Sammy Sam's line of sight, which caused him such excitement that he pointed at Socky with an outstretched arm and ran toward the two men.

"Socky, stop! Stop!" cried Sammy Sam. "I've got you!" Sammy Sam ran to the spot where Socky and the small man were, but he could not find them; they had disappeared into the crowd. Some shoppers were looking at Sammy Sam, but none approached him or asked him anything.

"I've got them, sir," said Sammy Sam on his cellphone, "but they've disappeared."

"Then you've not got them!" screamed Kong. According to Kate, Kong actually jumped up from his chair and pointed a threatening finger at an imaginary Sammy Sam in front of him.

"I did, I actually got them, sir. I was there and they were here, and I saw them; I had them in my sight, sir, but they've disappeared."

"No, you have not; you've not got them!"

"Yes, I did, sir; they were within my grasp, but they escaped, sir."

"That means you've not got them!"

"I wish you were here, sir; if you were you'd understand what I'm saying. I got them, sir; I really got them, sir."

"No, you didn't and that's final! Now go get them, I command you!"

"Yes sir, you can count on me, sir."

Sammy Sam started to dash about again, not really knowing where to go. Socky and the small man were looking at him from one floor above. They seemed pleased.

"Gee, this is fun," said the small man.

A shopper, a middle aged man who had been following the chase, approached Socky and asked, "Are you people doing a show, some kind of reality TV with a hidden camera?"

"Well, no," said Socky.

"Come on, tell me. You look familiar; I've seen you somewhere. You're an actor."

"I think you're mistaken," said Socky.

"We're secret agents," whispered the small man, hand covering his mouth and half his face

"Secret agents, really? Wow! This is exciting," said the shopper, his eyes lighting up. What about that guy down there, the one chasing you?"

"Oh, he's from the OSD," said the small man, hand still over his face

"The OSD, you mean . . ."

"Yes, the Orderland Security Department," said the small man.

"Wow! This is cool, really cool, and I'm in the middle of it!" The shopper punched the air with his fist. "But, hey, wait a minute . . . If he's from the OSD, then you must be . . . you must be the bad guys!"

"That's right," said the small man, still not showing his full face.

The shopper started to look serious. Then turning to Socky he said, "Hey, you look familiar; I've seen you somewhere."

"No, I don't think so."

"Yes, I have; I'm sure I have. Don't lie to me."

"Why should I lie to you?"

"Because you're a secret agent . . . Why are you looking at me like that? You're intimidating me."

"No, I'm not."

"Yes, you are; you're intimidating me. I've seen you somewhere; don't lie to me."

The shopper looked very frightened, like a cornered fox. He looked down one floor at Sammy Sam, as if seeking help. Then, with both hands cupped around his mouth for voice projection, he yelled, "Hey, officer! They're here! They're right here!"

Sammy Sam looked up and, seeing Socky and the small man, immediately dashed to the escalator and ran up to the floor above, all the while shouting, "Stop! Stop! I've got you!" When he arrived at the higher floor, Socky and the small man had disappeared. Sammy Sam looked around and saw the shopper, frightened speechless and pointing at something, but really at no particular thing. Then Sammy Sam saw Socky and the small man on the floor above. The small man waved to Sammy Sam, who immediately ran up the escalator. But, once again, Socky and the small man were gone.

"I got them, but they've escaped again, sir," said Sammy Sam, with a shaky grip on his cellphone and panting. The reply from Kong was so loud and unbearable that Sammy Sam jerked his cellphone away from his ear.

The next day, Sammy Sam, Sonny Song and Vento Voon assembled at the boardroom for an emergency meeting called by Kong. Socky was there too.

"Socky, I understand something strange happened yesterday," said Kong. "Why did you run away from Colonel Sam?"

"Run away? I didn't run away. Did he chase after me? Why did he chase after me?" said Socky. That unexpected reply threw Kong off balance, and he turned to Sammy Sam.

"You ran away from me," said Sammy Sam, thrusting himself forward in his seat.

"Why would I run away from you?" said Socky. "Did you chase after me?"

"Of course not, why would I chase after you?"

"If you had not chased after me, then I couldn't have been running away from you."

That stunned Sammy Sam momentarily. Then he recovered and said, "I didn't run after you, but you ran away from me."

"What are you saying, Colonel Sam? I don't get it," said Kong.

"I mean I didn't chase after him at all, but he was running away from me."

"Just what are you trying to say?" Turning to Socky, Kong continued, "Did you run away from Colonel Sam when he wasn't running after you?"

"How could that be possible?" said Socky.

"That's possible, because that was what happened," said Sammy Sam.

"If you were not chasing me, why did it matter to you that I appeared to be running away from you?" asked Socky. "Why did you bother? Why didn't you just let me run away? Why is my apparent running away an issue?"

Sammy Sam was stumped.

"It's not an issue, not a big issue at least," said Kong. "But we've received lots of queries from the public about the commotion yesterday."

"Commotion? What commotion?" asked Socky. "As far as I know, there was no commotion."

"No commotion? Nothing happened?" said Sammy Sam, thrusting forward again. "That must be the understatement of the year!"

"What happened then?" asked Socky.

"You were running away from me when I was not chasing after you," said Sammy Sam.

"We can't go on like this," said Kong. "How many times must we go round the world?"

"He took us three times round the world yesterday," said Socky, looking at Sammy Sam. That got Sammy Sam worked up straightaway, and he thrust forward again, hands on the table and arms spread apart, like a wrestler about to charge.

"Socky, who was the guy with you yesterday?" asked Sonny Song.

"Yeah, that small guy waving at me," said Sammy Sam.

"He's my friend."

"Yes, but who was he?" asked Sonny Song.

"He's my friend."

"I know he's your friend; tell us about him," said Sonny Song.

"But why should I tell you about my friend? It's personal; besides, I don't have his permission to disclose anything about him."

"No, no, I'm not asking you to say anything confidential about him," said Sonny Song. "Just tell us who he is."

"Yeah, just tell us who he is. What's the big deal?" said Vento Voon.

"He's my friend; I was just having a drink with him; just old friends meeting and talking. The rest is private and confidential and, if I may add, nothing interesting."

"Okay, never mind. But I'd like to meet your friend; I'd like to invite him for tea," said Kong, smiling slyly. "Your friend is our friend; we'd like to welcome him to our country."

"Oh, I don't know; I'm not sure he wants to have tea with anybody; he's a very private man."

"You wouldn't know if you hadn't asked him, would you? Please ask him; tell him it's a personal invitation from me," said Kong, the sly grin still hanging on his face.

"It's a personal invitation from the General; it's an invitation you can't refuse," said Sammy Sam, now duplicating Kong's sly grin.

"Me? I can't refuse? My friend's not me, anyway."

"C'mon Socky, give face to the General," said Sammy Sam, now unable to hide his glee.

*

A small crowd gathered at the roof garden at Croctopus HQ for a tea party. The OSD's Lenny Loon was there, as well as some beefy characters who seemed tense and not enjoying themselves. Kate was her usual self, a muffin in hand, talking happily to this one and that. I was enjoying myself too, and so was Roger. Kong was laughing every now and then, each laugh as loud as a rocket taking off.

"Where's Socky and his friend?" said Kong to Sonny Song. They did not have to wait long before Socky arrived at the roof garden with a small man.

"That's him; that's the small fella who waved at me," said Sammy Sam to Kong.

The small man had a face as round as the moon, on which he hung a pair of spectacles. He wore a safari suit, his paunch pushing the fabric. He was walking on platform shoes and his hair was blown high; there was an air of mischief about him. Socky brought him straight to Kong and introduced him.

187

"How do you do, General; I'm Kimmie," said the small man, who had a small mouth—just a little hole on his moon face.

"How do you do; I'm Kong."

"I think I'll call you General; I prefer it this way."

Kong was friendly, but he looked up and down Kimmie, clearly trying to size him up.

"We go back a long way," said Socky, "all the way back to school."

"Oh, that far back?" said Kong, still looking at Kimmie. "Actually, you look rather familiar but, of course, we haven't met before; this I'm sure."

"We were scouts at school," said Socky. "He was our dear leader."

Kong, Sammy Sam and Sonny Song looked stunned.

"Dear Leader?" said Kong.

While Kimmie and Kong were engaged in conversation, which was polite but guarded, Sammy Sam slipped quietly away. He held up his hand and gave a blinking hand signal to the beefy characters a short distance away, which caused them to move silently to take up their positions. Two guarded the exits; the rest spread out unobtrusively around Kimmie and Kong. Lenny Loon went over to Sammy Sam and they had a discussion.

"What's going on?" asked Lenny Loon.

"That's our pre-arranged signal to arrest our suspect; surely you remember?" said Sammy Sam.

"Who's our suspect?"

"That guy over there talking to the General."

"Why is he our suspect?"

"He's the one who waved at me in Croctopus Mall."

"Is that cause for arrest?"

"No, but look at him; doesn't he look suspicious? And he's addressed as Dear Leader."

"So what?"

188

"Look, are you going to arrest him or not?"

"Arrest him on what ground?"

"On the ground that he's our suspect."

"That's just beating about the bush."

"It's not beating about the bush. That guy's a terrorist suspect; I'm sure he knows something about Hidden Wagon." Sammy Sam's tone was firm, and he asked sternly, "Are you for us or against us?"

"Look, your suspicion is insufficient ground for arrest. We can't arrest him, at least not now," said Lenny Loon before giving a blinking hand signal to his men and walking away.

Sammy Sam was furious and he returned to Kong, apparently to report on his discussion with Lenny Loon. That caused Kong to excuse himself and go straight to Lenny Loon for some heated discussion. Kong gesticulated wildly with his hands and arms, and at times held his head firmly in his hands, as if trying to prevent his skull from exploding. Then he stormed off the roof garden.

Kimmie went over to Sammy Sam and gave a smirk before walking away.

Chapter 14

A state of siege descended upon Croctopus headquarters. A terrorist mole and a WMD were bad enough, but the appearance of Kimmie pushed matters way beyond limits. The morning after Kimmie's appearance, the terrorist hunters gathered at the boardroom for an emergency meeting. They waited for Kong to appear. To make matters worse, the air-conditioner was merciless, as if it was trying to show who the boss was.

"We must be in Siberia," I told Kate loudly.

"Anytime now, we could be in hell," said Sonny Song, "so we'd better not complain about the cold. You've got to appreciate what you have."

"Good morning," said Kong as he entered the room and headed for his seat, looking glum. "I'm sure I don't have to tell you the danger we're in. Anytime now, we could be in hell." That statement made Sonny Song sit up; pride welled up to his head. It was not every day that the boss said the same thing with exactly the same words; for some people it was like striking a prize in a lottery.

"Sir, that's what I've been telling them," said Sonny Song, who suddenly seemed taller than he used to be.

"Why do you need to tell them? I'm sure they knew it already," said Kong. Sonny Song seemed to suffer an immediate deflation and appeared slightly shorter than he used to be. Then Kong leaned forward in his chair as if he was going to make a speech, but did not proceed to do so, at least not immediately. He looked at everyone and, after a pause to heighten tension, said slowly, "When the circle is closed, boom!" He threw up his arms to outline an explosion, his eyes wide and looking intently at everyone. "I wonder whether the circle is closed by now."

"Sir, it could well be closed," said Vento Voon.

"That could be right, sir," said Sammy Sam.

"Sir, I tend to agree with this assessment," said Sonny Song

"What do you think, Ken?" said Kong. "You're the one monitoring Crouching Liar all the time."

"I get this unease about where we're heading. It's a strange feeling, but I can't explain it; something is gnawing at me inside. I think we ought to review this whole thing and see whether we're on the right path."

"What do you mean by this?" said Vento Voon. "How dare you imply that we're on the wrong path?

"I don't see why not," said Kate.

"Insubordination again!" said Sammy Sam. "This is most unbecoming of you. Don't you ever respect authority? This is not the way things are run here; you ought to know that."

"If you go on like this the entire hierarchy in the organization would collapse," said Sonny Song. "With the difficult task at hand we expect unity, but you never seem to know what's expected of you."

"Kate, I expect you to behave yourself," said Kong. "I don't want any more of this nonsense. We're on the right path, and don't you argue with me on this. Now, we've a mission to accomplish, so

I expect everyone to pull together. Unity is paramount; I've said it many times. Kate, you've caused enough distraction, and nobody's happy with your nonsense."

Nobody? I thought.

"But . . ." said Kate.

"Don't argue with me or tell me I'm wrong," said Kong.

How I wished Roger had been present to lend Kate and me the needed support. As the company's security consultant, his views would have carried a lot more weight than ours, and they would have been especially helpful as he too had been rather skeptical about the whole thing. Unfortunately, he was again out briefing the minister.

As someone who had been brought up in Orderland, I understood the culture of conformity, the clarion call to be united, the 'altogether now, don't rock the boat' exhortation, but I have always felt that such calls for unity must never be at the expense of the truth. I have never allowed myself to ignore the truth; it is such a counterproductive exercise. For me, the truth comes first and everything else second; every thought and action must flow from it, and nothing against it. And the truth is always based on fact, and not on what we liked or hoped. I go where the facts take me, however unpleasant the end might be. However, Kong swept all expressions of doubt aside when he said, "I don't want to hear any doubts about what we're doing; we must always be sure of ourselves; we can't win battles if we have doubts. Ken, tell us whether you think the circle is closed."

For a brief moment, I refused to answer a question that had not taken my views into account. I wanted my doubts to be addressed first. If we do not know the truth, how were we to move forward? I told myself that we go for the truth, and nothing but the truth. So I replied, "As I was saying, I think we need to . . ."

"Not what we need," said Kong, "Give me your assessment and I'll tell you what we need."

"For a proper assessment, we need to get to the truth," I said. "Therefore . . ."

"I don't want all this beating about the bush. Ken, are you going to give us your assessment or not?" said Kong.

"Certainly, but . . ."

"No but business! Give us your assessment. The reason I want your assessment is because you're the case officer, so give us your assessment."

"I will, but . . ."

"Just give us your bloody assessment!"

Sadly, I caved in and went along the path laid down by Kong. I do not know why or how it happened, but my subconscious mind must have told me that it was easier to fight another day; self preservation should come first, for without self preservation there would not be another day. And without another day, my believes and principles would be no more. So I blurted out, "I don't think the circle is closed. What has Socky learned about Orderland?"

I glanced at Kate and saw the total disappointment in her face, which I could remember to this day. I asked myself in my mind, was it a mere weakness or a moral collapse that she saw?

"Crouching Liar," said Kong.

"Sorry, Crouching Liar. What has he learned? He has learned about the undertaking business, something about the Social Welfare Extension Fund, a bit about the defense of the Croctopus headquarters, a bit about Croctopus Center, and that's about it. That's just scratching the surface of this country. To set off a WMD and cause maximum damage, he'd need to know where and when to set it off; that is, the best place and time to do it. He'd need to know what's most vital to this country and the time of the day we let our guard down. He'd also need to know the safest route and time to move the WMD into position. I don't think Socky . . . I mean, Crouching Liar knows that yet. The terrorists have, as far as we could figure, only one WMD here, and they'll surely want a knockout blow, or at least a heavy blow, with a single strike. Right now, I don't think they've enough intelligence to do that."

"Hmm . . . you've a point," said Kong, stroking his chin. "Kate, what do you think?"

"I still think we should review this whole thing."

"There you go again; that's not helpful at all," said Sammy Sam.

"Cut that out Kate, before I throw you out" said Kong. "We're over with that; don't you dare revisit this rubbish about reviewing where we're heading."

"I think Ken is being complacent," said Vento Voon. "As head of security, complacency is the last thing I want in Croctopus."

"Being correct is not the same as being complacent," Kate said. "It's essential to get the facts and the assessment right first."

"I don't like your attitude, your insubordination, which you seem to enjoy flaunting," said Vento Voon. "I don't want to waste any more time on your call or hint for a review. As for Ken's assessment, I'd say that complacency is a poison that we must not swallow, especially not in this security climate."

There was silence for a moment as everyone could see that Kong was thinking hard. Vento Voon leaned back on his seat and waited for Kong to guillotine Kate and me once and for all, and end all doubts and move on. Then Kong said, "You make sense, Ken."

Vento Voon deflated like a balloon. He said quickly, "But . . ."

"I now feel an immediate sense of relief," said Kong. "Crouching Liar has probably not closed the circle. But I also feel that we're at the losing end. Somehow, Crouching Liar is able to go about gathering intelligence, closing the circle step by step with impunity. I'm watching things unfold with a lot of frustration and worry."

"What's the OSD's assessment of the situation?" I asked.

"Ah, the OSD. Notice that Colonel Loon is not here," said Kong. "Well, I've left him out because we need to talk about him."

There was a slight stir in the room. "You see, I'm bothered by his refusal to arrest Kimmie. He should have arrested that man at the roof garden yesterday but he refused to, and I'm bothered by it, very bothered. This thing has been on my mind since; I couldn't eat or sleep yesterday. And I've had to struggle through my breakfast this morning; the hard-boiled egg is still stuck somewhere in my chest. So I'm a very, very unhappy man."

The air-conditioner started to cough like a sick man and a chill quickly made several laps round the room. Kate folded her arms to keep warm.

"You said Colonel Loon had refused to arrest Kimmie, but did he say why he had refused to do so?" I asked.

"He said there was no ground for arrest."

"Perhaps he could be right," I said.

"No ground? Now, that's a joke, sir," said Sammy Sam. "If there's no ground to arrest a terrorist, then there's no ground to arrest anyone for anything."

"Well, Kimmie didn't come with the word 'Terrorist' printed on his forehead, did he?" said Kate, as she made an imaginary label on her forehead with her fingers.

"But we all know he's a terrorist," said Sammy Sam.

"With Crouching Liar, Colonel Loon has a reason not to arrest him immediately; he has a US Senator uncle to protect him," said Vento Voon. "But not with Kimmie; he doesn't have such protection. We could've nabbed him."

"So we've a problem, a big problem," said Kong. "Colonel Loon is not as sharp as we had assumed. We had all along left it to the OSD to take the lead in the investigation, and we had played a supporting role. And what happened? Nothing! It has dawned on me that we can't leave it to the OSD; it'd be disastrous if we do."

"We're going to take a more active role in the investigation?" I asked. "We can't do it; we don't have the expertise and the police powers."

"We've no choice," said Kong. "Our country is in great danger; it could be destroyed any day now. We have to do something because it looks to me Colonel Loon is a lame duck."

"We may be taking a dangerous course," I said.

"More dangerous than having our country destroyed?" said Kong angrily.

"I think Ken has a point." said Kate. "As he has pointed out, we don't have the expertise and the police powers; we're neither the police nor the OSD. Besides, we're assuming the OSD is not doing very much, but I'm sure they're doing a lot more than we know. We've got to leave the investigation to the professionals."

"Enough of hesitation!" said Kong. "The investigation is going on like a lame duck. If we go on like this, Orderland would be destroyed."

"I agree with you, sir," said Vento Voon. "We've got to play a bigger role, a more aggressive role in the investigation." He looked like a limp balloon suddenly inflating with a rush of hot air. Life seemed to have returned to him.

"Sir, you're absolutely right," said Sammy Sam.

"No more lame ducks, sir," said Sonny Song.

"We've to be aggressive, a lot more aggressive," said Kong. "I think the first thing we should do is to invade Crouching Liar's lair. So far, we've been sort of moving around him, not really getting into his territory. We've got to go on the offensive, invade his territory."

"This is brilliant, sir," said Vento Voon.

"Absolutely brilliant, General," said Sammy Sam.

"Right on, sir. I'm with you, sir," said Sonny Song.

"Yes, but specifically what do you have in mind?" I asked.

"The General just said invade Crouching Liar's territory," said Sammy Sam.

"Yes, but how, in what way?" I said.

"Anybody has any idea?" asked Kong.

What bullshit is this? I thought.

As the terrorist hunters were cracking their heads, the boardroom telephone rang. Kate took it and said, "General, Master Fu is here for his appointment with you."

"Please tell him I'll be there in a moment," said Kong. Then after a moment's thought, he smiled, snapped his fingers and said, "I've got it. Do you all know who Master Fu is?"

"Is he a *feng shui* man?" I said.

"That's right, a geomancer and fortune teller," said Kong.

*

"Is he dangerous?" asked Master Fu.

"Well, we don't know enough about him, but I won't describe him as dangerous," I said, as I drove at my usual, unhurried speed.

"He might look dangerous to some people though," said Kate. "But if you've dealt with him you wouldn't think of him as dangerous."

"Deceptive huh?"

"Well, he doesn't seem like he's acting," said Kate. "His behavior looks quite natural to me."

"Wow, he's a natural; that's the most dangerous type. I've never been involved in an industrial espionage case before; this is exciting."

"We don't have proof of anything yet," I said. "We're going there hoping to find something."

"I hope to be of service to your great organization," said Master Fu.

I rang the doorbell and Socky opened the door almost immediately. "Spied you coming," he said with a smile.

Master Fu was taken aback by Socky's choice of the word. He must have thought that the last thing a spy should do was to remind people of spying. And as if to add to his suspicion, a trait of Socky caught his attention. "You look very familiar; have I seen you somewhere?" said Master Fu.

"No, I don't think so," said Socky, showing us the way into the house. "As I told Kate yesterday, I don't really need a geomancer for the house. This place looks fine to me; I feel nice and comfortable here."

"Well, there's always room for improvement; that's what the General said," replied Master Fu.

"I don't know. What do you want to do with this place?" said Socky. "Everything's laid out according to a certain order for my convenience. I really don't think I needed any improvement; I'm quite happy with things as they are."

"Things are not always what they seem; there's always some undercurrent that's not seen. A *feng shui* master like me would be able to detect it." Master Fu then produced a compass the size of a dinner plate, holding it in both hands and looking at it like a geologist taking readings from his instrument. He shifted about to align the needle and the markings.

"You've started work already," said Socky, sounding a little annoyed.

I had little doubt that Socky did not buy into this *feng shui* thing. He would not care to re-arrange his furniture according to Master Fu's recommendation. He was just being tolerant, if not amused, by a stranger's antics in his house. Fortunately, this whole exercise was the Kong's idea, otherwise I would have had to apologise to Socky immediately.

"Hmm . . . the orientation of the house doesn't appear to be very good; I'm rather concerned."

"Maybe I should turn the house around on its axis until the orientation is correct?"

"Ha ha, I'll see what I can do; there's no need for such a drastic action."

Kate and I took the opportunity to look around the living room, but we were not terribly excited by the ordinariness of the place. There was a book on a coffee table, a rack holding some newspapers, and a side table with a small, neat stack of magazines, the top one having a glossy cover with a setting sun and coconut trees by the sea. Well, even a mole would live an ordinary life at home, I thought with some amusement.

"This place is well kept; you're neat, Socky," said Kate, eyes not looking at Socky, but shifting about to take in the details.

"Thank you, I'm all alone here, so there's nobody else to mess things up for me."

"You may not be alone; the orientation of the house makes it open to uninvited guests," said Master Fu, knitting his eyebrows and looking concerned.

"Surely, you're not talking about yourself. What do you mean?"

"Spirits from another world find it easy to enter your house."

"That's scary," said Kate, folding her arms and raising her shoulders as if feeling a sudden chill.

"Seems that I may have company," said Socky, a hand over his mouth, trying to force a yawn.

"May I have a look in the kitchen and the backdoor? This is not good, not good at all." Master Fu headed straight for the kitchen without waiting for Socky's reply. At the entrance to the kitchen, he stopped abruptly, as if startled by something. He was motionless momentarily, save for his eyeballs, which darted about, as if trying to see the unseen. Then he trembled slightly as though he had sensed something, before steeling himself and saying gravely, "This place has been used."

"Of course, it has been used; I live here."

"It has been used by others."

"Others?" said Socky.

"Yes others, from the spirit world."

"Somebody has been stealing my food? Well, leftover pizzas mostly; not worth breaking in."

"The orientation of the backdoor is also not good; uninvited guests can come and go easily."

"I'm in trouble?"

"I'd better look upstairs." Master Fu headed out of the kitchen for the stairs as though it was his house. Kate and I took a final look around the kitchen. Well, what would a mole hide in the kitchen? Some chemicals for making explosives among innocent cooking ingredients? So far, nothing; the kitchen was well kept, but that was about it. The place was like any kitchen that you would expect to see in a middle income house. Why should a mole not live like us at home?

Socky showed us his bedroom and said, "Normally it's not this neat; I tidied up yesterday and this morning."

"Oh, don't be modest," I said, looking at the place from corner to corner. I paced about the room, feigning interest in its layout. The bed was big, and the mattress firm. Why should a mole not enjoy life? There was the wardrobe. I had this urge to look inside. I touched the door knob, but what should I say? "Hey, the mirror's really clean, there's not a single fingerprint on it."

However, I could not work up the courage to open the wardrobe door. How do you open your host's wardrobe without permission while he's in the room? I just stared at the mirror while still holding the door knob. After a while, I could not continue the pretense and just had to let go of the knob. Anyway, what did I expect to see inside the wardrobe? A cloak, dark glasses and a pen camera? Moles live a normal life at home, I told myself.

Kate realized my predicament and immediately sprang into action. "Hey, this is cute!" It was a picture of a cat.

Socky was distracted and turned around, whereupon Kate engaged him in a discussion about the cat in the picture. It was Socky's pet cat, which had died recently. But never mind about that; I took the opportunity to open the wardrobe and had a two-second view of the inside. What I saw was, well, clothes hung very neatly. There was no reason for a mole to keep incriminating items in his house that could be uncovered by a cursory inspection, I told myself. After the cat discussion, Kate paced about the room, picking up small items here and there and saying how pretty they were. She even looked behind the curtains, saying how much she liked the fabric. But, of course, nothing suspicious was on display.

Master Fu went over to the windows and looked out. "The windows have the same orientation as the front door."

"Spirits flying through the windows too?" said Socky, mocking surprise. "No wonder I feel I'm being followed these days."

"Do you feel your luck has been low, that you're somehow less lucky than you used to be?" asked Master Fu, hand rubbing his chin, as if thinking deeply.

"Well, yes, you've finally hit the nail on the head. Not that I've met with any major disaster, but things seem not to work out as I had expected. And like I've told you, I seem to have more than one shadow; someone has been shadowing me."

"There you are," said Master Fu. Surprisingly, to Socky's first useful statement, he did not add anything helpful. Instead, he proceeded to the bathroom to investigate, and he reappeared mumbling something and looking unhappy. Seeing that, Kate and I quickly entered the bathroom as if to find out what made Master Fu so unhappy. It was surprisingly spacious and orderly. I could have concluded that moles were picked for their tidy, meticulous habits.

Master Fu next investigated the study. There was a laptop on the writing desk. If only I could look into the files, but I was unable to figure out what excuse to give to switch on the thing. Even to this day I could not think of an excuse. I needed to do a piece of work or send an email suddenly? Really, there was no believable excuse I could have made to use the laptop. And even if I could somehow bluff my way to using that laptop, going through the files would take too long and expose my motive. I consoled myself that, short of stealing the laptop, even the best spy in the world could not have done better.

Master Fu worked his way around the house before finishing at where he started—the living room. "I don't need to investigate further; I've a good idea of your house's *feng shui*."

"That's a relief," said Socky in a bored, uninterested tone.

"Your place has really bad *feng shui*; you'll have to do something about it."

"I've got it; the house is pivoted on an axis of evil and I'll have to turn it around for better orientation."

"An axis of evil; ha ha, that's better than I could have put it. I'm glad you understand, sir. Your house is truly pivoted on an axis of evil but, of course, you can't really turn it around physically. You'll have to take steps that substitute for turning the house around."

"So what do you recommend? Buy a doll house and turn it about?"

"Ha ha, that's funny. But no, that's not the way. My advice is to rebuild the front entrance and windows so that they face a different direction from the existing one. In this way, the orientation of the house will be changed for the better."

"You mean the house faces one direction, but the front entrance and windows face another?"

"That's right."

"Wouldn't that make the house look funny?"

"Not so, lots of buildings here are done this way on a *feng shui* master's advice."

"Socky can't make the changes because this is not his house; the company is renting it from somebody," I said.

"Then we'll have to do the next best thing," said Master Fu, as he produced three mirrors, each in a hexagonal frame with some *I Ching* symbols, and gave them to Socky. "Hang them above the front door, the back door and your bedroom windows, facing out of the house. They'll deflect bad luck and spirits away from your house."

"That simple?"

*

"You found nothing? What do you mean you found nothing?" bellowed Kong.

"I mean we found nothing that could implicate Socky . . . I mean, Crouching Liar, with any terrorist activity," I said.

"How could that be? It's a terrorist's lair, and you found nothing in a terrorist's lair? This is incredible, just incredible, and I'm supposed to believe this?"

"I can confirm what Ken said; there was nothing in that house that was out of the ordinary," said Kate.

"Invading Crouching Liar's territory was a master stroke; it should have yielded the evidence for us to kick him out of this country," said Kong. "Now you're telling me you found nothing; it's such a disappointment!"

"But we really found nothing," I said.

"I don't want to hear this anymore; it's like throwing victory away when it's within your grasp."

It was a short meeting, as the failure to obtain any evidence from invading Socky's territory meant that there was nothing new to discuss. Anyway, Kong was too disappointed and angry to carry on any discussion. Kate and I were relieved to go off, as we were just as disappointed—with Kong rather than the failure to obtain any evidence against Socky. As we walked slowly to our department, Kate once again brought up her unhappiness with the way things were going.

"I'm sure you'll agree with me that the General's approach is wrong. He pronounces Socky guilty, and then tries to find the evidence to back his pronouncement. But it should have been the other way around—first find the solid evidence, then pronounce guilt."

"You're right, of course. And we get the blame for failing to find the evidence. Maybe there's no evidence at all."

"So, what shall we do? I think we've been too gradual, too gentle, in the way we try to bring about change. It has no effect on people with a closed mind. We can't get them to change direction this way."

"So, what do you propose we do?"

"I say we confront the General head-on. We march into his room, bang on the table, shake our fists, and tell him in the most direct way that he's doing it the wrong way and he has to seriously review this whole thing."

I raised my eyebrows and took a good look at Kate.

"I'm being a bit dramatic, of course, but you know what I mean."

I could not stop laughing at the drama that Kate had conjured up.

"Hey, stop laughing. How about it?"

"I understand where you're coming from; in fact, I agree with your assessment. There are gaps in the case against Socky. Nevertheless, if we proceed with your suggestion and shake our fists at the General, what do you think would happen?"

"We'd both be hung by our fingers and left to die in the hot sun."

"And would the General review this thing?"

"No, of course not."

"That's right, we know what would happen without even trying out your suggestion; it's not up to us to decide how the investigation should go. We could see gaps in the case and we know we're right, but the difficulty lies in persuading others to our point of view. And so far, I've no answer to this problem."

"But we can't just let things go on as usual; we could be chasing shadows."

"I hear you, I hear you, Kate. We could well be chasing shadows, but there's some coincidence surrounding Socky that's too neat to explain away, and the General just wouldn't ignore these evidence. Whatever we may feel, the big things are not up to us to decide. I'm a reasonable man, and I try to take the reasonable path. I suppose we'll have to wait for the right moment to make our move. In the meantime, we'll just have to be patient and try to change things slowly, one step at a time."

"But hoping things would change slowly is not reasonable. I don't want to be part of a future train wreck; we've got to get things changed quickly; we've lost valuable time already."

"I assure you I'm in total agreement with your assessment, but convincing the General is a different matter. We really have no choice; change in the company has always been top down. Our personal feelings go only so far; they don't count in the end if the General doesn't agree. Ultimately, it's up to him."

"There's too much unthinking deference to the top. I can't take this stifling conformism; I need fresh air."

Chapter 15

It was a lazy afternoon drive; traffic was moderate and the car cruised leisurely along the road like a satisfied hippo after a hearty meal. Cocooned in the air-conditioned comfort of the car, we were protected from the harsh equatorial sun. I pointed interesting sights to Socky, who was munching *kacang putih* out of a long paper cone.

"The lunch at Number One Chicken was super," said Socky, eyes droopy from the heavy meal. The glare from the midday sun added to the lethargy.

"Yeah, never fails to please. Every time I've had a lousy encounter in the office, I'd head for it."

"That's a good way to keep your sanity," said Socky, as he popped more *kacang putih* into his mouth. "A restaurant, like everything else, can have more than one function." As if surprised by his own wit, he turned briefly to me to watch my reaction, but I disappointed him as I was as inert as he was to be animated by any conversation.

"Where's Kimmie now?"

"He packed up and took the first available flight home. He didn't like the way he was treated at the roof garden."

"Well, I can't blame him; he received a hot reception instead of a warm one."

"He'll be back; he comes to Orderland quite often, but he won't go anywhere near Croctopus from now on."

"Hello, this is Ken." As always, I used the hands-free set for my cellphone while driving. "Socky wants to know more about our legal system, so I thought we could start with a visit to the Supreme Court."

"He wants to know about what?" said Kong excitedly at the other end. "Our legal system? That's it! He wants to know how we'll deal with him and his bunch of terrorists after they've exploded their WMD."

"Well, I'm not sure about that," I said.

"Well, I *am* sure; there's no other explanation; that no good terrorist mole is up to mischief again. He's closing the circle fast; soon he'll blow this country to rubble. If I could take him out of circulation, I'd do so immediately. Now listen, don't take him to the Supreme Court; we can't let him take one more step to close the circle. We'll deprive him of what could well be the last piece in the jigsaw; take him to the Offshore Court instead."

"The Offshore Court? But it has nothing to do with Orderland's legal system. You're not joking?"

"No, I'm not; take him to the Offshore Court. This way, he'll *not* learn about our legal system; we must stop him from learning about our legal system at all costs. He must not feel that he has learnt enough about this country and think that the circle is closed. We must keep disrupting his plan, make him feel that there are gaps in his knowledge of Orderland. Why, in his mind our legal system could be the last gap for him to close. He has gone far enough with his research; we can't take any more risks with him."

207

"I'm not sure I can persuade him to go to the Offshore Court instead of the Supreme Court. I mean, our legal system has been commended by people from other countries; it's been held up as a model for others in some studies. So I don't think Socky will exchange that for the Offshore Court."

"It's not up to him; it's up to us! You don't need to persuade him. I say go to the Offshore Court, and that's an order!"

"But . . ."

"The Offshore Court!"

"Well, okay . . . but . . ."

"The Offshore Court!"

"If that's what you want . . ."

"I presume it's the General?" said Socky, after he was sure I had disconnected the call. "What does he want? Sounds like he's trying to tell us what to do."

"The General suggests we go to the Offshore Court instead of the Supreme Court."

"But, surely, the Supreme Court is the better place to visit, don't you think so? After all, the Offshore Court has nothing to do with Orderland's legal system."

"Well, for some reason he thought you should visit the Offshore Court."

"He didn't say why?"

"No, he just thought that's the better place for you to visit. You know the General, sometimes it's difficult to understand why he makes certain decisions; it's instinctive, not based on reason, I suppose."

"I'm disappointed, it's an irrational decision." Socky shook his head. "Say, can't we go to the Supreme Court without telling him?"

"We don't have the time to go to the Supreme Court and the Offshore Court, and when we are back at HQ the General is sure to ask you about the Offshore Court."

"So we've no choice?" Socky popped the last *kacang putih* into his mouth and crumpled the paper cone into a ball so deliberately that it was as if he was trying to squeeze somebody's neck.

As I changed direction and headed for the Offshore Court, Socky played with the ball of crumpled paper, lost in thought, as though he was trying to figure a way out to go to the Supreme Court instead. "We're now on the road where the Offshore Court is; we'll be there soon," I said. "Do you know that this road is over a hundred years old?"

"Really? It looks new to me."

"Ha ha, it was not always like this. Over a hundred years ago, it was a dirt track with only two houses. The first house was built by a Chinese merchant called Kang. Later, an Indian merchant built the other house; his name was Aroomugum, often shortened to Aroo. Both became very wealthy; they donated large sums to philanthropic causes and became famous. They even paid for the road to be paved, saving the government some money. They became community leaders and are mentioned in the history books that students study today."

"It's right that they should be remembered," said Socky, holding the crumpled paper, but not playing with it anymore.

"After our country became independent, the road was widened and extended to become the road you now see. And in their honor the road was renamed Kang Aroo Road."

"They deserved the honor."

"Yes, they certainly do. Unfortunately, the two houses were demolished when the area was developed. That's progress for us; we lost a bit of our heritage."

"It's a shame."

"It sure is. We've demolished quite a lot of our old buildings in the name of progress."

"It's a shame," repeated Socky, but more emphatically and shaking his head this time. "I've always believed that if we really want to pay attention to history; we've got to remember the people and how they had lived, remember their way of life, and keep the historical sites too."

"That's right, a historical site is not just a location; there's got to be something standing there to tell its history. If there's nothing there to remind us of what had happened, it would not be much of a historical site."

"Now that you've told me about the history of this road, it feels different traveling on it. I could almost expect to see Messieurs Kang and Aroo walking here and waving to us. Unfortunately, it won't be the same for visitors who don't know its history." The car speeded up a little as the mood inside became lighter. "At first, I was puzzled when I saw the name as we turned onto the road," said Socky. "Couldn't make out whether it was a Chinese or an Indian name; now I know."

"People use the road name for the Offshore Court."

"Really?"

"Of course, it's just an unofficial name. The official name is still the Offshore Court, but the official name somehow didn't catch on with the people. I mean, Offshore Court sounds functional, like a description of something rather than a name."

"That's true, I don't like the official name either," said Socky. "It's too ordinary, as though no effort had been taken to come up with a proper name."

"If you don't name something right, the people would just give it their own name, and the official name would be found only in official documents and not in everyday speech."

"What's the people's name for the Offshore Court?" asked Socky, suddenly realizing that I had not mentioned it.

"Kang Aroo Court."

We soon arrived at the Offshore Court. The architecture was uninspiring; the building looked purely functional, like many buildings in Orderland. Socky sized up the place on the outside, and scribbled something on his notebook. There were a few people going about their business. Then I saw a familiar figure walking toward us.

"Hey, look who's here," I said.

"Surprise, surprise," said Socky, looking straight ahead and saying no more.

"What are you doing here?" I asked.

"The General asked me to come and help you show Socky around," said Sonny Song, sounding as if his sudden appearance was the most natural thing in the world.

"Why does Ken need any help?" said Socky. "We're just going to walk around and have a look. In fact, we almost went somewhere else."

"Well, I had a bit of spare time, so the General asked me to come; two heads are better than one." Sonny Song forced a grin. "I'd like to have a look too; could learn something, you know."

"You don't sound like you know this place well, so how could you help Ken?" Socky returned a forced grin.

"I've always had lots of ideas, so even if I don't know much about something I could still contribute."

We walked into the building slowly, without enthusiasm, as if transported reluctantly on a conveyor belt. The inside of the building was as uninspiring as the outside. I looked cursorily at the notices on a bulletin board, while Socky scribbled something on his notebook, not writing much though. Sonny Song looked left and right, up and down, also showing little interest in the place.

"What's the function of the Offshore Court?" asked Socky.

"It's for offshore cases," said Sonny Song. "Orderland wanted to position itself as a legal hub, so the Offshore Court was established."

"It's a facility that people in other countries may use to hold their court hearings," I said. "They've to pay for the use, of course. We also earn from support services, such as interpretation.

We'll even provide the judges, if needed. Our hotels earn too, as the hearings could last many days."

"It's like the arbitration courts in some countries?" asked Socky.

"Well, the idea is similar, but the Offshore Court goes further; it's not limited to commercial cases," I said. "It hears criminal and even constitutional cases; in fact, cases of any kind; there's no limit to what it can hear. Of course, the law applied in each case would be the relevant law, usually the law of the country using the facility, not Orderland law."

"So a trial in the Offshore Court will proceed as if it's being heard in the country using the facility," said Socky.

"That's right," said Sonny Song, beating me to it.

"That means the trial has nothing to do with Orderland?" said Socky.

"That's right," I said. "We only provide the court, the physical structure, as well as support services, and earn good money from them."

"Why would any government use the Offshore Court for criminal or constitutional cases? I'm sure every country has its own courts."

"Sometimes, it may be politically inconvenient to hear such a case in their own country, so they could hold the trial here, away from their public's eye," I said.

"And a terrorist could be brought from another country to the Offshore Court for trial," said Socky. "That would be convenient for some countries."

"I see, you're thinking way ahead of us," said Sonny Song. "You're interested specifically in trials for terrorists?"

Socky gave him a puzzled look, but did not answer.

"Excuse me, I've got to make a call," said Sonny Song, as he went out of hearing range and whipped out his cellphone to make his call.

"He's asking questions about trials for terrorists in the Offshore Court?" said an excited Kong, who had activated the conference mode of the telephone for the benefit of Kate.

"Yes, he's definitely on to something. My guess is he's trying to find out what would happen to his terrorist friends and him if they were caught."

"Stick close to him, and report to me once you're back."

The three of us went on an unguided tour of the place, peeping into courtrooms here and there, Socky not writing much on his notebook. Sonny Song looked bored; he was more interested in Socky than the Offshore Court. The visit was uneventful; none of us was happy or satisfied. Finally, we walked out of the building into the sunlight.

"You asked about having terrorists tried at the Offshore Court," said Sonny Song to Socky.

"What about it?"

"What did you have in mind?"

"Nothing, really."

"How could it be?"

"Why not? It was something that came to my mind, nothing more. That's why I didn't go further."

A man came up and handed each of us a pamphlet before walking away.

"This is about a case tried here, at the Offshore Court, some time ago," I said, looking at the pamphlet. "The young man had tried to smuggle drugs into his country and was caught at his country's airport. The whole smuggling attempt and his arrest had nothing to do with Orderland, but he was tried in the Offshore Court here under the law of his country, and was sentenced to death by hanging for drug trafficking. Everything except the trial happened outside Orderland."

"He's appealing, I presume," said Socky.

"He did appeal and it was also heard in the Offshore Court. Unfortunately for him, his appeal was dismissed, and he was hanged not long ago," I said.

"I see that he was only twenty-five years old; how could the court do that?" said Socky, looking at the pamphlet.

"Well, the law of his country provided for the mandatory death sentence for drug trafficking, so the Offshore Court had no choice," I said. "Once he was found guilty, the court had to sentence him to death; it had no discretion to give an alternative sentence."

"He knew the penalty; he went back to his country carrying the drugs with his eyes open, and was caught at the airport. It was his fault," said Sonny Song.

"It might have been his fault, but are you saying a country can inflict any punishment on an offender so long as it had declared the punishment beforehand?" said Socky.

"Of course, that guy had a choice not to smuggle drugs."

"So a country is entitled to chop off the hands of petty thieves or whip an adulterer to death so long as people had a choice not to break the law?" Socky looked indignant. "Is there no limit to punishment?"

"Well, drug smugglers deserve death; they destroy the lives of innocent people. A country must protect its people against such a danger," said Sonny Song.

"So why can't a country impose a substantial prison term instead of the death sentence?"

"The death sentence is the best deterrence," said Sonny Song.

"I'm not sure about that," said Socky. "But even if it's the most effective deterrence, is there no limit to punishment? Is the heaviest punishment absolutely necessary?"

"Surely, a country should use the most effective deterrence," said Sonny Song.

"Then why shouldn't a country use the most effective deterrence for all offences? Why not apply capital punishment to petty thefts too?"

"It's up to each country to impose the punishment for each crime."

"That's not answering my question. Surely, there's a limit to how much punishment you can mete out to an offender. That's why you can't sentence a petty thief to death. And it's not just because the law says so; it's because it'd offend against our sense of justice. Even an offender needs to be treated with justice."

"Look, do you realize that drugs could destroy our economy? Every drug addict is unproductive. If even five percent of our population is hooked on drugs, our GDP, our gross domestic product, would plummet. I'm not prepared to see our economy destroyed. I say hang the drug traffickers before they destroy us."

"Isn't this going too far? Hanging people to protect the economy?"

"A country has the sovereign right to impose any sentence on an offender. Why are you so concerned about punishment for an offender? You don't seem to like heavy punishment for criminals. Is there a reason for it?"

"I think you didn't get what I'm trying to say," said Socky. "Look over there." He pointed to a sculpture not far away. "See that sculpture of a blindfolded lady with a scale and a sword? She's the personification of law and justice. The blindfold tells us she's impartial; the sword is to enforce the law. But what I find most interesting is the scale she's holding with her other hand. It means fairness, the very basis of justice; it means weighing the evidence and deciding according to it. And just as important, it also means balancing the crime with the right punishment. Justice is about fairness. For me, the scale and the blindfold are the most inspiring parts of the law, far more than the sword.

215

"So what are you trying to say?" said Sonny Song, gazing at the sculpture.

"The punishment must fit the crime," said Socky, "That's what I'm trying to say. Sentencing a small fry drug smuggler to death is punishment totally disproportionate to the crime. That guy didn't commit any violent crime; he didn't kill anybody."

"Well, the law prescribes the mandatory capital punishment for the offence; surely, in such a case the court can't decide whether it's fair or not," said Sonny Song. "There's only one sentence for the offence."

"Yes, but the law-makers, the legislators, can change the sentence," said Socky.

"Anyway, drugs kill," said Sonny Song. "So the capital punishment is fair."

"Can you be sure the small-time smuggler actually killed anyone?" said Socky. "Look, if you shoot a man and he survives, you can't even be charged for murder. That guy didn't kill anybody; he was caught at the airport. Addicts who die are those who overdose themselves, or who take drugs with other harmful substances, such as alcohol, creating a lethal cocktail. They die largely of their own recklessness; there's a lot of personal responsibility here."

"So the smuggler is not at fault?" said Sonny Song.

"I didn't say that," said Socky. "Don't erect a straw man to demolish; the issue here is more than a straw man."

"What Socky's trying to say is that law-makers can't just use the sword and forget about the scale; justice is never like that," I said. "There has to be a balance; the punishment must fit the crime. Any thug can wield a sword, but justice never forgets its scale."

"Socky, I keep wondering why you're so concerned with saving criminals," said Sonny Song. "Every government has the duty to get rid of society's rotten apples to protect the people."

"If you equate people with apples, then you're treating them as commodities," said Socky. "You can't use the death sentence so freely to buy security for the country; it's like using the death sentence as a premium for some kind of insurance; the premium's too high. Besides, maximizing security has nothing to do with justice. I'd rather equate human life with a sacred flame. You see, the mother of all human flames was first lighted about two thousand generations ago. With each human life, a new flame is lighted from an existing one, which goes all the way back to the mother flame. Every sacred flame must be handled with the greatest care and respect, lest we extinguish it carelessly. We should not extinguish a sacred flame like we throw away a rotten apple, without a second thought."

"I agree that each human life is like a sacred flame, but if we have to extinguish it for the sake of deterrence, so be it," said Sonny Song.

"Then what's so sacred about your flame?" said Socky.

"Well, as I've said, it's important that we get rid of the rotten apples."

"Let me put it this way," said Socky, "would you rather be treated as an apple or as a sacred flame?"

"I believe the government should, indeed must, keep society safe from criminals."

"That's not answering the question," said Socky. "The question is: safety at what cost? Should law-makers throw away the scales of justice for no higher purpose than having excessive insurance for the people?"

"Why are you so concerned with a criminal's life?" said Sonny Song. "Is it in your interest to save all criminals from the gallows? Maybe that's what you really want; the interesting question is "Why?" Why are you so anxious that we should not execute criminals? What about terrorists? Shouldn't they be executed?"

"Now, let's not go that far; we're talking about small fry smugglers," said Socky. "What I find amazing is that you keep giving excuses for the hanging of a small-time drug smuggler, but you don't even stop to think deeply about whether it's right or wrong to do so. Don't you question your actions?"

217

"The issue is straightforward; society comes first," said Sonny Song.

A woman came up and handed each of us a pamphlet with the title *Endless Night*.

"It's the case we're talking about," I said. "It's a poem about the drug smuggler who was hanged."

Endless Night

We deny him
the rest of his life.
This we do
to keep our world nice.

We make him pay
the ultimate price.
For we most fear
our own secret vice.

We give ourselves
the sovereign right
to make him walk
the endless night.
He rocked so boldly
our wholesome dream.
Now his loved ones do
The endless scream.

We're the world's best,
Even in a hanging fest.
We're the world's best;
We gave him no rest.

When I got home, I was still bothered by the drug smuggler's case. Socky was right—do we not question our actions? I went to bed a little earlier than usual, trying to sleep the troublesome thoughts away. I tossed and turned for some time before finally sleeping. Then the dream began.

I was seated at a table, looking at some documents. Across the table was a man whom I had never met before. The stranger looked nice and friendly. But the air was hot and oppressive.

"The insurance policy I'm selling is the best in the world," said the man. "It offers the best protection. And best of all, no money is payable." He paused for my reaction. By the confidence he exuded he seemed to know how I would react.

My face lighted up and, without further questions, signed at the dotted line at the bottom of the page. Then I stood up smiling, and was about to leave when the man said there was a minor detail that we had to discuss. So I sat down on the edge of the seat, expecting to settle the minor detail in a moment or two. Then I noticed the man now looked different. It's the same man, but he looked different; his features now looked hardened and fearsome. I felt a chill and held my breath; it was strange that joy could turn into fear so quickly.

The man said, "Now, I hope you understand that nothing is free." But he quickly assured me that he would keep his promise and not take money for the insurance policy, the best in the world. He seemed to have done this many times and knew how to handle me.

"I'm happy with your assurance that no money is payable." I do not know why I said this; maybe I was trying to tell him that I was satisfied, and then leave, but he put his hand on my arm and somehow I felt I was being held down.

"You can take it from me that no money is payable. Still, nothing is free." The man looked at me with hard, piercing eyes. "There's just a minor detail concerning payment, and we've to settle it before you go. But rest assured, I will take no money; I'm a man of my word."

"So what do you want? Who are you?" I asked in a now anxious voice. I swallowed a lump of saliva and waited for his reply.

"If you really need to know, I'm the Devil."

Cold sweat oozed from every pore of my body; I could hardly breathe in the hot, oppressive condition. I just wanted to go off, to be released.

"As I've said, nothing is free; I hope you understand that."

I did not reply, but just sat motionless and looked at him, fearing what was to come.

"The premium for the insurance policy, the world's best, is payable annually with a human life. Now, I won't dictate to you how you should obtain and deliver the premium; I'm a reasonable person. But you'll have to deliver it one way or another; I leave it entirely to you. I want to assure you that there's no need to pay the first premium immediately; it can be deferred till later, even years later. The terms are very reasonable; you pay nothing at the beginning, but payment will eventually have to be made, for nothing is free."

By now, my clothes were soaked in sweat.

"I'd like to reconsider this thing; perhaps I don't need the world's best insurance policy after all; maybe the second best policy would do."

"Why do you want the second best policy when you could have the best?"

"Well, I'm not sure if you'll understand this; you see, the cost . . . the premium is kind of unacceptable to me."

"Why is it unacceptable to you? Everything has a price, I'm sure you'll agree. And this policy, the best in the world, won't cost you a cent. This is reasonable, I'm sure you'll agree."

"The price is too high, just too high." I shook my head as I said it.

"Too high? What are you talking about? It won't cost you a cent, I assure you."

"But it must be paid for in human lives. Surely . . ."

"Does that trouble you?"

"Sure as hell it does. The price to pay is just not acceptable."

"I don't understand you. Look, you pay nothing at the beginning. Why don't you stop worrying and accept it? Once you've enjoyed the benefits you'll come round to accepting it. The price to pay is not as prohibitive as you have assumed. I assure you, there's nothing to worry about. You'll get used to it; people get used to everything."

"Look, I'm not some kind of psychopath; I won't pay for anything with human lives."

"What do you mean? I don't understand you at all! You've made a pact with me, the Devil, and you can't back out of it. Nobody backs out of a pact with me. I've been very patient with you; let me remind you that you entered the pact of your own free will!" The Devil pointed a hard finger at me; his stare was hard as stone.

I woke up with a start, breathing hard. The clock indicated it was still early morning, but the air was already stifling and oppressive.

Chapter 16

I managed to back out of the tight situation, albeit with a great deal of difficulty. I was angry and relieved. The two emotions working on me at the same time was not something rare, and perhaps it was the same for others too. Who the devil does he think he is? I thought. The stupid, inconsiderate driver who parked his car illegally too near my lot almost prevented me from reversing my car out of it. Why are some people so self-centered? Are they not aware that there are other people in this world? The stupid driver needed no brain to see the problem he would have caused others when he parked his car illegally; he needed only eyes to see the problem he would have caused. Yet he could not even see with his eyes something right in front of him. If such a person were to run a business, he would almost certainly fail because he would run the business solely for himself and not for his customers. I told myself not to waste any more time on this and drove quickly to Croctopus HQ. I disliked being late for anything. When I arrived, Socky was waiting for me at the main gate. I was supposed to pick him up and go to Croctopus Mall, so I was surprised to find Kong there, talking loudly and gesticulating energetically. At the receiving end of Kong's onslaught was a man whom I recognized as the chief executive officer of one of Croctopus's subsidiaries. I parked my car by the side of the road and alighted to meet them.

"Tell me, Ken, should we employ a thousand workers to work for a year to lose ten million dollars?" asked Kong, looking extremely agitated.

I was not sure why he asked such a question, but the answer seemed obvious, so maybe it was not a question at all. However, I had to pretend that it was, and so I replied, "Well, of course we shouldn't."

"Don't you agree?" said Kong to the CEO.

"Yes, of course, I have to agree, General, but we didn't work with the intention of losing any money. Anyway, the loss was just ten million dollars, a small sum compared to the size of the company. It was well within our means to absorb."

"That's not the point," said Kong. "The point is should we employ a thousand workers to work for a year to lose ten million dollars?"

"If you put it that way, I suppose we shouldn't, sir, but . . ."

"That's enough," said Kong, raising his hand like a policeman stopping traffic. "Croctopus is the largest corporation in Orderland. We're a multinational corporation, with tentacles reaching out to many countries. Within Orderland, we've a stranglehold on many important industries and businesses. We've connections to the highest places here; we've no equal in this country. We're like the big, bad crocodile in the river; we eat anything we want, and nobody eats us. In this country we always win, we don't lose. Now listen carefully, we do not lose! You understand? We do not lose! So, when you suffer a loss of ten million dollars, where do you expect me to hide my face? Everybody's laughing at me!"

"It's really not a big sum, sir," said the CEO.

"I've told you that's not the point! The point is we just do not lose. We're Croctopus, the animal with a crocodile head and tentacles of an octopus; we're the meanest, most feared creature in the country—one that everyone is afraid of. Do you understand me?"

"Yes, I understand you, sir, but . . ."

"Look at that *kacang putih* man over there," said Kong.

The *kacang putih* man, dressed in all white, noticed that we were looking at him. He smiled at us and held up an empty paper cone hopefully, but we were not about to buy any nuts. Kong was certainly not in the mood to put up with anything he thought was a nut case.

"How much profit do you think he earns in a year?" asked Kong.

"Well, I don't really know, sir," said the CEO.

"Perhaps twenty thousand to thirty thousand dollars?" said Kong.

"I suppose that's about right, sir."

"That means this one-man show earns a greater profit than your company, which employs a thousand workers, doesn't it?"

"Well, I can't deny that, sir, but . . ."

"In that case, why don't I wind up your company and you sell *kacang putih*?"

The CEO did not answer because it was not really a question. Both Socky and I felt really sorry for him. One day he was the CEO of a company with a thousand workers, the next day he could be a *kacang putih* man selling nuts in cones made of recycled paper. What a horrible threat from Kong. Still, from a purely management point of view, it made sense. But I decided it was not the time and place to contemplate any management case study. It was a time to be merciful, and so I decided not to be a spectator at the CEO's roasting. I excused myself and drove away with Socky.

"The CEO's at HQ taking flak from Kong and we're on our way to his store at Croctopus Mall for damage control," said Socky. "Shouldn't the CEO be with us?"

"Yes, but it seems the General wants him at HQ to take flak."

"How did all this happen? I still don't get it, although it looks like very poor planning to me. Anyway, couldn't they have revised the price of the game box they were selling?"

"I know it's absurd to sell the game box at below cost, but they couldn't change the price. They had contracted with the manufacturers to sell at that price, and they were not allowed to change it. So when they opened the store this morning they had to sell it at below cost."

"Phew!" said Socky, shaking his head. "So, the more they sell, the more money they'd lose. They're real losers, but I still can't see how they came to fix the price below cost."

"I really don't know; maybe they had failed to take into account some cost factors in their initial calculations, or they had wanted to sell below cost to gain market share and sales got out of hand. Anyway, about an hour ago they decided to stop the sale of the game box until they could sort out the mess; that's why we're on our way to the store to help them close it temporarily."

"So, when we arrive at the store what are we supposed to do? What can we do?"

"I don't know."

We soon arrived at Croctopus Mall and went to the store in a hurry. The place was packed with noisy customers, all clamoring for the same item—the under-priced game box. The customers were pushing and shoving, and grabbing as many pieces of the game box as they could possibly carry, and arguing loudly with the harried sales people.

"Please, the game box is not for sale," said a woman, looking disheveled and trying to cope with the overwhelming demand.

"But they're on your shelves, so they must be for sale," said a woman customer with eight boxes in her trolley.

"No, they're for display only; they're not for sale."

"Why, that's ridiculous. Why do you display them if they're not for sale?"

"They're for show."

"That's not an acceptable answer."

The store manager rushed up to them and said, "Please don't buy from us . . . please don't buy from us." Without waiting for a reaction to his strange request, he rushed off to other customers randomly and repeated the plea to them. Socky and I looked at each other in amazement and went about the store, unsure whether to tell customers not to buy the game box. After a while, we bumped into the store manager.

"Please don't buy from us . . . please don't buy from us."

"Hey, I'm Ken, don't you recognize me?"

"Oh, I'm sorry, Ken. And you must be Socky. This is a bad day, a very bad day."

"I thought you're closing the store today? That's why we're asked to come here to help you do it," I said.

"We've tried; we announced that the store would be closing, but the customers wouldn't budge," said the manager, wiping sweat from his forehead. "I'm glad you're both here; we need help immediately. Please tell the customers not to buy the game box from us. Thanks, got to be off to get things in order." Then off he went pleading with customers, "Please don't buy from us . . . please don't buy from us."

A middle-age man carrying six boxes bumped into Socky. Just for fun, Socky said with the most serious face he could muster, "Please don't buy from us."

The middle-age man stared at Socky for a while and said, "You're threatening me."

"No, I'm not threatening you; I'm just urging you not to buy from us."

"Why should you do that?"

"It's a bit difficult to explain, but we'd be happy if you don't buy from us."

"No, you're threatening me; you want my boxes." The middle-age man looked frightened.

"I'm not threatening you."

"See, you're threatening me. You can't hide that threatening tone and look of yours. I've seen you before." The middle-age man backed off, turned around and disappeared into the crowd.

I looked on in amazement at the chaos and said, "Come on, let's go; there's nothing we can do. Besides, I don't like telling customers not to buy from us."

"Yeah, makes us look kind of stupid," said Socky, shaking his head.

We drove back to Croctopus HQ, all the time talking about the absurd situation at the game box store and wondering aloud why we were sent to salvage an impossible situation. Kong and the CEO were nowhere in sight by then. The CEO could be at the store taking flak from customers after taking it from Kong. As we entered the lift Socky said, "It would be a relief for the CEO to take flak from customers rather than the General."

"Hopefully, we're done with the game box business; I don't want to think about it anymore," I said.

As we came out of the lift, Kate rushed to us and said, "Thank goodness, both of you are here. I've been taking flak from that woman, and I need support; she's really a hard nut to crack. The way it's going, one of us will sink to the bottom of the ocean and never re-surface."

"What's going on?" I asked.

"It's about the game box business," said Kate.

"Ken doesn't want to think about it anymore," said Socky with a chuckle. "And I'll throw a fit if anyone talks to me about it."

"Fit or no fit, both of you just have to help me. I know everyone's up to here with the game box business," said Kate, bringing her hand up to her eyebrows, "but it's not finished yet."

"So, what's happening now?" I said.

"It's that woman, the immoveable object; I feel like strangling her with my bare hands."

"Which woman is it that you want to murder?"

"The deputy CEO of the game box company, Mrs Chan," said Kate with a long sigh. "I've been asked by the General to help her sort things out, and I've just come out of a meeting with her and some of the staff. We're taking a short break for her to take her vitamin pills and do her daily meditation. When the meeting re-convenes in a few minutes, I want you to go in with me."

"You want me to come along too, right?" said Socky.

"Yes, of course, thanks."

"But you haven't told us the whole story," I said.

"You see, the company has a mountain of game boxes, which it doesn't want to sell because the more it sells, the more money it loses. But I've told them to sell and cut losses because the boxes have already been paid for; they're sunk costs. And it's no use keeping them—they'll be obsolete in a short time."

"You're right, of course," I said.

"But they want to keep the boxes because they don't want to sell at a loss," said Kate.

"That's stupid," said Socky.

"Yes, but that's not all; Mrs Chan wants to buy a warehouse to keep the boxes."

"What? That's ridiculous," I said. "Three stupid decisions in a row; no wonder they're in such trouble. First, they priced the game box below cost, then they refused to sell them to cut losses, and now they want to incur a further cost buying a warehouse to keep the boxes."

"Mrs Chan has a certain warehouse in mind," said Kate. "The important thing now is to stop her from buying it."

"Right," I said, "but she must be quite a stubborn person. I'm sure you must have listed all the reasons why she shouldn't go ahead with the purchase of the warehouse."

"That's right. I tell you, she is stubborn."

"If an intelligent person like you couldn't persuade her, I don't see what Socky and I can do."

"Never mind about that, I need support; we'll think of something as we go along; three heads are better than one. But we must stop the purchase of the warehouse. It's time for the meeting, let's go."

We walked briskly into the boardroom. Mrs Chan was not there yet, but the other game box company people were. An air of gloom hung quietly but heavily over them. No one spoke; some flipped through their notes and pretended to read. One or two made muted coughs so that they still looked alive to others. One man looked intently at the door, as if bracing himself for a storm to crash through it. The dispirited lot did not have to wait long. Mrs Chan, about sixty years old, soon appeared like an apparition and took her seat, looking reinvigorated after her vitamin pills and meditation, and ready for a long, hard battle.

"I see you've called for reinforcement," said Mrs Chan, eyes shooting daggers at Kate.

"Well, I've consulted some people for a second opinion. This is Ken, you've met him. And this is Socky, who is working with us on several projects."

"We'll see what your reinforcement can do for you." The others around the four of us were stunned into complete silence at Mrs Chan's confrontational remark. None of them even dared shuffle any papers or let out a muted cough.

"As I was saying before we took our break, we've no choice but to purchase the warehouse, which is a small one with a good price. I repeat, we've absolutely no choice. We can't continue selling the game boxes because the more we sell, the more we lose. Our only alternative is to keep the boxes until such time when we can raise the price."

"When and in what circumstances can the price be raised?" Kate asked.

"I really don't know, but what I do know is that we cannot sell things at a loss."

"That means you may have to keep the boxes indefinitely," said Kate.

"I hope not."

"You can't base your decision on hope," said Kate, "especially with electronic products, which are in a highly competitive market and become obsolete quickly."

"Neither can we base our decision on selling at a loss," said Mrs Chan sternly.

"Okay, you still have some time to decide what to do with the boxes. The immediate issue is whether to purchase a warehouse," I said.

"The issue is not whether to purchase a warehouse; the issue is whether the offer price for the warehouse is acceptable to us, and I think we have a very good price right now."

"But you could lease some warehouse space," said Socky.

"That'll be money down the drain. Warehouse prices have come down considerably. It's really worth our money to buy a warehouse. After all, we don't know how long we'll have to store the boxes."

"But your people don't have any experience running a warehouse," said Kate.

"What experience do we need, really? It's just a big, empty space with four walls and a roof."

"Well, you can never be too sure about things you don't know," I said.

"But what we can be sure of is that with a warehouse all our immediate problems will be solved. We'll just store all the boxes in the warehouse for the time being."

"That's like sweeping everything under the carpet," said Kate.

"How could you say that? Young lady, that's totally uncalled for. We're not trying to sweep anything under the carpet! We're trying to solve a difficult problem, a very urgent and difficult problem. Now that we've a solution at hand, you come up with a ridiculous, insulting statement. Young people nowadays just shoot their mouth off without thinking."

"Well, I tend to agree with Kate," said Socky. "It's warehousing your problems; you're not solving them, you're just putting them on hold for the day that will not likely come."

"How dare you put it this way? You're older than Kate and you should know better what not to say. My goodness, people nowadays . . . It seems like you're threatening me!" Mrs Chan looked like a kettle puffing out steam and its cover rattling.

"No, I'm not threatening you; I'm just putting things in the proper perspective." Socky was clearly annoyed at the change of subject, but he tried to remain calm.

"Of course, you're threatening me; you look threatening and I feel threatened."

"I don't look threatening and I'm not threatening you."

"Yes, you are; you're threatening me. You're an intruder, and you're here to threaten me; that's your task here. You've not given any constructive suggestion at all, which makes me wonder why you're sitting in this room. Tell me honestly, why are you here?"

"Socky is not threatening you," said Kate. "And he has kindly agreed to be here to help us arrive at the correct decision."

"Yes, he is most certainly threatening me; I could feel it right down to my bones. The big, bad wolf is threatening me."

231

"No, I'm not. I'm neither threatening you nor am I a wolf of any sort."

"Yes, you are. You are!"

"Now . . ." I was trying to restore some sanity to the situation when I was cut off.

"Haven't I seen you before?" said Mrs Chan, eyes narrowing and looking at Socky suspiciously. "Tell me, where have I seen you? You're a most unpleasant man and it's most unpleasant talking to you."

"Now, let's not go off on a tangent," I said. "We're talking about buying a warehouse."

"That's right; we should stick to talking about the warehouse," said Kate.

"None of us in this room knows anything about running a warehouse," I said. "We don't even know simple things like how many people to employ to run it and how much to budget for the warehouse. That would include budgeting for contractors to clean the place. To me, a warehouse means dirt, lots of dirt. There are hidden problems and costs and we don't even know what they are."

"Dirt? What do you mean?" said Mrs Chan, suddenly looking uneasy, her fingers fiddling her collar as if it had suddenly tightened around her neck.

"I mean what I said. Have you ever seen a warehouse without dirt? There'll be dirt swirling all over the place; vast quantities of it, and we'll have to spend a lot of time and money cleaning up."

"Would there be really so much dirt?" said Mrs Chan. "I mean, would dirt give us a problem?" This time, it was a genuine question, although not a necessary one. It seemed Mrs Chan wanted an assurance rather than information. Amazingly, before I could draw my second breath, the air thick with confrontation disappeared, replaced by one that reminded me of having lukewarm, tepid tea on a cloudy, lazy afternoon.

Notwithstanding the sudden change to a more agreeable atmosphere, I smelled blood. In the midst of the thick, swirling dust before my mind's eye, I sensed something shifting about, like a frightened prey for me to seize. I felt like a tiger going for the kill. "You see, dirt and warehouses go hand in hand; they're like Siamese twins. You can't have a warehouse without dirt; they come together and are inseparable. You understand me? When you say you want a warehouse, you're also saying you want dirt. Am I not right to say this? But are you prepared to put up with all that dirt? I mean, just imagine, choking dirt hanging about the place all the time, like an unwelcomed fog. Do you want to deal with dirt day in, day out?"

"Dirt, I've never thought about that." Mrs Chan became silent and contemplative, her mind somewhere beyond the boardroom.

"Yes, within a short time, all the crates would be coated with dirt, and I dare say a very thick layer of dirt. Imagine that."

"Don't ask me to imagine anything now. Dirt, that's horrible! Horrible! Horrible!"

"Yes, dirt, stifling dirt. You can imagine dirt swirling in the warehouse. You may have to put on a gas mask to inspect the things inside. And even if you've been in the warehouse for a short time, you can't come out of it without dirt clinging onto your clothes—and skin. By the way, are you allergic to dirt?"

"Am I . . . Don't tell me anymore! Enough!"

"But I've to tell you what to expect; I've to tell you the truth. Warehouses and dirt go together; you take them as one. You're asking for dirt, and you want to pay good money for it. Dirt should be upper most in your mind. Think about vacuuming your house; cleaning up a warehouse would be a hundred times worse."

Mrs Chan put her palm on her chest just below the neck and started to breathe heavily, which stunned everyone. Her facial muscles tightened, as though they were trying to squeeze her face shut. Then sweat oozed from her pores and soaked her like rain soaking laundry hung out to dry. She wiped her face and neck with tissues and then with a small handkerchief, which quickly became soggy and unusable. Then she started to cough and choke, her hand still on her chest. I stood up and approached her, followed by Kate and Socky. The rest were glued to their seats, too stunned and confused to do or say anything. Mrs Chan put up her hand to stop me from delaying what she had to do. With great effort, she stretched out a shaky arm and reached unsteadily for a button to call her secretary. It was as if that was the one thing that would save her life; as if all the training and experience in her entire life were in preparation for that moment.

Then with the greatest of effort, Mrs Chan said in a voice that was shaky and desperate and seemed near death, "Susan, cancel the meeting with the agent for the warehouse owners; we're not buying it." Then she slumped back on her seat, mouth open and eyes staring at the ceiling.

That ended the big fright for Kate. At the lift lobby she turned to me and said, "Ken, that was brilliant; it was just brilliant. I could never have thought of it. You literally attacked her with dirt. It really choked her off from any desire to buy the warehouse."

"Well, let's just say dirt is a personal problem for me."

Socky said he had had enough nonsense for the day and wanted to get away from the game box company. We drove to Number One Chicken. However, as we alighted from the car and took a slow walk to the restaurant, we were still talking about the game box company and the day's events. We just could not stop thinking and talking about what had happened.

"I can't believe what's happening in the game box company; it has really opened my eyes," said Socky. "I mean, it's the worst-run company I've ever come across in my life."

"There are a number of other subsidiaries that are run badly," I said, "although you've probably seen the worst."

"What I don't understand is this: Croctopus is the biggest corporation in the country, yet there are pockets within it that are so

234

badly run. Makes me wonder how Croctopus came to be the biggest corporation in Orderland." Socky kept shaking his head.

"Well, what I know is that long ago, before our time, Croctopus was indeed the best-run corporation in the country. But after it attained dominant position in almost all of its businesses in the country, it became bureaucratic and lethargic, and started to go downhill. It continues to remain on top only because of its size and connections."

"Shouldn't something be done about all the nonsense that's going on?"

Kate sensed an opportunity. "Let me ask you something, Socky. If Croctopus mishandles a case, and you know very well that it's going in the wrong direction, what would you do?"

"I'd tell whoever's in charge that we're heading the wrong way and we ought to change direction."

"What happens if the one in charge is the General?"

"I'd still do the same thing. Of course, I'd prepare myself to take a lot of flak."

Kate looked at me, like finally seeing a ray of hope, and said, "What say you, Ken? So, how about it?"

"Do you think the General would change course?"

"Well, he might not, especially when his mind is made up," said Socky. "But, I'd still do it."

"What if you get the sack for trying, and the General doesn't change course, and proceeds as before?" I said, looking at Socky and then at Kate.

"Well, what can I say?" said Socky. "I'd have sacrificed myself in vain. Nonetheless, I think I'd still do it. I suppose it's just me; I'm like that."

"I would, too," said Kate.

"Hey, why are you both asking me this?" said Socky. "Do I know the case?"

"Well, Kate thought the company's not doing something right, and I think she might have a point, but confronting the General and telling him he's wrong is a different thing altogether."

"I know the General's a difficult person," said Socky, "but I don't think you need be afraid of telling him the truth."

"It's not that I'm afraid," I said, "but the General expects us to be team-players, to be loyal and united in the face of adversity, not to squabble among ourselves."

"I think the General just doesn't like to be told he's wrong; I think he's afraid to be wrong," said Kate.

"Ha ha, I won't comment on that," I said. But I could see how things would go if we were to confront him directly. We'll all be shown the door and he'd continue as before. Our effort at making him see our point of view would just be wasted. I think we'll have to change the General slowly, not through a head-on confrontation, but through a subtle process of making him see things our way. We can be effective only if we're around to be effective; non-existent people cannot make their mark."

We disappeared into Number One Chicken, still arguing.

Chapter 17

When I returned home from work, I felt that things in the house had been tempered with, as if an intruder had broken in and searched the place. Things seemed in place at first sight; the intruder must have taken care to return everything to its original place, or so he thought. But it was my house, and I knew that things were not exactly the same as when I had left for the office in the morning. At first I could not tell exactly what was misplaced, then I noticed that the newspapers were not in the rack. In fact, there was nothing in the rack, when there should have been several days' newspapers in it. I was sure I had put the day's newspapers into the rack on the way out in the morning, as it was my habit, and the rack was not even empty then. A newspaper thief had broken in? That was not possible, I thought. Who would bother to break into a house to steal newspapers? Some other things must have been taken. Then I felt a presence, a certain disturbance in the air. I froze.

"We'll continue later, bye," said Arm on her cellphone. "Looking for the newspapers? I've thrown them away; this place was a mess."

Suppressing any expression of surprise, I said, "It wasn't a mess." I walked to the kitchen to get a drink; Arm followed me there, but kept a distance.

"Mother told me to return; she asked me to forgive you," said Arm. When there was no reply from me after a pause, she repeated, "I said Mother asked me to return and to forgive you."

"Why didn't she ask me to forgive you?" I replied.

"What? How could you? How could you say such a thing? You're always like that; you haven't changed! I'm doing my best to patch things up and you're reopening old wounds. You've to understand that a lot of give and take is needed between husband and wife. I've tolerated a lot of your nonsense; it's time you appreciated that. Mother asked me to forgive you, and I have. The least you should do is to appreciate this. But did you? No, you didn't. When are you going to understand you've to play your part in building up a good relationship? Maybe you came from a family that doesn't care very much about relationships, but mine does. And you can see the difference between us. I wish . . ."

Arm carried on for about forty-five minutes before storming off to the kitchen.

Later in the evening, I took my briefcase to the desk in the study, hoping to finish some work. Since my daughter Mei was born, I had refrained from bringing work home, preferring to spend time with her, and later with Min too. I did not always succeed in keeping work from home, for there was often urgent work, but I had managed to keep it to a trickle. As soon as I sat down at my desk that evening, I realized that I no longer needed to ferry Mei and Min between Arm and me, now that she was back; it was good for the children now that the family was back together again. I felt happy for them and I let the feeling linger on. Then I decided not to

238

open the briefcase. Maybe it was an excuse not to work, I thought at first; but soon concluded that I really had wanted to celebrate for my children. So I spent the evening reading leisurely until my eyes became heavy, and I went to bed.

Then the dream started. I was on a plane. The flight was uncomfortable, made worse by Kong sitting next to me. He looked agitated and gesticulated with his usual energy. But he was talking without sound, even though he was, as often, excited and appeared to be talking loudly. The only sound was the background hum from the plane engines. It did not seem weird to me that Kong was talking without sound. People often talked without sound in dreams; even I in my dream seemed to understand that. Kong wagged his finger at me, and suddenly I could hear him—his voice was very distant, almost inaudible. I looked at him and listened intently, and could just manage to hear him say repeatedly, "Don't you dare say I'm wrong!"

Then, without warning, the plane shook violently as it approached the runway in a frighteningly quick descent, and landed with a heavy thud, like a goose whose power of flight had failed. Everyone was scared white. The plane hurtled down the runway with a harrowing momentum; the pilots had lost control! As the wheels screeched and friction burned up the tires, leaving long lines of track on the ground, a frightening roar rushed into the cabin. The passengers asked themselves whether the plane would become their collective coffin. The roaring engines, the screeching tires and the rushing wind coalesced into a deafening, terrifying call of death. I felt for the seatbelt instinctively. It seemed that my time was up; there was no appeal; I felt the cruelty of fate. Then I realized that it was not Kong who was sitting next to me. It was Arm. Strange, I thought in my dream, how could I have made such a mistake? I did not think very much; people in dreams do not think very much. I took another look. Arm was wearing a tiger-striped suit. I felt I had been in the same situation before, but could not figure out when and where before. I turned to take another look at Arm, hoping to jolt my mind into remembering. To my surprise, she was not there anymore. Instead, to my shock, a tiger was on the seat! It stared at me with killer eyes and gave a menacing snarl. I broke out in cold sweat and my body went limp.

At that most desperate moment, when I was at a total loss as to what to do, I realized that Socky was on the seat between the tiger and me. How did Socky come between the tiger and me? I did not think very much, just relieved that I was now not the target of the tiger, though it was very bad for Socky. The tiger extended a paw and made a swipe at Socky, but missed. It was strange the tiger missed such an easy target, but I did not think much about it; I was just thankful I was not the object of the tiger's attention. The other passengers seemed totally unaware of the tiger; instead they were bracing themselves in anticipation of a frightening crash. The tiger seemed unsettled by the momentum of the runaway plane, and seemed to feel that Socky was responsible for its discomfort. It bared its teeth and clawed at Socky several times. Socky's back was pressing against me as he tried to move away from the tiger. That in turn caused me to press my back hard against the wall of the plane. I used my elbow desperately to hit the windowpane, but was unable to crack open an escape route. Strangely, despite the tiger clawing at him, Socky was unhurt. Then the heads of Mei and Min popped up from the seats in front, looking curiously at the tiger. I stood up quickly and pressed the two tiny heads down with my hands. The tiger seemed unaware of their presence. I felt we were all going to die; there was no hope. Yet all the tiger wanted to do was to claw at Socky; it could not comprehend what was going on. To the tiger, Socky, and not the runaway plane was the problem.

The plane crashed with a frightening force; the sound of a thousand thunderclaps rocked the cabin. Pandemonium exploded like an angry volcano spewing hot lava everywhere. People stampeded for the exits; they screamed without sound. Then I felt the heat; the plane was going to explode! The high-grade fuel was going to make the cabin a collective coffin for all. The stewards and stewardesses were trying desperately to guide the passengers to the exits, but no one listened, no one cared. The people fused into a single mass, with screaming heads and flailing arms sticking out from the fused body. Socky was gone, but the tiger was still there, blocking my path to the nearest exit. I was desperate and my mind was racing to find a solution. Then I realized the mass of body had disappeared. Where were Arm, Mei and Min? Nobody was around except the tiger and me; they must have left the plane. Before I could decide what to do next, the tiger leapt from its seat and ran to an exit and jumped out. I followed the tiger to the exit, but was afraid to jump; it was too high above ground. I stood rooted at the exit and surveyed the scene below.

People were frantically running away from the plane. The tiger, behind them, was running in powerful strides. I was transfixed by the sight and forgot about the danger and did not make any attempt to escape from the plane. Then, inexplicably, the tiger turned into a goose, and the people turned around and started to chase the goose, which somehow managed to elude its pursuers. The people seemed to have forgotten about the burning plane; there was a goose running about wildly, and all they wanted to do was to chase it. Why did they chase the goose? I did not think about it; neither did the pursuers. They did not even stop to discuss the question; the mob simply chased—the goose was there, so they chased it, as if triggered by instinct. Even though the frightened bird appeared clumsy, the pursuers failed to catch it. It was always one step ahead and managed to elude capture as if it knew exactly when to make an evasive twist or turn. The scene was unreal.

Then I woke up, wet all over. In the moonlight, I saw Arm sleeping soundly; all was peaceful for her. I could not sleep, staying awake till about an hour before my usual wakeup time before dozing off from fatigue. So I overslept and had to rush as soon as I got out of bed. Fortunately, it was the school holidays and there was no need to worry about the kids going to school late. By the time I had washed and was taking the first bite of my peanut butter sandwich, Arm was already awake.

"You were tossing and turning the whole night; I had a hard time sleeping," she said. "I'll be tired the whole day; you should've been more considerate and turned lightly."

I did not reply. As I would most certainly be late for office, I rushed out of the house, before stopping on my tracks. Arm was screaming as though the house was on fire. So I rushed back in, and found Arm standing on a chair, screaming and pointing excitedly at something.

"There's a mouse over there," said Arm. "It dashed across the floor, then climbed up to the sink and got out through the window."

"It must have finished the night shift and gone home to sleep," I said. "It won't bother you anymore; the sun has come up."

"Are you sure?"

"Of course."

"Anyway, we'll have to call the exterminators; it could come for another visit."

"Go ahead," I said on the way out of the house. Why was a tigress afraid of a mouse? I could not figure it out. Maybe a mouse scurrying about conjured the image of a runaway penis darting about everywhere, which would have been most dangerous and frightening to a woman.

I tried to drive fast to the office but to no avail, as leaving the house at that hour meant bumping along in rush-hour traffic. I arrived at the office half an hour late. As soon as I was at my desk, Kate came over to tell me that Kong was calling a meeting, which would start in another five minutes. "There's still time for coffee," I said before heading straight for the pantry. By the time we reached the boardroom, the rest of the Croctopus terrorist hunters were there.

242

"I've received disturbing news early this morning," said Kong. "Crouching Liar bumped into Sammy this morning and told Sammy casually that he would be starting research on banking in Orderland."

And he had to call an emergency meeting early this morning because of this, I thought. While Kong was talking, Kate scribbled something on a piece of paper and handed it to me. I read the message: What's the big deal? That startled me, but I managed to compose myself quickly and gave little away. I wanted to crumple the paper, but stopped as it would be obvious that she had handed me something trivial. So I folded it nicely and kept it in my file and moved my lips silently to convey, "Thank you."

"What's the big deal?" asked Kong. "Ken, could you tell us?" Kate gave me a little smile.

"That's where we all keep our money," I said.

Before I could say further, Kong cut in, "The banks are the bedrock of our financial system; without banks we can't do business the modern way. We must defend our banks against all attacks at all costs."

"At all costs?" I asked.

"Of course," said Kong. "The whole country—everyone—must make whatever sacrifices needed to defend this most important institution of ours. We must all defend our banks."

You're nuts or what? I thought. In my mind's eye I saw thousands of peasants rising up in arms and storming a bank, with Kate leading the charge. "Would the peasants . . . I mean, the poor sacrifice anything to defend our banks?" I asked.

"If they know what's good for them," said Kong. "In the private sector of the economy, the banks come first. All of us, wealthy and poor, must do our utmost to defend our banks."

"And defend Croctopus Bank most of all," said Sammy Sam.

You're all mad, I thought. In my mind's eye, I saw the peasants crashing the gate, and Kate was holding a tattered flag up high and waving it wildly.

"Yes, that's right; we've to defend it at all costs," said Kong. "Croctopus Bank is the largest local bank in the country; if it's put out of action in a terrorist strike, the whole of Orderland would be plunged into chaos."

"Banks in most countries are the same, more or less," I said. "So why would any terrorist need to study the banking system in Orderland?"

"They want to hit banks in the right place and at the right time to cause maximum damage," said Kong.

"They could do that simply by striking at the Croctopus Bank headquarters on a business day," said Kate. "They don't need to research banking in Orderland."

"The General knows what he's talking about," said Vento Voon.

I am not sure about that, I thought. By now, smoke was billowing everywhere, and one peasant with an eye patch was seating on the chairman's seat, chomping a cigar.

"You're absolutely right, sir," said Sonny Song.

"You and Ken don't get it," said Sonny Song. "General, perhaps you could explain it further; some people need more elaboration."

"I don't need to explain it further," said Kong. "It's obvious."

"So what do you propose we do?" asked Roger.

"I could feel our terrorist friend closing the circle on us, with his finger on the button, itching to press it," Kong said. "We've to stop him from doing any research on real banking in Orderland. Ken, I want you to bring him to Whisper Park and show him Croctopus Bank's takeover of the business there. That's about all the banking he should learn."

You are talking crap, I thought. "That's a strange place to study banking in the country," I pleaded.

"It's not; the takeover is part of banking business," said Kong.

244

"I'm afraid I've to agree with Ken," said Kate. "Whisper Park is not the place to start. I mean, we'll look like deliberately trying to place obstacles to any research on banking."

"No, we won't," said Kong with unexplained confidence. "Bring him to Whisper Park."

*

The sun's rays could not punch through the thick layer of white clouds, which sailed silently across the sky from East to West like a long line of battleships. As it was a weekday, there were not many picnickers there; a few heads bobbed up and down in the sea, chasing a red ball, faint shouting and laughter in the distance from the swimmers in the game. A few bodies were sprawled on the beach here and there, their owners, who looked like tourists, trying to soak up whatever sunlight there might be. A woman was reading under a beach umbrella, a glass of drink with a bent straw next to her. The purpose of the umbrella in the tepid sunlight was unclear. Two little boys were walking on the beach, picking seashells with childish delight. On an adjacent field, several people were flying kites of various colors and designs. The leaves atop a line of coconut trees swayed like hula dancers, while a fluttering kite was entangled on a treetop like a struggling insect trapped in a spider web. The sea breeze blew as though a thousand persons were whispering at the same time.

"So, this is Whisper Park," said Socky, surveying the place. "It's a lovely place for a picnic, but what has it got to do with banking in Orderland? I'm confused."

"Look over there," I said, trying to keep a straight face while pointing to a small, shabby brick structure.

"That's a public lavatory," said Socky. "We come all the way to study a public lavatory? Surely, this has nothing to do with banking in Orderland?"

We walked toward the brick structure at a reluctant pace. An old man was dozing contentedly at a counter between the entrances to the gents and the ladies. A box with a slot for coins was before him. It was obvious that operations of the lavatory were way behind the times.

"This building belongs to this old man," I said. "It was built by his grandfather and handed down the generations. So this public lavatory has been here for three generations, from the time Whisper Park was opened."

"So the takings from this lavatory housed, fed and clothed his family for three generations?"

"That's right; you're clever. His grandfather slept here all his life, then his father slept here all his life, and now he sleeps here all his life."

"Will one of his children take over from him and continue the long doze through the generations?"

"No, his children will be saved from such a fate. They are being saved by Croctopus Bank; that's why we're here. After trying for three generations, from the time of his grandfather, the bank has finally persuaded his family to sell this lavatory."

"The bank is trying to run a public lavatory? Now, this does not smell right."

"No, no, don't worry, Socky; there's no money in public lavatory, at least not enough for a bank to bother with. The bank intends to demolish the building and use the land for some other, more profitable, purpose. I don't know what it will be, but definitely not a public lavatory."

"Phew! I'm relieved."

"The bank had a little celebration after the deal was done."

"When will it take over this place?" asked Socky, looking at the old man. "He doesn't seem concerned."

"No he has a good deal; he'll be paid a handsome sum. The bank takes over tomorrow; but it's a condition of the sale that the lavatory continue to operate for another year and he be employed by the bank as a cashier for the one year. He'll still be sitting at that counter for the next one year; he said he needed the time to adjust to a new life. The bank bent backward to accommodate him. Three generations of tenacity, three generations of hard work hard work by dedicated bank executives; that's how much it took to take over this lavatory."

"So, today he's the boss; tomorrow he'll be an employee," said Socky, looking at the old man. "But he'll continue his long doze."

My cellphone rang; it was Kate on the line. "Ken, could you go over to Croctopus Bank headquarters straightaway? A minor crisis has developed over the bank's announcement to increase charges tomorrow. Seems like the whole country is against it."

"Yes, it has been in the news over the last few days," I said.

"A crowd of protesters is at the bank headquarters right now; the General wants you to go over there to help the staff calm the situation."

"Hmm . . . It was also announced at the same time that the entry charge to the Whisper Park lavatory here would be increased, but I don't see protesters here," I told Kate.

"Don't be funny; it's not the same. Anyway, there were protests in the Internet, over the radio and in the newspapers over the plan to increase the lavatory charge."

"But no protest crowd here. Maybe I should remain here to help out in case a bunch of protesters turn up." I did not really feel like going off to Croctopus Bank headquarters to meet a crowd of protesters.

"I said don't be funny. Now go to the bank headquarters straightaway, and that's an order . . . from the General."

"Yes, madam," I said, standing to attention and giving a salute. "Socky, let's go; I'll explain to you in the car."

By the time we got to Croctopus Bank headquarters, the crowd had become boisterous; people were waving their fists and chanting slogans. Some carried placards with the words "Blood Suckers" splashed in red, as though the words were written in blood. We could not get through the crowd.

"They just take our money any time they feel like it," said a man to us. We just smiled and tried to find a way forward.

A fat woman came to us and said, "We're poor and they are rich, but they keep taking from us."

"Yeah, that's right!" shouted an angry young man. "And that's wrong!"

An old man came up to Socky and said, "Hey, I remember you, I've seen you somewhere."

"Really? I think you've got the wrong person," said Socky.

"No, no, I've seen you somewhere. I remember you, but I don't remember where I've seen you or who you are," said the old man.

"Then you don't remember me."

"No, I remember you. You must be someone important or famous; that's why I remember you. Hey, it's very nice of you and your friend to come and help us. We need help; we're the small guys. Someone important and famous like you will give us a voice."

Socky and I tried for quite a while to get into the Croctopus Bank headquarters, but were unable to get through the crowd and police line. After a few hours, the police managed to disperse the protesters peacefully.

*

Three days later, Socky and I were back at Whisper Park. "Just three days after the takeover and we've to do a report on it," said Socky, before popping some *kacang putih* into his mouth. "And we've to say whether efficiency here has improved. I think this is ridiculous."

"Yes, it certainly is. But I'm curious about what you think. So, do you think efficiency has improved?"

"Ha! Everything has remained exactly the same, as you can see for yourself," said Socky, looking at the old man sleeping at the counter.

"The bank has just announced that efficiency at the lavatory had improved greatly," I said, showing Socky a newspaper report.

"This is absurd, how can it be? Nothing has changed; it's the same old man sleeping all day here."

"They've also announced that efficiency at the bank had improved." I pointed to an adjacent report. "I heard over the radio that opposition to the increase in bank charges had dropped because of the report. People are starting to accept that the increase in charges was necessary; the improvement in the bank's efficiency is accepted as proof."

"The report is nonsense; how could efficiency in the bank improve in two or three days? The bank is talking nonsense." As Socky got more agitated, his rate of eating *kacang putih* increased. "The efficiency of the bank remains the same as before, just as the efficiency of this lavatory here has remained the same. Nothing has changed in the bank and the lavatory."

I popped some *kacang putih* into my mouth, almost without realizing it as I was engaged in thinking deeply about the lavatory. "You see, improvement in efficiency is brought about by an increase in revenue for the same amount of work."

"But there has been no improvement or even change in work method; everything has remained the same."

"Well, the number of people using this lavatory has remained the same or has even dropped due to the increase in the charge. Yet, the takings have increased by virtue of the increase in the charge. There's no improvement in work method whatsoever; the old man is sleeping as before. But as far as the bank is concerned there's an improvement in the lavatory's efficiency because usage has remained the same or even dropped, but takings have increased."

"Hmm . . . You're right, clever," said Socky, raising a finger to emphasize the point. "But what people don't know is that the efficiency didn't come from a change in work method; it's the same old man sleeping the whole day. In fact, this lavatory serves the same or even a smaller number of people."

"And it's the same with the supposed increase in banking efficiency, although there's no change in work method," I said, popping the last *kacang putih* into my mouth and crumpling the paper cone. "The increase in bank charges has caused a drop in usage while increasing revenue."

"So fewer people are served while the bank earns more, and that's efficiency," said Socky, shaking his head.

*

Socky and I were at the lobby of Croctopus Bank headquarters. "Hi Mark, we're early; glad to see you here; saves us a trip up to your floor. Socky, this is Mr Mark Mak, the vice-president of property leasing."

Mark Mak was a fat, serious man. He seemed not too happy with the unplanned meeting. After shaking hands, he said, "Actually, I'm on my way to deal with an unexpected situation, and on the way I ran into a second unexpected situation—both of you."

"Mark, this is our report on the Whisper Park lavatory takeover," I said, handing over the file.

"This file looks rather thin; I had expected a more substantial report," said Mark Mak.

"That's not possible. How much can we write about a lavatory?" said Socky.

"In Croctopus, we take our work seriously," said Mark Mak.

"Let me see him!" a man shouted. A woman was trying to stop him from going further.

"It's okay, I'll see him," said Mark Mak.

"I'm Raju; we spoke earlier on the phone. I'm here to discuss the new rent collection procedure."

"I've told you on the phone that the new procedure had come straight from the board of directors, and we can't make an exception for you," said Mark Mak.

"I'm not asking the bank to make me an exception; I'm asking it to revoke the directive for everyone."

"Why should we do that?" said Mark Mak.

"It's unfair and wrong!" said Raju, unable to contain his anger. "How could you collect three months' rent in advance? Stick to the monthly collection."

"The bank is collecting three months' rent each time?" I said.

"Yes!" said Raju. "That's not right."

"We've the right to do so; it's in the agreement that we may change the procedure on the collection of rent," said Mark Mak.

"Changing from a monthly payment to a three-monthly payment goes beyond procedure," said Raju.

"No, it does not."

"Yes, it does."

"Can I help?" I said.

"Thank you, I'd like to hear from you," said Raju.

"No, you may not help, Ken," said Mark Mak. "The decision is made at the highest level, and nobody can change it. Not you, not me, not anybody."

"But, surely, you could let the board of directors know what this gentleman is saying," said Socky.

"It's not only me; all the tenants are upset," said Raju.

"Why is the bank asking for rent to be paid three-monthly in advance?" I asked.

"Efficiency," said Mark Mak. "It's more efficient to collect rent every three months in advance than to collect it monthly. It's too much of a hassle to collect monthly."

"Too much of a hassle? The bank actually thinks collecting big money is too much of a hassle?" said Socky.

"The bank is so fat and comfortable that collecting big money is a hassle," said Raju.

"Now, I think you don't understand the situation," said Mark Mak.

"What is the situation?" asked Raju.

"The situation is that the board's decision is final," said Mark Mak.

"Oh, come on," said Socky, "a commercial decision like this one need not be final."

"But it's final; I know it is final. Now, if you'd excuse me, I've something important to attend to." Mark Mak walked off, leaving the three of us dumbfounded.

"You know something?" said Socky. "I agree with you, Mr Raju. I think banks in Croctopus are too fat and comfortable. Any corporation that finds collecting big money a hassle is too fat and comfortable, that's for sure."

"Exactly!" said Raju, smacking his hand on his file for emphasis.

"Which means that there are too few banks in Croctopus," I said. "There's no competition; the banks are not hungry."

Not having got what he wanted, Raju went off dejected and angry. Socky suggested that, as we were already in the building and had about an hour to spare, we look around the place; he wanted to learn a bit more about banking in Orderland. As we were talking and walking to the inner part of the building, a tall, well-groomed figure appeared. She was one of the bank's credit managers, Bo, an energetic woman in her twenties whose surname I had forgotten. She was on her way to meet a prospective client, and I took the

252

opportunity to request that Socky and I be allowed to attend the meeting. In the small conference room, Bo, after some pleasantries, commenced discussion with the prospective client.

"Mr Low, as you are new to the bank, I suggest you start off with a small loan of five thousand dollars," said Bo.

"Five thousand dollars? That's rather low, isn't it? You can hardly do anything with five thousand dollars," said Mr Low.

"That's just the start," assured Bo quickly. "The amount can be increased in the future." They haggled over the loan amount for a while, but Bo was adamant that the amount could not be increased. Socky and I felt sorry for Mr Low, but we did not interfere, as it was really not our business.

"All right, I'll agree to five thousand dollars for a start."

"Great," said Bo with a broad grin. "Now, there's the question of security."

"You need security for the paltry sum of five thousand dollars?" Mr Low raised his eyebrows.

"Oh, don't you worry, Mr Low. All you have to do is open a fixed deposit account with us with five thousand dollars, and that'll solve the problem."

"I deposit five thousand dollars with you? And you lend five thousand dollars to me with my own money? And I pay you interest on my money? Is this a joke or something?" The meeting did not survive for another minute. Socky decided that he had had enough of the banking business in Orderland, and fled Croctopus Bank headquarters, never to return. In the car, Socky kept shaking his head.

"Now I'm beginning to understand why Kate and you asked me the other day, after the meeting with Mrs Chan, about what I'd do if the company was heading in the wrong direction," said Socky. "Croctopus is full of holes. You were right, the company remains on top only because of its size and connections. You ought to do something about such nonsense, Ken. I don't know what case Kate and you were talking about the other day, but I suggest both of you go straight to the General and tell him he's wrong and ask him to change course. Come on, I'll buy you a drink if you do that."

"Thank you very much, Socky, but the General won't change his mind; the exercise would only get us into trouble for nothing."

Chapter 18

Kong called a meeting of Croctopus terrorist hunters in the afternoon, soon after lunch. That was unusual of him, for he preferred morning meetings. But Kate was not complaining; at least, she would not be at the mercy of old man air-conditioner. The afternoon was hot and oppressive—the air-conditioner seemed to have lost the struggle with the equatorial sun. Old man, give us some arctic winds, I pleaded in my mind. Kate looked at me, seated next to her as usual. I sat there like a statue. When I noticed Kate looking at me, I stirred and scribbled something on a piece of paper and handed it to her. It read: Any toothpicks for my eyelids? Kate gave me a kick beneath the table. She had done that so many times that she could keep her body above the table top perfectly still. But, probably because of drowsiness arising from a heavy lunch, she misjudged the force this time, and I got a nasty whack. I looked down to hide my grimace and also pretended to scratch my leg, when I was actually rubbing it to soothe the pain. Roger also hardly stirred in his seat, his eyes staring into infinity, although the wall ahead was not so far away.

"Ken, Kate and I had lunch at Number One Chicken; it was a good one," said Roger, probably trying to wake himself up with some jaw exercise.

"I'm glad you had a good lunch; mine was a disaster," said Kong. "There was so much salt in everything that I've been drinking like a camel."

"General, the chicken I had wasn't particularly good either; that makes two of us, sir," said Sammy Sam.

"The roast beef I had was horrible, sir," said Sonny Song, "the worst I've had in a long time."

"Sir, we'll never go to back to that restaurant again," said Vento Voon. "The fish I had was over-cooked; they really didn't know how to cook fish, sir."

"Nothing is as bad as having a ton of salt inside you sucking all the water out of your body," said Kong, who proceeded to gulp down a glass of iced water. "I called this meeting partly because we're slowly getting strangled to death by our terrorist mole; he's like a python having us for lunch. He gets the intelligence he wants, but we're nowhere near nailing him. The evidence we have is good enough for us, of course, but not good enough for the OSD. If this keeps up, he'll soon, and I mean soon, close the circle and Orderland will go up in smoke . . . boom!" Kong whacked his fist against the palm of his other hand, and waited a while for the effect to sink in.

"Anything from the OSD?" I asked.

"Nothing from Colonel Loon. He's so secretive; he never tells us anything other than bits and pieces of information that he thinks we really must have."

"I wonder how far is the OSD ahead of us," said Roger.

"I really don't know," said Kong.

"They ought to be ahead of us," said Kate. "We're still at square one."

"Now, that's not fair at all," said Vento Voon, wagging his finger. "How could you say such a thing? It's very unbecoming of you. You've got to learn how to behave. Under the General's leadership, we've made great strides in our investigation."

"That's right," said Sammy Sam. "Kate, I'm surprised and disappointed that you can't appreciate all the good work that has been done; you're still in the dark about where we are. Don't you know? One wrong move by Crouching Liar any time now and he's finished."

"Right, you're hopelessly lost, Kate," said Sonny Song. "We're just waiting for that one wrong move, and it could happen soon."

"I can't agree with this assessment," said Kate. "We've been beating about the bush; we don't even know where we're heading. I think we should review this whole thing, analyze our every step right from the beginning."

"Such impertinence! Such impudence!" said Vento Voon. "Reviewing the case from the beginning would be a complete waste of time. I say we press on."

"Press on to where?" said Kate.

"Press on straight ahead," said Vento Voon.

"Straight ahead to where?" said Kate.

"Now, don't be funny," said Vento Voon. "You've crossed the line; your conduct is unbecoming of a subordinate; it's outright insubordination, if I may say so."

You may not say so, I thought.

"What are you talking about?" said Roger. "What's this insubordination thing that I hear of so often? I don't understand it."

"Kate is just giving her views," I said, "and I think she may have a point."

"You too?" said Vento Voon. "Since when did you go over to the other side?"

"Enough of this!" commanded Kong. There was immediate silence. "Kate, I don't want any more of such behavior from you.

257

Either you learn to respect authority or I'd show you the way out of this organization. And Ken, you should have known better than try to defend such insubordination. If you don't know what is or is not acceptable here, you'd have to follow Kate out of here. We're facing great adversity; our country is in danger; we have to stand united in our mission or our enemy will win. I expect loyalty and steadfastness from all of you. I don't want anyone to sow the seeds of doubt in us. We've wasted enough time on your nonsense, Kate. I'm not giving you a long dressing down today only because I've something very important to discuss. I've a piece of good news. Kate, you're saved by the good news, so you'd better be thankful."

"I'm most grateful," said Kate. Kong and the senior executive vice-presidents looked at her suspiciously, not knowing whether she was truly grateful or she was trying to be funny.

Now, I called this meeting because a window of opportunity has opened up suddenly," said Kong, as he stood up and paced about the room. "It's a precious opportunity, and this time we must not waste it. I want something to come out of it."

"Sir, we're going to nail him this time," said Sammy Sam.

"I hope so; we've wasted enough opportunities," said Kong.

"You can depend on me, sir," said Sammy Sam.

Don't make my toes laugh, I thought.

"General, I've never let you down," said Sonny Song. "What's the window of opportunity, sir?"

"Sir, send me," said Vento Voon.

Enough, guys, this is not a circus, I thought.

"I've just learnt from our terrorist mole that his aunt, one Mrs Dangle, is coming to town," said Kong.

"Crouching Liar's aunt is coming?" said Vento Voon. "That's great; it's really a window of opportunity for us, sir."

"According to him, she's the only relative he keeps in touch with regularly," said Kong. "So, she must mean a lot to him. I suppose she's his only reliable channel for news about his family, if he wanted to learn anything about them."

*

The van left Orderland Airport and headed toward town. Mrs Dangle, alert and happy, talked animatedly. Socky smiled all the time; I had never seen him happier. Kate seemed to be infected by the pair's gaiety and was very happy too, although there was no special reason for her to be that happy. I was driving more slowly than usual because I was also absorbed in the conversation. Vento Voon, in the front seat, did not say much, but I could sense that he was listening to the conversation very intently.

"This is my second visit to Orderland," said Mrs Dangle.

"Really? That's a surprise; you've never told me that," said Socky.

"My first visit was ten years ago; I enjoyed myself very much."

"Oh, welcome back," said Kate. "I hope you'll enjoy yourself even more this time."

"I will, I most certainly will."

"This van will be at your disposal during your stay here," I said, "and I'll be your chauffeur."

"That's very kind of you and the company; I feel so welcome. I can't thank you all enough."

"This is by the order of the General," said Vento Voon.

"It's so kind and generous of him. Please convey my thanks to him, my dear man."

"I certainly will; rest assured that I'll inform him that I've told you of his generosity and you've conveyed your thanks."

"The last time, I enjoyed the drive from the airport to town very much; the view was just fantastic." Mrs Dangle looked out the window expectantly. "I can still remember how it was ten years

259

ago; I'll never forget it. It was just fantastic. And now I'm going to experience this once again; it's such a thrill, a real privilege."

"Our country has made great economic strides in the last ten years," said Vento Voon. "Lots of buildings have sprung up; I'm sure the view will be even better now."

"Well, the drive to town is quite nice, but I never knew it's so thrilling," I said.

"Me too," said Kate. "I think I'll watch you while you're watching the passing scenery; I'd like to know what exactly gives you such a thrill."

"You don't think it's a nice drive?" asked Mrs Dangle, before looking out the window again.

"Well, it's a nice drive," said Kate, "but you seem to find it a lot more thrilling than we do. Maybe we've been taking things here for granted."

"She has a very good eye for beauty," said Socky. "She's a photography enthusiast and she takes very good pictures, I can assure you of this."

"I see, that explains it; you see things that people miss," I said.

"She sees lots of things that people miss," said Socky.

"I suppose beauty is subjective to some extent," I said. "You could see beauty when we couldn't. May I ask what do you find is the best part of the drive to town?"

"The best part, the most thrilling part, is the view from the summit of Mountt Riverside," said Mrs Dangle, looking at us for a response.

"Mountt Riverside is a fairly low hill," I said.

"Yes, that's why the view of the city skyline is so thrilling," said Mrs Dangle. "If it's higher, the view would be completely different; it wouldn't be a view of the skyline, but a bird's eye view instead, certainly still beautiful, but different."

"I've never thought of it this way," I said.

"It's not a matter of thinking; it's a matter of appreciating beauty out there, no thinking is required. The same thing can look beautiful from different angles. The skyline from the summit of Mount Riverside is just right, simply dramatic. A little too low or too high, the drama would be gone."

"And you saw it ten years ago," said Socky.

"Yes, it was so dramatic that it was captured in my mind like a photograph."

"You managed to take some photos from atop Mount Riverside the last time?" I asked.

"Yes, I did; I took day and night shots. But it's not just the static view. There are static views of city skylines in other places that are quite dramatic too, but yours is unique."

"Unique? The only one of its kind in the world? How so?" I asked.

"It's how the skyline comes into view as you drive up Mount Riverside; that's a knockout. The drive from the airport to Mount Riverside passes through the countryside, trees everywhere, nothing but trees. As you go up the slope of Mount Riverside you see the sky, but it's still the countryside, and you expect more of the same. Then the car reaches the summit and all of a sudden . . . wham! A great city comes into view! It's like one of those adventure movies where people go deep into the jungle to look for a lost city, and when they've gone in deep enough and thought they were lost, the lost city suddenly comes into view at a distance; absolutely dramatic. I've traveled all over the world and, I can tell you, nothing comes close. The summit of Mount Riverside is truly the gateway to your country."

The van negotiated a bent and glided round a curve before Mount Riverside came into view. Mrs Dangle shifted in her seat, obviously excited by the prospect of re-visiting the top of the hill to take a look at the cherished Orderland skyline for the first time in ten years. She held her camera very steadily with her hands on her laps, ready for the skyline to pop into view, the inside of the car becoming quiet. As the van proceeded up the slope, Kate and Socky looked at Mrs Dangle in anticipation, while I looked at her through the rear view mirror. The van lost some momentum as it neared the summit; it sounded like it was really exerting to its limits.

"Here it comes," I said. Mrs Dangle did not respond; she gazed intently out the window, camera now raised chest-height.

As the van reached the summit, Mrs Dangle gave out a shriek as if she had seen something horrible, and she exclaimed, "Oh, my God! What happened? Where is it? Where is it?"

"Where's what?" asked Socky, his voice full of concern. "Are you okay?"

Mrs Dangle choked, and with a great effort managed to say, "The skyline, the Orderland skyline . . ."

"Well . . . ," said Socky, looking confused and unable to complete his sentence.

"The skyline is gone; the Orderland skyline's gone!" Mrs Dangle was almost in panic. Then she turned white and slumped on her seat.

"Mrs Dangle, are you all right?" said Kate, shaking Mrs Dangle gently. "She has fainted."

I immediately pulled the van to the side of the road and opened the windows to let in fresh air.

"How is she?" I asked as I turned my head to the rear of the van. To the relief of everyone, Mrs Dangle stirred and opened her eyes.

"Mrs Dangle," called Kate.

"Are you all right?" asked Socky.

"The skyline is gone." Though the voice was weak, it still conveyed the disappointment clearly.

"What do you mean, Mrs Dangle?" I said. "It's still here; not to worry, the skyline's still here. It's not possible for the skyline to disappear into thin air, so there's nothing to worry about. Keep calm, everything will be alright. You'll get your skyline, Mrs Dangle, I assure you."

"No, it's gone. Gone! My God, your beautiful skyline is gone." Mrs Dangle was almost in tears.

Everyone looked in the direction Mrs Damgle was pointing. There stood a massive, rectangular building dressed entirely in what looked like gray bathroom tiles.

"Well, this building came up after your last visit ten years ago," I said sheepishly. "I'm sorry it blocked almost the entire skyline."

"You exchanged your beautiful, unique skyline for this?"

"Well . . . ," I said, not knowing how to reply.

"But this . . . the summit of Mount Riverside with its magnificent view is or, rather, was the gateway to Orderland, like the gateway to a lost city deep in the jungle."

"You're very imaginative," said Vento Voon. "That building is the Croctopus Hotel."

"It looks like a government housing block with bathroom tiles on the outside," said Mrs Dangle.

"It's a five-star hotel, the finest in Orderland," said Vento Voon. "We're very proud of it; it's the most beautiful, most magnificent hotel in the country. It's also the most expensive; service is first class. The Croctopus Hotel is the favorite of visiting VIPs from all over the world. It's just out of this world."

"It certainly doesn't look magnificent to me. Anyway, I don't care if it's a ten-star hotel; give me back the lost city in the jungle."

"I'm glad you've regained your feisty self," said Socky. "For a while, we were really worried."

"By the way, those tiles are not bathroom tiles; they're very expensive tiles," said Vento Voon. "If I remember correctly, they're the most expensive tiles adorning the walls of any hotel in Orderland."

"That may be so, but they look like bathroom tiles, and that's what matters."

"I'm beginning to see what you mean," I said. "This place really was the gateway to Orderland. The skyline was so dramatic, day and night; a pity it's gone. Every time I passed this place, I'd feel something was missing, and it'd gnaw on me for the rest of the journey. I couldn't explain it; now I know what's missing."

"You're right, Mrs Dangle; I understand now," said Kate. "As you reach the summit, the city appears so suddenly at a distance. It takes your breath away and knocks you off your feet. Of course, the drama is gone now."

"Now, let's not get sentimental," said Vento Voon. "We can't stop progress."

"Is this progress? Exchanging the gateway to Orderland for a government housing block with bathroom tiles on the outside is progress?"

"Mrs Dangle, you're allowing your imagination to run wild," said Vento Voon. "That building is not a government housing block, and the tiles are not bathroom tiles. I hope you'd understand it's not our policy to stop progress. We cannot allow sentimental feelings to stop our drive forward."

"You don't take time out to ask what progress is. Was what you've done—exchanging the gateway to your country for a government housing block with bathroom tiles on the outside—progress? Are you paying too high a price for such so-called progress?"

"Well, a hotel is something real, something concrete; that's progress, surely," replied Vento Voon. "A skyline is just a view. If we don't have it anymore, so be it. And the gateway to Orderland, well, it was just a gateway, wasn't it? Couldn't have been that important, surely; definitely it couldn't have been as important as a five-star hotel."

"Years ago, when a developer wanted to build a hotel near the Sydney Opera House, practically the whole city, maybe the whole country, were up in arms," said Mrs Dangle. "The protest was so thunderous that the plan was shelved forever. Surely you've read about this?"

"But in our case we did nothing," said Kate. "We lost our skyline and the gateway to the country without putting up a fight."

"Well, it's not as if the skyline has been wiped out," said Vento Voon. "You can still see it from Croctopus Hotel."

"It's not the same as a lost city popping out in the distance suddenly! The drama was what knocked you off your feet!" said Mrs Dangle. "And can anyone go into the hotel just to take a look at the skyline?"

"No, of course not; only hotel guests may do so," said Vento Voon. "I fully understand the hotel's stand. They're running a business, not a charity."

"So now tourists get to view the skyline, but not the locals?"

"Well, that's life. The hotel is not running a charity."

"This is amazing, absolutely amazing; what disservice you've done to yourselves," said Mrs Dangle, shaking her head. "Anyway, the view from the hotel is static, no lost city coming into view dramatically."

"I'm afraid we were not farsighted enough and we also didn't feel we had ownership of the piece of real estate, so we left it to the bureaucrats to do what they liked. That building with er . . . the toilet tiles came up when we were not paying attention, when we looked away momentarily" I said. "If only the people in this country had been more like you, Mrs Dangle."

The car sped down Mount Rvierside, Mrs Dangle having recovered from her shock, though not from her disappointment. There was silence in the van for a while. Kate and I seemed to feel sorry for Mrs Dangle, and for Orderland, too. Socky was relieved that his aunt now appeared all right. Vento Voon was rather unhappy that nobody seemed to see his point. Then Kate seemed to realize something.

"If we know something is wrong, we should never allow it to go on," said Kate. "We should let the people involved know that it's wrong."

"I've explained why it was not wrong to build Croctopus Hotel," said Vento Voon, who sounded annoyed.

"Sorry, actually I'm just telling Ken about something that we've been discussing."

"Well, I can't say you're wrong, Kate," I replied. "In fact, I've come to agree with your assessment of the situation. Still, some things are not up to us, just like the building of Croctopus Hotel."

Chapter 19

Kate and I knew why Kong had called the meeting; we did try to escape it by giving some excuses, but none worked. So we sat in the boardroom like condemned prisoners waiting for the executioner. Even old man air-conditioner seemed to pity us and behaved itself by acting like a good air-conditioner should—not a cough came from it. Sammy Sam seemed to relish the agony that Kate and I were going through. The two of us tried to behave as if nothing was happening, of course, but we were too quiet and still. The smirk on Sammy Sam's face expressed his feelings for all to see.

"If I could kick him in the butt, I would," whispered Kate to me, while using her nose to point to Sammy Sam.

I nodded with a serious face and replied in a voice audible to all, "I would, too."

Sammy Sam looked at us with suspicious eyes; he obviously felt that we were talking about him, but had no proof to confront us. Sonny Song looked on unhappily, having the same thoughts as

Sammy Sam. "What are you two talking about?" said Sammy Sam, unable to contain himself anymore. "Care to share your thoughts?"

"Oh, it's something personal," said Kate.

"Nothing to do with the office?" said Sammy Sam.

"No," said Kate.

"Then you shouldn't be discussing it here."

"Why not?" said Kate. "The meeting hasn't started."

"I know," said Sammy Sam, "but our minds ought to be engrossed in our work whenever we're here, especially so when we're dealing with a most dangerous situation. Our country could be blown up anytime."

"The trouble with you two is that you don't seem to understand the gravity of the situation," said Sonny Song.

"I'm sure they do," said Roger.

Kong entered the boardroom looking most unhappy. The chorus of morning greetings from all present failed to change his mood. Sammy Sam looked happy that Kong had arrived and was full of anticipation, as if Kong was about to deliver a blow on his behalf against Kate and me.

"As you can see, I'm a most unhappy man," said Kong. "Mrs Dangle could well be our last chance to catch our terrorist mole with a smoking gun before he closes the circle and blows us up. But it came to nothing—naught, zero! I'm not used to this; I'm not used to losing, let alone losing all the time! Could anyone explain to me what happened in the strange case of Mrs Dangle's visit?"

"Obviously, there was failure along the way," said Sammy Sam. "The question is where did failure occur and who failed?"

"Ken, you've a lot to answer," said Kong. "Why did we fail?"

"And who failed?" said Sammy Sam.

"As far as I could see, Mrs Dangle was not involved in any terrorist network; she was not a terrorist," I said. "That being the case, we obviously couldn't find a smoking gun on her. There was no way we could have squeezed blood out of stone."

"What an excuse you're giving," said Sammy Sam, almost leaping out of his seat and flying across the table at me.

"It's not an excuse," said Kate, "It's good observation and deduction."

"Oh, come on," sneered Sammy Sam.

"The fact that we didn't find any smoking gun could be due to there being no smoking gun," said Roger. "There's no reason to insist that we had failed."

"That's not reasonable," said Sammy Sam. "Mrs Dangle is our terrorist mole's aunt and the sole relative he keeps in touch with."

"Well, that may be the case, but it doesn't mean she's a terrorist," I said.

"That doesn't mean she isn't," retorted Sammy Sam immediately.

"That's not the point," said Kate. "The point is that she's not necessarily a terrorist."

"Don't give excuses," said Sammy Sam. "You failed to find the smoking gun, and it could well be our last chance before this country gets blown up."

"I'm afraid there was no smoking gun to find," I said.

"That's ridiculous," said Sammy Sam. "Had I been there, I would have found the smoking gun, and our terrorist mole would have been arrested or on his way home."

"But Colonel Voon was there, and he didn't find any smoking gun," said Kate, as she extended her arm in Vento Voon's direction, like a host introducing a guest coming onto the stage.

"Hmm . . . , yes, how come you didn't find anything, Colonel Voon?" asked Kong.

"Well, er . . . ," said Vento Voon, sliding down his chair a little. "The problem is that . . . You see . . ." Vento Voon shifted about to give himself that precious few seconds to think. He then opened his file and shuffled his papers as if looking for something.

269

"Yes, what have you got to say?" said Kong.

"You see . . . it's difficult with Mrs Dangle," said Vento Voon. "I mean, she's a problem . . . Believe me, she's one hell of a problem." He stopped to let someone else continue.

"So did you miss a smoking gun?" asked Kong.

That was, of course, a problematic question. It would have been suicide for Vento Voon to admit that he had missed finding a smoking gun. On the other hand, if he had said there was no smoking gun, it would have been a slap on Sammy Sam's face.

"Well, there apparently was no smoking gun," said Vento Voon, delivering the slap and saving himself. Sammy Sam kept very quiet and still, as if trying hard to balance his head, lest it should fall off his shoulders.

"I'm frustrated!" said Kong. "I've a bunch of incompetent people chasing after a very dangerous terrorist! Is there anything we can do to get a smoking gun? We don't want to encourage our terrorist mole to poke his nose into something important. We just want him to snoop around something unimportant and make a slip, and thereby reveal a smoking gun. It's that simple, and you people can't even manage that. You're a bunch of jokers."

"We want him to poke around unimportant stuff in the hope that he would reveal something important?" I said.

"That's being too hopeful," added Kate quickly, as if knowing that I would be afraid to thrust the knife.

"Of course not!" said Kong. "I don't like the way you both put it. Kate, you don't seem to understand the meaning of insubordination. I've told you time and again insubordination has no place here. I don't like such nonsense from you; you know where to draw the line. I've not shown you the door so far only because I believe in giving people the freedom to express themselves, and also because you've been too deeply involved in the case; but you've got to know where the 'out of bounds' markers are. You seem very incapable of knowing what can be said and what cannot be said. We

270

have rules here; some written, some not. But rules are rules, even if unwritten. Do I have your assurance that such things won't happen again?"

"Yes, that's going way too far," said Sammy Sam. "You've got to give the General due respect."

"Why don't you let Kate answer my question?" said Kong.

"Sure, you have my assurance that I'll try not to offend you," said Kate. "Actually, I've never . . ."

"Now, let's get back to the real business; we've wasted enough time already. Throwing our terrorist mole a harmless bait is the only way to go; we can't expose ourselves too much. The real question is what harmless bait can we throw him?" said Kong.

"Excellent analysis, sir," said Sonny Song. "The problem is that everything about Croctopus is important."

"That's true, everything we do is important," said Sammy Sam.

"Well, the Croctopus Country Club is about to be completed," said Kong. "We could ask Crouching Liar to help out."

"That's really unimportant work," I said. "Are you sure he'll agree?"

"It doesn't matter what he thinks; it's not up to him," said Kong. "I think it's a good idea. I'll ask him to help out at the country club. Of course, it means Kate and you will have to be in whatever club committee he's in."

*

"I call this meeting to order," said Bobby Boon. "I'm honored to have been given this great responsibility, although I'm very busy in the Annual Ball Committee. As this is the first meeting of the Croctopus Country Club membership subcommittee, let me first give you a short briefing on our mission and tasks."

Bobby Boon then proceeded to give a half-hour speech, repeating himself often to emphasize points he deemed important.

As it was just after lunch, all the others at the table, twelve in all, were fighting to keep awake. I passed Kate a note with the message, "This is an emergency; I need toothpicks." Kate read the note without betraying anything, dug into her purse and calmly handed me two sealed toothpicks, careful to hide them from view. That took me by surprise, but I took the props calmly, and moved my lips to convey a silent 'thank you' so as to make things look real and hide the farce. Heavy though my eyelids were, I did not use the toothpicks, of course. Meanwhile, Socky made no effort to hide his boredom, yawning hard and wide several times.

After he had finished, Bobby Boon asked, "Are there any questions?" There followed a period of silence before he continued, "Socky, you always had questions; how come you've no questions this time?"

"I really have no questions," said Socky, eyelids and moustache drooping.

"You mean I've been so very thorough?" said Bobby Boon.

"Very," said Kate.

"I suppose I can give myself a pat on the back. Okay, what I said earlier was the starter; now for the main course."

"Oh no," mumbled Socky, as he slapped his face.

"What's that?" asked Bobby Boon.

"Oh, nothing." Socky placed his hand at the nape of his neck and twisted his head about, as if to loosen something. Then he said, "There's this pain in my neck."

"Now, we start at the beginning," said Bobby Boon.

"I thought we had already finished with the beginning," said Kate. "It was a pretty long beginning, so let's not have another beginning."

"I'm saying we proceed with the beginning of the main course. We now start with the admission of members."

"We're the admissions subcommittee; we should have started with the admission of members," said Kate.

272

"Don't try to be clever; this borders on insubordination. Haven't the General warned you many times to behave yourself?" said Bobby Boon, staring at Kate for an uncomfortable few seconds before continuing. "Now, as all of you already know, the Croctopus Country Club is only for the management and staff of Croctopus; it's not open to the public."

"So it's automatic membership for Croctopus employees?" I asked.

"No, it's not," said Bobby Boon. "You know that nothing in this world is free. And what are apparently free will be taken for granted or, worse, abused. This is the wisdom that generations of Croctopus leaders, our legendary captains of industry, have imparted to us, and we have always followed it."

"So what is the admission fee?" I asked quickly, hoping to prevent another speech.

"That's what we're here to decide. Now, I've given some thought to this. I believe we should have a two-tier fee structure; one for top management and another for the lower ranks. This way, we can fix fees so that those who are not so well-off will not find it a burden to be members."

"That's very kind of you, sir," said a woman in white.

"We must always have a thought for the less well-off," said Bobby Boon. He stopped for a moment to let the kindness of the company warm the hearts of all present. "Everyone in the company is important. We must all work together and play together. The club is the place for all of Croctopus to come together and enjoy themselves; it's a shiny example of what we believe in." There was a bit of appreciative clapping by some of the subcommittee members. Bobby Boon let the clapping continue until the barely audible sound of the very last clap. "The General has instructed me to ensure that the entrance fee for the lower ranks is kept to the minimum. After all, we want everyone in the company to join the club; fees are only to ensure that people don't take things for granted or abuse the facilities."

"So nominal admission fees?" I asked.

"I'm thinking of a nominal admission fee of $20 for the lower ranks," said Bobby Boon.

"Splendid," said a man in blue to another round of appreciative applause, which was again allowed to continue until the kinetic energy expired.

"What about those you called top management?" I said. "And who are they, anyway?"

"Top management should pay $200—ten times more," said Bobby Boon.

"That's fair," said the woman in white.

"Yeah," said the man in blue.

"Actually, $200 is a very small sum for top management," I said.

"I think so too," said Kate.

"We're not trying to make money. The idea is to show that top management pays more."

"Who are the people deemed to be in top management?" said Socky.

"Oh, I see that you're interested in the top management of Croctopus," said Bobby Boon. "Is there any reason why you're interested in our top management?"

"I'm not really interested in the top management; it's just the logical next question."

"Oh, come on, tell us why are you interested in our top management," pressed Bobby Boon.

"I've told you I'm not interested in the top management."

"You expect me to believe that?"

"Yes."

The two of them went back and forth while the rest looked on either in undisguised impatience or transparent incomprehension.

"Why are you so interested in my supposed interest in the top management?"

"I'm interested in what's in your mind," Bobby Boon pressed on.

"Why don't we get on with the real issues: admission fees and the question of who are deemed in the top management?" said Kate.

"I'm trying to get Socky to say why he's interested in our top management. "You know better than to interrupt me on this, Kate."

"I'm not interested in the top management," said Socky. "I'll repeat this each time you ask me."

"I think we should carry on with the meeting," I said.

"We *are* proceeding with the meeting," said Bobby Boon. "Anyway, I've given the composition of the top management a lot of thought. I think it should comprise senior executive vice presidents and above."

"That's logical," said a woman in black, nodding.

"Of course, we've to do this logically. So, logically there has to be two classes of membership—one for people who pay $20 and another for those who pay $200. We'll call them ordinary membership for those paying $20 and elite membership for the people paying $200."

"I don't like this idea," I said immediately.

"Yeah, me too," said Kate.

"Count me in," said Socky. "Why should there be two classes of membership?"

"Because there will be two classes of people paying different fees."

"Does the club constitution provide for two classes of membership?" I asked.

"No, it doesn't," said Bobby Boon, "but, of course, it provides that the club may decide on admission fees."

"In that case, it's unconstitutional to have two classes of membership," I said.

"Well, officially all will be called ordinary members," said Bobby Boon, "but those paying $200 will be issued with a different membership card, namely, the elite card."

"The distinction looks to me unnecessary, besides being unconstitutional," I said. "I mean, what's the big deal about paying a $200 admission fee?"

"It's ten times what the lower ranks pay," said Bobby Boon.

"But it's still a very small sum. And in any case, why should we have two classes of members? Why don't we just make everyone pay $20? Let's have a single admission fee."

"I support that," said Kate.

"I agree too; it's a very good idea," said Socky. This two-tier fee structure is, as Ken said, unnecessary; it serves no purpose."

"On the contrary, it demonstrates that the well-off pay more," said Bobby Boon. "And this is important to us. We've to show that we care for the less well-off."

"Two classes of membership are not only unnecessary and unconstitutional, they're counterproductive," I said.

"Making the rich pay more is never counterproductive," said Bobby Boon.

"This looks like a big show to me," said Kate.

"Okay, can a person choose to pay $200 for the elite card?" I asked Bobby Boon.

"No, of course not," replied Bobby Boon immediately. "If we allow people to choose, there'd be too much confusion; we've got to make things simple. I mean, the last thing we want in the club is confusion over its management; we've got to streamline things."

"Why shouldn't people be allowed to choose?" I said.

"Yes, I'm sure some wouldn't mind paying $200," said Kate.

"No, no, no, this wouldn't work at all," said Bobby Boon.

"Excuse me, I don't know about the others, but I'm confused," said the woman in white.

"Yeah, this is all very confusing," said the man in blue.

276

"Wouldn't you say it's logical to make the rich pay more?" asked Bobby Boon.

"Well, it's logical, of course," said the man in blue.

"Good! Then you agree with me. Let's not waste any more time on this; let's move on; we haven't got all day."

"But we've not resolved the issue yet," said Kate.

"I had discussed the two-class membership with the General before the meeting, and he liked the idea," said Bobby Boon.

"So no more discussion?" said Kate.

"We've already discussed. Besides, as I've said, we haven't got all day; we need to move on. Now, we've to be logical in our approach, and be fair too, because fairness is important. I repeat, fairness is important. So, elite members will have to be given certain rights and privileges; it's only logical, they're paying more."

"So that's the reason for having two classes of membership," I said.

"What are you trying to imply? As I've said before, and I'll say it one last time for people who didn't pay attention, we need two classes of membership because there'll be two admission fees. And we need two admission fees because we need to show that the top management have to shoulder a heavier burden."

"It's unconstitutional, unnecessary and counterproductive," I said.

"I disagree, and don't get emotional, Ken. What I'm suggesting had already been approved by the General."

"So what rights and privileges do you want for the top management?" asked the woman in black.

"It's not what I want," said Bobby Boon. "It's what is fair to those who will have to pay more."

"So what rights and privileges do you have in mind?" asked the man in blue.

"Well, I don't have the full list yet," said Bobby Boon. "But definitely they must include priority in the use of club facilities.

Also, the management committee should be reserved for the elite members."

"Special rights and privileges for the elites!" said Kate. "That's not fair!"

"Yes, that's not fair at all," I said. "Priority in the use of club facilities is bad enough, but reservation of the management committee for the elites smacks of . . . well, elitism. There's absolutely no reason for it, especially when people can't even choose to pay more to get the elite card."

"Don't get emotional," said Bobby Boon. "We've to be realistic. Running a country club is not the same as having a birthday party, you know. It's not easy; we need people who know what they're doing, otherwise the club will collapse. We need talent for the job. Can you imagine one of the lower ranks willing to become club president?"

"I can," I said.

"Come on, let's be honest," said Bobby Boon. "Don't say things just for argument's sake. I just can't imagine someone from the lower ranks coming forward to be president."

"I don't think Ken is saying things just for argument's sake; he means what he says," said Kate.

"How do you know? You're always siding each other."

"Let's not go off course," said Socky. "Ken says someone outside the company's top management should be allowed to be club president, and I agree with him."

"It's all nice and well to go for simplistic fairness and equality but, hey, let's be realistic. For me, this point is non-negotiable. Those who contribute more must be given certain rights and privileges; it's only fair."

"So people outside the top management have no say on whom is to be in the management committee?" said a woman in red.

"No, no, let me assure you that's not what I have in mind. I want to be fair to the lower ranks. All members will get to vote for the management committee."

"That's very reassuring," said the woman in black.

"Then what are we arguing about?" said the man in blue. "If everyone can vote for candidates for management committee posts, then there'd be no difference between the two classes of membership. I don't understand this."

"Well, while every member gets to vote, only the elite members may be nominated for election to the management committee," said Bobby Boon. "Of course, if members don't think an elite member is suitable to be in the management committee, they don't have to vote for him. So every member, even the ordinary members, gets to vote. We're very fair."

"That's not fair," I said.

"Why not? It looks fair to me; it is fair" said Bobby Boon.

"An ordinary member cannot be in the management committee even if he wants to. And as you've said, he or she can't even choose to pay the higher fee of $200 so as to be an elite member."

"You've got to calm down, Ken. As I've already explained, number one, we've to be fair to those paying more; number two, we need talented people to run the club, otherwise it'd collapse. And number three, I assure you, ordinary members can serve in any of the subcommittees."

"I'm not convinced; it's still unconstitutional, unnecessary, counterproductive and unfair," I said. "It's like you're trying to create a caste system for the club."

"What are you trying to say? You're out of order."

"You don't seem to get the point. You're trying to create a two-caste system in the club, and members can't even choose which caste they want to belong to."

"Look, I'm not trying to create anything, but there're certain facts of life you can't ignore. Besides, we should really have only qualified people in the management committee."

"Facts of life?" Ken paused before shaking his head and looking at Kate. "Okay, why don't we be fair to the top management and let them pay only $20 for admission?"

"Yeah, $20 for all," said Socky.

"Right, we must be fair to the top management," said Kate.

"That's not right," said Bobby Boon, "Top management should pay more."

"Excuse me, I'm confused," said the woman in white. "Why are both sides trying to outdo each other in fairness?"

"I propose that we have one admission fee and one class of membership," I said.

"I've already informed the General that we're having two classes of membership, and he has approved it."

"Shouldn't we put Ken's proposal to a vote?" said Kate.

"The decision still lies with the management committee; we're just a subcommittee," said Bobby Boon.

"But shouldn't we submit our recommendations only after we've decided on them by vote?" I said.

"Now, don't confuse the others in this subcommittee. We don't vote unless I call for a vote, and I'm not calling for a vote anytime soon."

"Then what are we here for?" asked Kate.

"We're here to give feedback and constructive criticisms to the management committee."

"We're not here to decide on membership admission?" I said.

"I didn't say that; don't put words in my mouth."

"Surely, action speaks louder than words," I said.

"Now, we've wasted enough time arguing. Let's not get bogged down by minor details. We haven't got all day," said Bobby Boon.

"I don't think we should proceed with further action until we've settled the admission issue," I said.

"I don't see any issue here. The top management has volunteered to pay more. How could receiving more money, happily paid, be an issue? Anyway, this is a good time to adjourn this meeting; we've talked enough for the day. I'll fix the date for the next meeting later and let you all know. Meeting adjourned." Bobby Boon packed his things into his file and fled the room, as if it was on fire.

Kate, Socky and I were dumbfounded at the speed of Bobby Boon's exit. We remained at our seats, refusing to accept that the meeting had ended. The rest of the subcommittee trooped out of the room in a daze.

"So, what now?" the woman in red said to the man in blue as they were going out. There was no answer from him. After a while, Kate, Socky and I went off to Number One Chicken to continue our discussion.

"This idea of having two classes of membership with one class having special rights and privileges is grotesque, especially when no member can choose which class to belong to" I said. "I can't imagine a club like that."

"There's no need to imagine," said Kate, "it's actually happening."

"Can't they see how ridiculous this idea is?" I said. "The damage this would do to morale is clear as daylight."

"Well, some people don't know daylight when they see it," said Kate.

"Why are they so blind?" said Socky.

"For too long they've been in their small, exclusive enclave, shielded from the world outside, shielded even from sunlight," I said. "Surrounded by a fat layer of yes-men, they run this place by remote control."

"Croctopus is really full of holes," said Socky.

"We need to stop this nonsense," I said, before chewing my chicken with unnecessary vigor.

"I say we shake our fists at them," said Socky.

"Yes!" I said. "It's up to us to show them that they're wrong!"

"Ken . . . ," said Kate, surprised, but clearly delighted. She could not stop smiling. It was as if she had hit the jackpot in a lottery.

"I'm surprised at this sudden change, my friend," said Socky.

"Actually, Ken has a great sense of justice," said Kate. "He can take a lot of nonsense personally, but he doesn't stand for the small guys getting shoved aside. The trouble is we've people who think they're somehow above the ordinary folks and ought to be treated special. What we have here is like feudalism—there are the feudal lords and there are the peasants."

*

Socky went from person to person in the reading room. A number of them signed the petition without needing much persuasion; some gave him a nod or a smile. "Thank you very much," said Socky with an appreciative smile.

"I should thank you for taking the trouble," said the young woman. "I can't imagine a club reserving the management committee for an elite membership. And why do we need elite members? I mean, what would the rest be? Please do what you can; you have my full support."

I entered the reading room and searched with my eyes before locating Socky. "How's the going?" I said.

"I've got fifty signatures so far." Socky held up the list of signatures to show me.

"Anyone refused to sign?"

"Yes, quite a few, actually. They said they were afraid they'd get into trouble with the top management."

"Sad, isn't it? It's up to them to act, but they're not doing it."

"Yes, I'm surprised by the number who said they were afraid to sign. But I'm still optimistic about getting a good number of signatures. How's the going for Kate and you?"

"The same as you; a number refused to sign, but we're encouraged by what we have so far."

I went to the public relations department to get more people to sign up, while Socky headed for the gym to try his luck there. He was crossing a courtyard when he saw a woman, about mid-forties, walking his way. He approached her with a smile and requested for her signature.

"No, I don't want trouble," said the woman, shaking her head.

"Oh, don't worry," said Socky, "you won't get into trouble for signing a petition."

"Oh yes, I will."

"No, you will not."

"Oh yes, I will."

"Have you ever heard of anyone getting into trouble for signing a petition?"

"No, but that's because this has never been done before. As far as I know, this is the first time someone is going around collecting signatures for a petition. I'd rather be safe." The woman folded her arms, locking up her hands so that they would not be able to take Socky's pen and petition.

"You want to let the top management walk all over you?"

"The company has been good to us; I'll accept whatever may be the top management's decision. I'm happy just to use the facilities. In the old days, we didn't even have such facilities. So I'm thankful for what we have; I'm not interested in how the management committee is formed."

"But any member should have the right to be elected to the management committee, which should not be reserved for the top management."

"I said I'm not interested in how the management committee is formed." The woman looked as if she was about to beg for mercy.

"Don't reject the petition out of hand; think carefully."

"No, no, no, my mind is made up; I don't want trouble." The woman waved both her hands to signify 'no'.

"Believe me, your fear is unfounded."

"You look familiar . . . I've seen you somewhere before. Are you some kind of troublemaker?"

"Of course not, I'm just trying to help you."

"I don't need help. Anyway, why are you so kind? What's your motive?" The woman's lips quivered and her face turned pale.

"My motive is to stop a grotesque two-class structure, with special rights and privileges reserved for the elite class."

"What's your ulterior motive?"

"I've no ulterior motive; I'm just trying to do what's right."

"You look familiar; I've seen you before. You look like a troublemaker to me." The woman took a step back and made an about turn before fleeing.

Socky looked at her in disbelief as the sound of her hurried footsteps faded away. He looked in the direction of her retreat a little while longer, as if trying to make sure what had happened was real. Then he shook his head and proceeded to the gym.

*

"What's going on? I want an explanation from both of you, and it better be good," yelled Kong.

"I'm sorry, I don't get it. What exactly do you want us to explain?" I said.

"You should know what I want you both to explain."

"Actually, we don't," said Kate.

Kong thought the meeting to confront us was so important that he had asked his secretary in to take down every word we said.

284

Years later, the secretary, after getting dismissed by Kong, was to become a valuable source of inside information for me.

"We can't believe what's taking place," said Sammy Sam. "That's why an explanation is called for."

"You were supposed to keep an eye on our terrorist mole," said Kong, "Instead, you've both joined him to start a rebellion against Croctopus! This is treason!"

"Yes indeed, sir. This is intolerable," said Sonny Song. "Insubordination is bad enough; rebellion is most definitely treason!"

"We've been keeping watch on Socky," I said. "Nobody can accuse us of not doing that. And while we're on this matter, I'd like a review of the case."

"I don't want you to change the subject. You've both joined him to start a rebellion against Croctopus," said Kong, pointing a finger in the direction of Kate and me.

"We're not part of any rebellion," said Kate.

"There's a rebellion going on, and you're both part of it," said Bobby Boon.

"Just what are you talking about?" I said.

"Don't act innocent," said Bobby Boon. "The three of you were collecting signatures for a petition against the admission rules in the Croctopus Country Club."

"That's no rebellion," I said. "That's just an attempt to let you know that there are many people who are against a two-class membership, with special rights and privileges reserved for so-called elite members."

"You should have expressed your views through the proper channels," said Bobby Boon. "That's the Croctopus way of doing things; surely, you must know that."

"First, the so-called proper channels refused to hold a vote on the issue," I said. "And secondly, the so-called proper channels are not the only channels of communication with Croctopus management."

"I find your actions preposterous," said Bobby Boon. "If you don't go through the proper channels, then what are the proper channels for?"

"Maybe they're there to kill our views," I said.

"Preposterous!" said Sammy Sam. "And why should you be ganging up with Crouching Liar?"

"We're not ganging up with him," said Kate. "We happen to agree that a two-class membership for the club is bad."

"You agree with a terrorist?" said Sonny Song. "I never knew such a day would come."

"You're not arguing rationally," I said.

"Ganging up with a terrorist is rational?" said Sonny Song.

"There's no cogency in your argument at all," I said. "You're just taking potshots any old how."

"You can't deny that you're ganging up with a terrorist and working against the interests of the company and the country," said Bobby Boon.

"What kind of stupidity is this?" said Kate.

"How dare you . . . We're not stupid; we're smarter than you think," said Sammy Sam. "Whose side are you on?"

"I've heard enough!" said Kong. "The meeting is adjourned. Ken, Kate, you two go back to your desks."

After we left, Kong addressed the senior executive vice presidents, with the secretary taking every note he said.

"Gentlemen, I hope you understand that the situation has taken a completely new and dangerous turn." Kong waited for the message to sink in before continuing. "First, our terrorist mole has gone on the offensive. He's no longer merely collecting intelligence; he's now fomenting a rebellion. If he succeeds, there'd be open insurrection in the company and maybe even in the country. And the total confusion would open up the perfect opportunity for him to detonate his WMD."

"Excellent analysis, sir" said Vento Voon.

"Absolutely spot on, sir," said Bobby Boon, not to be outdone by the man who replaced him.

"I'm in absolute agreement with you, General," said Sammy Sam, erecting his body smartly, as if he was about to stand up and give a salute.

"General, your analysis is always way ahead of everyone's," said Sonny Song.

"Secondly, it's now revealed to us that Ken and Kate have weak characters, easily deceived by our terrorist mole. They're not like us, unwavering in our stand; once we've decided on something, nothing can make us change our mind. This is our strength, which they don't have. They'd always listen to the other side, and this is their weakness because they could be swayed in the process. They don't have our toughness; we hit first and ask questions later. But they ask an endless stream of questions. Even when we've decided on something, they continue to ask questions. They lack that single-minded toughness. I only wish we had assigned people who could block out all doubts in their mind. In this life-and-death struggle, we can't have doubters, but unfortunately we have two in our midst. This not only weakens our effort, it also puts us in danger because the two of them might not see obvious dangers and alert us."

"You are right, sir; they're very weak people," said Vento Voon.

"I've also noticed that Ken has changed. He used to be a team player, but he's no more that now. And as for Kate, she was rather rebellious in the past, but she's a lot worst now. Both now argue too much and that's bad."

"What shall we do with them, sir?" said Vento Voon. "Shall we take them off the case?"

"That's a good idea, sir," said Sammy Sam.

"I think we've no choice, sir," said Sonny Song.

"This may not be a good idea, sir," said Bobby Boon. "Taking both of them off the case will alert our terrorist mole, sir."

"That's true," said Kong. "We can't afford to alert Crouching Liar at this dangerous stage." Bobby Boon's head seemed to have swelled a little. He waited for further endorsements of his genius.

"General, it'll be too dangerous to keep Ken and Kate in the case," said Vento Voon, sensing danger to himself.

"You've a point," said Kong, hand rubbing his chin, thinking hard.

"General! We absolutely cannot afford to alert our terrorist mole that we're on his trail," said Bobby Boon. "This is absolutely crucial, sir. I repeat, absolutely crucial."

"Sir! We can no longer depend on Ken and Kate," said Vento Voon. "If we do so the whole company and the country would go up in smoke; I guarantee you this, sir."

"Sir! If our terrorist mole becomes aware that we're after him, I guarantee you that'd be the end of Croctopus and Orderland," said Bobby Boon. "I'm certain of that, sir"

"General! I'm absolutely convinced that we must take Ken and Kate off the case," said Vento Voon.

"Sir! I'm absolutely sure that we must not let our terrorist mole have even a whiff of what we're doing," said Bobby Boon. "I'm absolutely sure of this, sir; absolutely sure, sir."

"I think you're right," said Kong. "Removing Ken and Kate abruptly would be sending a big signal that we're on to something. Besides, our terrorist mole trusts them as friends, so we can't replace them easily. It'd take a new team too long to gain Crouching Liar's trust, and we just don't have the time to spare. I'm afraid we've to keep them on the case, although they're our weak link. We really don't have a choice; we've to leave them where they are, at least for now."

Bobby Boon's head swelled further, his chest puffed up. He looked as if he was ready to do a victory lap round the boardroom. Vento Voon, however, looked like he had been flattened by a huge boulder.

"That's one question we've settled," said Kong. "Now, the more important problem is that our terrorist mole has gone on the offensive. So we can't go on as before, carrying on heroically on our own. We need to launch a sustained offensive against him to smash his network and find Hidden Wagon. And to do so, we need help from outside."

"Yes, we should ask the OSD for more help, sir," said Vento Voon.

"We've not had any decent help from them," said Kong. "Colonel Loon is a lame duck. The situation has entered a dangerous phase, and it looks like we've lost the initiative. We must seek help from outside, but not from the OSD."

"To whom can we turn to?" asked Sonny Song.

Chapter 20

Kate was nibbling a chocolate muffin when I came to her desk holding a cup of coffee. I took a sip and looked at the muffin. "How many muffins do you eat a year?" I asked.

"Not more than the number of cups of coffee you take."

"Hah, you never change."

"Why should I?"

I paused for a while and said, "You know something? Do you feel a change in the air?"

"You just said I never change."

"I don't mean you; I mean Kong and his senior bunch. They seem to be leaving us out of the loop. Don't you feel it?"

"Yes," said Kate, suspending her chewing and changing to serious mode. "I think it's due to the petition that Socky and we are working on."

"Must be, I'm unable to think of any other cause. I mean, the petition seems to agitate them greatly."

"That's silly, isn't it? The country club and our work are separate matters; we know the difference; they should know that."

"They don't separate anything; everything's 'them and us'. If we're with Socky on one thing, then we become 'them'. The General and that bunch are driven by instinct. Once they sensed danger to themselves, they instinctively shut down their reasoning faculty and change to survival mode."

"It's a pain working with these people."

"I think we should discuss how to tell the General that he's wrong and that we should change direction. The problem now is that they seem to be keeping us out of the loop."

"We can still march into the General's room and pound on his desk and shake our fists, and demand a hearing." Kate suddenly appeared energetic.

"All right, but we'll probably have only one chance to do it; we'll have to prepare well." We headed for the lift to attend a meeting.

"Do you think they're just keeping up appearances, pretending to keep us in the case by feeding us a bit of information every now and then?" asked Kate.

"Looks like it; I suppose they want to ease us off the case rather than chop us off."

"Now, why would they want to ease us off? They've never been this kind or subtle to anyone before. If they don't want us, I'd expect them to give us the chop."

When we arrived at the boardroom, nobody was there.

"Old man, be kind to us this morning," I said as I looked at the air-condition outlet.

Then Roger came in and, after exchanging greetings, said, "I heard something's happening."

"What's up?" I said.

"I don't really know; it has something to do with a secret weapon."

"Hidden Wagon?" I asked.

"No, I don't think so; it's about a secret weapon that we could use to fight terrorists."

Vento Voon, Sammy Sam and Sonny Song came in.

"What's brewing?" asked Roger.

"Seems like we've acquired a secret weapon," said Vento Voon.

"Any idea what secret weapon we're talking about?" said Roger.

"No idea whatsoever," said Vento Voon. "We've to wait for the General."

We did not have to wait long. The door opened and Kong came in with a man in his middle or late forties, who was built like a wrestler and, strangely, had a pair of dark glasses wrapped around his eyes. He looked deadly serious, like a wrestler who had just stepped into the ring.

"The General has a bodyguard," I whispered to Kate.

"Please shut up," whispered Kate, "they can hear you."

"No, they can't"

"Please shut up, will you? You're unusually brave today."

"You're all anxiously waiting for the secret weapon to be unveiled," said Kong with a half-grin.

"Yes sir," said Sammy Sam, "you can read us very well."

"What secret weapon do you all have in mind?" said Kong. "Tell me, I'd like to know; I don't think any of you would be able to get it right."

"We really have no idea, sir," said Sonny Song.

"Think," said Kong, his crooked forefinger poking at his temple several times.

"A portable X-ray machine or a long-range listening device?" guessed Vento Voon.

Kong looked unimpressed and did not bother to reply. Then he said, "Oh, I haven't introduced you to our guest. This is Colonel Rudic Flow."

"He's here to present the secret weapon?" asked Vento Voon.

"No, he *is* the secret weapon," said Kong, clearly waiting for a reaction from the terrorist hunters.

"He sure looks like one," I whispered to Kate

"Colonel Flow was at one time with the army, but he now runs a consultancy based in Washington D. C. He's a much sought-after expert on terrorism and the WMD threat; he has advised many governments."

"Then how come I've never heard of him before?" whispered Kate, louder than I did.

"Keep quiet."

"We're most fortunate Colonel Flow has agreed to help us," said Kong. Rudic Flow sat motionless, like a prize-fighter on display; all eyes were on him. Behind his dark glasses, he presumably did not bat an eyelid at the introduction.

"Colonel Flow certainly has impressive credentials; I'm sure everyone here would agree," I said. "Colonel Flow, if I may ask, what specifically will you be doing in Croctopus?"

"Now, wait a minute," said Kong quickly, "Colonel Flow can't give details at this juncture."

"So why are we meeting him? I mean, what's the purpose of this meeting?" asked Kate.

"You're all here so that I can introduce to you Colonel Flow."

"But is there anything that Colonel Flow can do that Roger can't?" asked Kate.

"Don't be rude," said Vento Voon.

"I'm not . . ."

"Yes, Kate, don't be rude," admonished Kong. "While we have full confidence in Roger, he specialises in the security of installations, whereas Colonel Flow specialises in terrorism and the WMD threat. His expertise is what we sorely need right now."

"But terrorists target installations and buildings, so we still end up needing Roger's expertise," I said.

"Yes, of course, but let me put it this way. Shall I say, Roger advises us on how to defend ourselves, whereas Colonel Flow pursues the quarry," said Kong. "That is to say, Roger is for defense, whereas Colonel Flow is for attack. You get my point?"

"Well, you sure look like an attacker to me, Colonel Flow," I said. "Do you know whom or where to attack? We've been on this case for some time and we don't seem to know how to go about attacking."

"How could you say this?" said Vento Voon. "You're becoming more like Kate as each day passes. Your conduct is most unbecoming of an officer of this company."

"Yeah, seems like Kate and you are making a sport out of insubordination," said Sammy Sam.

"You're lucky that the addition of Colonel Flow to our team has lifted my spirits and I'm in a very good mood today, Ken," said Kong. "Otherwise, I would have shown you the way out of the company. Surely, you know who our quarry is?"

"Well, what I'm trying to say is, if we're so sure, why haven't we attacked?" I said.

"Don't try to be clever, Ken," said Vento Voon.

"It's a valid question," said Kate. "I was about to ask it myself."

"You're siding with Ken for no good reason," said Sonny Song. "You're doing it just because you're both good friends. Besides, you just enjoy defying your superiors."

Kate was about to reply when Kong cut in and said, "Don't interrupt unnecessarily, Kate; you should know that I dislike interruptions. Now, Colonel Flow is here for a specific task—a showdown with Crouching Liar."

"A showdown?" I said.

"Yes, a showdown."

"I mean, a showdown in what way?" I asked.

"I haven't told you everything about Colonel Flow's expertise. Besides terrorism and the WMD threat, Colonel Flow has considerable expertise in interrogation. He's an expert on interrogation techniques; he has many years' experience as an investigator in the army."

"Wow, that's fearsome," I said calmly.

"What do you mean by 'fearsome'?" said Sonny Song. "Colonel Flow is on our side."

"Just making an observation," I said. "So the showdown will be Colonel Flow's interrogation of Socky?"

"That's right," said Kong.

Noticing that Rudic Flow had been sitting erect without saying a word, Kate asked, "Say, is that why you wear dark glasses indoors? It's easier to interrogate with dark glasses on?"

"What are you trying to imply?" said Sammy Sam.

"Imply? I'm just asking a straightforward question," said Kate.

Then Rudic Flow moved his lips and, in a commanding voice, said, "Dark glasses are a very useful tool for interrogation. The eye is very human, so I take that away during the start of an interrogation. This deprives the suspect of a potential source of comfort."

"Awesome," I said.

"Dark glasses also make me look like I have insect eyes. This makes the suspect subconsciously feel that he's confronted by a giant insect that's about to devour him for lunch. Very distressing."

"Shock and awe," I said.

"Also, eyes betray our thoughts. Dark glasses prevent the suspect from knowing what I'm thinking. Sometimes during interrogation, I'd need to lie to the suspect and dark glasses would enable me to do so. The suspect wouldn't know when I'm lying and when I'm telling the truth. So dark glasses are essential for such a task. However, when I've worked myself up to blinding anger and hatred, when my eyes are those of a pitiless killer, I'll take off the glasses."

"Phew," I said, "I wouldn't want to be at the receiving end of your interrogation."

"I haven't told you everything about why Colonel Flow is here," said Kong. "Perhaps you'd like to tell them yourself, Colonel Flow?"

Rudic Flow adjusted himself on his seat and leaned forward a little. He said, "I've been pursuing the quarry, whom you call Crouching Liar, for years. Perhaps that was why he decided to leave the United States and come here to work."

"So now we have the proof to send Crouching Liar packing," said Vento Voon.

"But the fact that Socky is not behind bars in the United States would seem to show that Colonel Flow doesn't have the proof," I said.

"That's an insult to Colonel Flow," said Vento Voon.

"Ken is just making a logical inference," said Kate.

"Don't defend somebody just because he's your good friend," said Sonny Song.

Before Kate could respond, Kong said, "Colonel Flow, would you let us have the proof so that we could send our terrorist mole packing and save our country?"

"What I have is insufficient to amount to proof," said Rudic Flow. Kate turned up her nose at Sonny Song, who seemed to be trying hard not to let steam shoot out of his ears. "What I need is to interrogate Crouching Liar once, just once. It's difficult to do that in the United States because his uncle is a senator and the law is, shall I say, rather protective of criminals. But about a week ago, it dawned on me that I might have the chance to do it here. Orderland is so far from the United States that the interrogation would have been over and Crouching Liar nailed by his skin before his uncle knows what had happened to him. Also, I presume the OSD would look the other way when I interrogate my prey. That's why when I learned that he was in your country, I packed my bags immediately and took the first flight here. This is the window of opportunity that I've been waiting for."

"Your one chance in years," said Kong.

"Yes, and I'll need only one session with him," said Colonel Flow.

"You're that confident?" I said.

"Yes."

"Colonel Flow is an expert in interrogation, remember this," said Kong. "It'll be the final showdown."

"This showdown must be kept an absolute secret; not a word must leak out," said Vento Voon.

"It doesn't matter," said Rudic Flow. "Nobody can prepare against my interrogation."

"That awesome?" said Kate.

"Colonel Flow, when do you want to interrogate Crouching Liar?" said Kong.

"In the next few days. I need just a little preparation, basically to gather information about what he had been up to in Orderland."

"Ken and Kate will brief you," said Kong. "Just let them know whatever you need." Turning to the senior executive vice-presidents who were sitting together, Kong continued, "The three of you take turns to sit in at the briefing."

"Yes sir," said the three senior executive vice-presidents in unison.

"I don't think we need to trouble them; they don't need to sit in," I said. "Kate and I can brief Colonel Flow; we know Socky's movements more than anyone else; we don't need any help."

"No, I want at least one of them to sit in," said Kong. "Two heads are better than one, or rather three heads are better than two. They sit in; no arguments over this." Kong was getting excited and, as usual when he became excited, he switched to barking mode.

"I don't want any delay in our preparation for the interrogation; I want maximum effort from everyone. Is that clear?"

"Yes sir," said the three senior executive vice-presidents loud and clear.

"Shouldn't we inform the OSD?" I said.

"Yes, I almost forgot. Colonel Voon, once I've decided on the showdown date, call Colonel Loon and let him know," said Kong.

"But, General, I thought you had wanted to keep the OSD out of this case," said Vento Voon.

"But not for the interrogation," I said.

"Why not?" said Vento Voon. "The OSD is more hindrance than help; the General said this."

"The interrogation could get a bit rough," said Kong. "I'd rather not have anyone, least of all the one being interrogated, accuse us of doing anything illegal. Colonel Loon has police powers; his presence at the interrogation will keep things legal."

Vento Voon deflated like a balloon; his chest seemed to have pumped out all the air, and he slid down his chair a little.

"Where will the interrogation be?" I said.

"We'll use the meeting room on this floor at the end of the corridor. Colonel Sam, rearrange the furniture to make it suitable for interrogation," ordered Kong. "Colonel Flow, you'll have to advise us on the furniture arrangement; we have no experience in interrogation. Colonel Sam, how much time do you need?"

"Well, I don't need more than a few days."

"A few days?" said Kong, raising his eyebrows. "Colonel Flow wants to interrogate our terrorist mole in the next few days! Why do you need a few days? Get it done by end of tomorrow."

"Yes sir!"

Kong rubbed his hands in anticipation and continued, "I can't wait for the showdown; we'll get rid of our terrorist mole once and for all. Colonel Flow, the future of Croctopus and Orderland depends on you. I know you can do it."

"Everything depends on the showdown?" I said. "We're looking for a silver bullet to solve a problem that requires painstaking efforts over a long period."

"Don't doubt Colonel Flow," admonished Vento Voon.

"I don't doubt Colonel Flow's expertise," said Kong. "In a few days, Hidden Wagon will be found and Crouching Liar sent packing home, if not arrested and put behind bars. Colonel Flow, all our hopes are on you; I know you'll not fail us."

After the meeting ended, Kate, Roger and I continued with our discussion as we headed for Croctopus Café to refresh ourselves. "The General is placing all his hopes on Rudic Flow," I said.

"Well, Flow said he had been tracking Socky for years," said Roger. "But he hasn't shown us why he's so confident."

"Was it all a bluff?" said Kate. "As you said at the meeting, if Flow had evidence that he was a terrorist, Socky would have been behind bars already; he wouldn't be in Orderland at all."

"But Flow seemed very confident that he would need just one session with Socky to nail him," said Roger. "How could he be so confident unless he had something?"

*

"To our success!" said Kong, holding up his glass in a jubilant mood. Kate, Roger and I held up our glasses, but without any sign of jubilation. Vento Voon, Sammy Sam and Sonny Song were as jubilant as Kong was. Rudic Flow, without the dark glasses that evening, had loosened up, but just a little. It was as though he had taken off his mask, and he smiled a little every now and then, but was still inscrutable. And he was nowhere as jubilant as Kong and the senior executive vice-presidents were. The General was in a celebratory mood and seemed determined to have a good time that evening. Other than the lounge staff, there were no other persons there, as the Croctopus Country Club had yet to open officially. Kong and we were there to test the operations before the opening and to have first use of the facilities. After a few drinks, Kong broke into song loudly, and the senior executive vice-presidents sang along. As more drinks were poured, Rudic Flow's smiles became broader. Then more loud singing from Kong, with his senior bunch in support. It was a rowdy affair, with Kong seemingly trying to bring the roof down.

"I'm a very happy man," said Kong.

"I can see that," said Rudic Flow.

"You cannot imagine how frustrated I had been before you came. But now, I'm very happy. Do you know why? Let me tell you. In another day or two, Crouching Liar will be gone, and so too Hidden Wagon. Cheers!"

Kong broke into song again; the senior executive vice-presidents gave him solid vocal backing.

"Why are you so quiet, Ken?" asked Kong.

"I'm enjoying my drink."

"Aren't you happy that we'll close the case soon?"

"I hope so."

"Hope so?" said Sammy Sam. "Colonel Flow, Ken doesn't have confidence in you."

"He didn't say that," said Kate.

"Oh, come on," said Sonny Song, "let Ken defend himself."

"There's nothing to defend," I said.

"Cheers! I've not been so happy for so long," said Kong, holding up his glass.

"Cheers!" all of us shouted.

"Colonel Flow, I'm so glad you're here to help us," said Kong. "Without you, I don't know how long this case would drag on. But now, things are different. All our hopes are on you now, don't fail us. I know you can do it; I've full confidence in you. Cheers!"

"Cheers!" we all shouted again.

"How do you feel at this moment, Colonel Flow?" asked Kong.

"I feel like a soldier on the eve of battle, having a final drink with comrades."

"Yes, the battle will be the final one," said Kong.

"Yes, either the enemy falls or I fall," said Rudic Flow. "Only one of us will return home."

"Cheers to our victory!" said Kong, raising his glass high. There was more rowdy singing by Kong and the senior executive vice-presidents. They continued drinking and toasting. This went on till late into the night. Finally, Kong and his senior bunch staggered to the exit, while Rudic Flow was still very much sober. Kate, Roger and I were relieved that it was time to go home. Kong gave a good-natured slap on the back of the club manager, who also looked relieved that he could finally close the club for the evening. Somehow, Kong's slap looked very funny to the senior executive vice-presidents, and they all gave a hearty laugh, as though the club manager had made a fool of himself.

"Very good, the club passed my test!" proclaimed Kong to the club manager. That, too, seemed very funny to the senior executive vice presidents, and they gave another round of hearty laughter. "Don't worry about us, I've asked the company drivers to send us back." That triggered another round of loud laughter from the senior executive vice-presidents. Then they and Kong staggered to the row of cars and disappeared clumsily inside. Kong was still singing as he went off. Kate, Roger and I watched the cars go off into the night before leaving with lots of unanswered questions in our heads.

Chapter 21

I took a deep breath and opened the door to the boardroom and looked inside, expecting to see terrorist hunters in battle formation, but nobody was there. I walked in, followed by Kate and Roger. We were too tense and excited to sit down; after all, this was to be the showdown, the final battle. So we paced about in the confined space, wondering where the others were and talking about how the event would unfold.

"Strange to arrive all ready for a battle, and then finding an empty place," I said.

"Is this really going to be the final battle?" asked Kate.

After a brief pause, I replied, "The General thinks so, but I don't know. Is Rudic Flow that good? Could he deliver on his boast? I mean, how could anyone be so sure about the outcome of an interrogation? After all, he can't subject Socky to any form of torture."

"He seems very confident about nailing Socky," said Roger. "I'm not sure what tricks he has up his sleeves, but I can't think of any."

"What role will we play in the showdown?" asked Kate.

"Seems like it's going to be the Rudic Flow show, brought to you by the General," I said. "We'll be the spectators."

The door opened and in came the three senior executive vice-presidents and the Orderland Security Department's Lenny Loon, all looking even more tense and excited than we were.

"Are you all ready for battle?" asked Vento Voon in high spirits.

"We're ready, although it seems Rudic Flow is going to do all the fighting," I said. "After all, he is the secret weapon."

"And he's going to flush out Crouching Liar and get him to reveal the location of Hidden Wagon," said Sammy Sam.

"After today, our terrorist mole will be finished," said Sonny Song. "This is a great day."

The door opened again, and Kong walked in, followed by Rudic Flow, with his insect-eyes dark glasses. Not surprisingly, they, too, looked tense.

After we had taken our seats, Kong said, "This is a great day." Sonny Song swelled with pride, having anticipated Kong's sentiment to the last word. "I had a good breakfast, almost perfect; the day started very well for me. Did you all have a good breakfast?"

"Yes sir," said the senior executive vice-presidents collectively.

"Good, I want to make sure we're all ready before marching into the battlefield."

"It's just a walk down the corridor," said Kate. Kong looked annoyed; the senior executive vice-presidents glared at her. Fortunately for Kate, the task ahead was, for Kong, a momentous one and he probably did not want to be side-tracked by a minor irritation.

Kong addressed us like a commander addressing his troops about to go into battle, "Fellow soldiers, loyal citizens of Orderland, we have waited a long time for this day. For too long we have been frustrated by a slippery, elusive enemy. But, finally, the day has arrived. In a few moments, we shall march into the battlefield. We shall draw our weapons and meet the enemy; we shall fight him without mercy and without any expectation of mercy from him. And we shall not return until the enemy is vanquished."

Kong stood up and paced about the room. He said, "We could have sent our terrorist mole packing long ago but, for one reason or another, we couldn't do it. Even now, our hands are tied behind our back. We feel frustrated, although it's not our fault." Kong paced about some more. He stopped at Kate's chair and took his time to cast his eyes on each one in the room. "But now things have changed. Now, we have our secret weapon, Colonel Rudic Flow, who will nail Crouching Liar by his skin before the day is over." Kong resumed pacing about before arriving at his starting pointing, his own seat. "Think about it; before the day is over, we'll score a decisive victory, one that has eluded us for so long." Kong, still standing, turned to Rudic Flow and, in a voice overflowing with emotion, said, "Colonel Flow, all our hopes are on you; I know you will not fail us."

Rudic Flow, his eyes masked by his insect-eyes glasses and looking grim, said, "I shall nail him by his skin." He pressed his fingers, producing loud crackling sounds. He actually looked fearsome.

Kong, his eyes with a trace of mist, said in a calm but commanding voice, "Comrades, are you ready?"

The senior executive vice-presidents, in a single, determined voice, answered, "Yes, sir!"

Kong remained silent for a moment, as if to let us, his battle group, calm ourselves. Then, in a low voice hoarse with emotion, he said, "Let's go."

He turned to face the door and waited for the rest of us to get into formation behind him. Sammy Sam, as if following a battle drill, moved ahead to open the door. Kong was about to lead the march out when the music started.

"What the hell is that?" said Kong.

"Looks like someone is testing the new sound system," I said.

"Tell them to stop it immediately!"

I took out my cellphone quickly and gave some instructions, and the music stopped. All the while the battle formation stood at the ready. After a few moments of silence, Kong marched out, followed by the rest of us. The battle formation trooped down the corridor and arrived at the 'battlefield', the interrogation room, in a matter of seconds. Sammy Sam was ahead and he opened the door quickly, and the formation marched in without a break. It was a big room in semi-darkness, as all the curtains were drawn and the lights dimmed. We took up our positions immediately; that is, we proceeded to sit down at our designated seats, with Kong at the center, flanked by the rest of us. Next to him was an empty seat. Rudic Flow sat behind alone, hidden by darkness. In front of the panel of interrogators, and a short distance away, was a single chair, which was illuminated by a spotlight. Kong waited for everyone to settle in their seats before leaning slightly to one side and pressed a button. "Ask him to come in," said Kong in a steady voice.

"Yes sir," said a woman over the speaker.

In a short while, the door opened. But nobody came in. There was a bit of confused head movements among the panel of interrogators in semi-darkness. Kong looked surprised. However, a few moments later, Socky appeared, walking in slowly. In the dim light, he looked like a big, bad villain, very threatening.

"What the hell is this?" said Socky with a steady gaze.

"Good morning, Socky," said Kong, his voice as cold as arctic ice, made worse in the dimmed and enclosed space. "Please take a seat." Kong's voice bounced about the room, producing menacing reverberations.

Socky looked around and saw the single chair in front of the panel, but he did not take it.

"What's the matter? Please take a seat," said Kong.

Socky looked at the chair and said, "Why should I take that seat?"

"You'll understand soon enough; please, take your seat."

"I'm not taking that seat."

"Please, don't make things difficult for us right at the start of the meeting. It's only a seat; please take it, it's your seat."

After further hesitation, Socky took the seat slowly; he looked up briefly and unhappily at the spotlight before staring at the panel of interrogators.

"Did you have a good breakfast?" asked Kong.

"Yes, thank you."

"Good, you'll need the energy."

"I want to know what's going on," said Socky in a firm voice.

"We're here for a discussion."

"It doesn't look like we're going to have a discussion."

"We're here to talk about you; we need to clear certain doubts."

Socky did not answer, but fixed his gaze at the panel. Suddenly, the air-conditioner started to groan, which startled everyone. There were some uncomfortable head movements among the panel. Kong turned to me and said, "What's going on?"

"The old man's at it again."

"Can't you do something about it?"

I took out my cellphone quickly and, in a low voice, gave some instructions.

"As I said, Socky, before the interruption, we're here to clear some doubts about you. In fact, before the day is over, we want to clear all our doubts about you once and for all."

"This must be the most unfriendly room in the whole of Croctopus, and you want to clear your doubts in this room?"

"We're only doing what must be done. Before we proceed further, I'd like to introduce to you some people." Kong looked

306

at Lenny Loon and continued, "You've met Colonel Loon before, but I've to tell you now that he's from the Orderland Security Department."

Socky raised his eyebrows and said, "What's the OSD doing here?"

"He's here because the OSD is interested in you."

"This must be a joke, of course."

"I can assure you this is no joke. And I'm sure, deep in your heart, you too know it's no joke."

"Deep in my heart, this is a circus," said Socky angrily. "Ken, what's going on?"

Before I could respond, Kong quickly cut me off by raising his hand, like a traffic policeman stopping traffic. "I'll handle this," said Kong. "Now, Socky, let me introduce to you the man who will help you to help us clear our doubts about you."

Kong turned bodily to Rudic Flow, who got up from his seat in the dark and stepped forward and took the seat next to Kong. At that moment, the air-conditioner gave a loud groan and blasted chill air into the room. Kate folded her arms to keep warm, and I held my collar completely shut in an attempt to retain body heat. Socky froze, as if he had seen a ghost.

"Good morning, Socky," said Rudic Flow, his voice cold and menacing. "Or do you prefer that I call you by your real name?" Rudic Flow gave a blood-curdling laugh that resonated frightfully in the enclosed space. Kate rubbed her upper arms with her hands, as if trying to make her goose bumps subside.

"It's you," said Socky, his voice as cold as ice.

Kong sat up in his seat, surprised. He stared at Socky, and then turned to Rudic Flow, as if expecting an answer. But there was no answer. There were excited head movements among the panel of interrogators in semi-darkness.

"We haven't really got started and we're taken by surprise already," I whispered to Kate.

"What a start," she replied.

Kong regained his composure and said, "You know each other? And Socky has a real name?"

"I'm using my real name; I've no other name," said Socky. "We're ancient enemies."

There was a murmur and some head movements among the panel.

"Ancient enemies?" said Kong raising his eyebrows.

"That's right, ancient enemies," said Rudic Flow, smiling menacingly, but without explaining his statement.

"He's the bully whom I kicked out of school," said Socky. Kong turned pale, and confused heads among the panel moved about uncomfortably. The air-conditioner started to cough and sneeze; a cruel chill made a lap round the room.

"I've waited almost a lifetime for this," said Rudic Flow. "Today, you shall pay for what you did to me."

"Wait a minute," I interrupted, "is this a personal vendetta? I thought we're here for some important work concerning the company and the country." Everyone looked at me.

"What the hell are you trying to do, Ken?" said Kong. "Don't interrupt Colonel Flow! We press on!"

"Today, I shall unmask you and make you beg for mercy," said Rudic Flow.

"Unmask me? I don't wear a mask; what you see is what you get."

"Liar!" screamed Rudic Flow, a finger pointing accusatively at Socky.

"That's not good enough; I'm not a liar even if you say so."

"Liar! Liar! Liar!" screamed Rudic Flow, arm outstretched and forefinger aimed straight at his target. "You're a terrorist mole!"

Socky was taken aback; everyone waited for his response. The air-conditioner gave a boom and forced out an avalanche of chill air. "So, now I understand; everything's falling into place," said Socky.

"Yes, you now know that we're aware of your dark secrets," said Rudic Flow. "Are you surprised?" He gave a bloodcurdling laugh, so frightful that Kate folded her arms again, as if in self-preservation.

"Surprised? Yes, surprised; I didn't know you had joined the circus." Socky's reply caused an immediate change in Rudic Flow's facial expression—from menacing smile to bloodthirsty stare, possible even with his dark glasses covering his eyes.

"Before I strip you naked and expose your dirty secrets to the world, I want you to beg me for mercy. Go on, beg now! Beg!"

"Wait a minute," I said, "I think this is not right."

"Keep quiet, Ken!" said Kong. "Don't interrupt!"

"How dare you interrupt?" said Vento Voon. "Shut up!"

"What's this begging business all about?" I said.

"Shut up!" said Sammy Sam.

"Why should Ken shut up?" said Kate.

"Both of you shut up!" said Sammy Sam.

Lenny Loon walked over to me and, in a low, conspiratorial voice, said, "Colonel Flow is trying to impose his dominance over Socky. An interrogator has to do this at the start of the interrogation. Believe me, I know what I'm talking about; so keep quiet, will you?"

That restored a semblance of order in the panel.

"Why are you not begging me?" said Rudic Flow. "On your knees!"

"And if I don't do as you wish, what are you going to do?" said Socky with a smirk. "Burst like a balloon?" Socky gave a loud, taunting laugh, which infuriated Rudic Flow so much that he shook with anger.

"I'm going to make you pay for your defiance!" Rudic Flow pointed a finger sternly at Socky.

"Pay? I've ten dollars in my pocket; shall I give it to you?"

Rudic Flow slammed his fist on the table and screamed, "Shut up! How dare you defy me?"

"Shut up?" said Socky. "Don't you want me to beg you? Hey, I've a better idea. Why don't *you* beg me instead, before I expose your little secret?"

"I've no secret, little or great," said Rudic Flow.

"Don't be too sure, pal," said Socky.

"He has a secret?" Kate whispered to me.

"I don't know, Socky could be bluffing."

Socky smiled coldly and said, "Remember the days when we were in school?"

"Shut up!" screamed Rudic Flow, followed by an icy cold stare.

"Don't be funny, Socky," warned Vento Voon. "You're the one being interrogated."

"Hey, aren't you all here to learn about our dirty little secrets?" said Socky. "Don't you want to know about Rudic Flow's darkest secret, a secret he's so ashamed of that he has pushed it to the farthest recesses of his mind?"

"I don't have such a secret."

"Oh yes, you have, you liar!"

"Watch it, Socky; I'm warning you," said Vento Voon. "You're the one being interrogated, not Colonel Flow."

"Stupid," Kate whispered to me. "He actually expects Socky to play the role designated by them."

"You dare not learn the truth?" said Socky.

"We've no fear of the truth, but you're out of order," said Vento Voon.

"Out of order? You're telling the one getting interrogated that he's out of order?" I said. "I always thought that that should be reserved for the interrogators."

"Whose side are you on, Ken?" said Sammy Sam angrily.

"You're out of order!" said Sonny Song, aiming a finger straight at me.

"Order! I want order!" said Kong, slamming the table with his fist.

As Rudic Flow was about to speak, Socky said, "Don't you all want to know the truth about Rudic Flow? His darkest secret?"

"Say it quickly," said Kate.

"At school, Rudic Flow was a real nasty bully, but he only picked on students much younger than he was. He never bullied anyone his age, or even one a year younger."

"That's a lie!" said Rudic Flow.

"Oh no, it's the absolute truth," said Socky.

"Wait a minute," said Kong, "is this relevant?"

"Of course, it's relevant," said Socky. "You'll see as we proceed further."

"Socky, please continue quickly," said Kate.

"Wait a minute . . . ," said Vento Voon.

"Go on, Socky, don't stop," I said.

"Picking on the little guys shows your character, doesn't it?" said Socky. "Your character is flawed, but there's more to it; there's another reason why you picked on kids much younger than yourself; it's your darkest secret."

"I'm warning you," said Rudic Flow, pointing a threatening finger at Socky.

"Carry on, Socky," I said.

"Quick, Socky, go on," said Kate anxiously.

"Do you know why Rudic Flow only picked on the little guys? Do you all want to know?"

"Shut up!" said Rudic Flow.

"That's not possible now; I've piqued the interest of everyone here. They're now too curious about your past to want to stop me." Socky gave a loud, menacing laugh, which seemed to rock the interrogation room. Then he continued, "Rudic Flow, you couldn't fight kids your age; you were hopeless. You were fat and soft and a coward; you couldn't take on anyone your age!" Socky let out a laugh so loud that Rudic Flow, a man built like a menacing wrestler, slunk down in his seat. The air-conditioner rumbled and poured out freezing air, which cascaded mercilessly onto the panel of interrogators. "Your darkest secret is out; this is the end of you, Rudic Flow," said Socky.

"Wait a minute," said Kong, "you can't do this to him. He's here to make sure it's the end of you."

Socky jumped up, pointed a triumphal finger at Rudic Flow, and said, "No! Today is the end of Rudic Flow!"

"You can't do this to him," said Kong. "You can't do this to us!"

"Oh yes, I can," said Socky.

"No, you can't! All our hopes are on him; our company and our country depend on him. You can't do this; too much is at stake!"

"I was not fat and soft and a coward, you liar! Tell them I wasn't."

"You were fat and soft and a coward!"

"No, I wasn't!"

"Yes, you were!"

"No, I wasn't! I wasn't!" Rudic Flow buried his head in his hands. Kong jumped out of his seat, but after that did not know what to do. The senior executive vice-presidents and Lenny Loon looked at one another in confusion. Kate, Roger and I watched the spectacle unfold open-mouthed.

"Now, what Colonel Flow was in school was no big deal," said Kong.

"Oh yes, it was. Before he became a bully and picked on much younger kids he was teased no end. It went on for years; it's a big shame as far as he's concerned. It's his darkest secret. There was more oil in him than muscles, bones and flesh put together."

"That's not true!" screamed Rudic Flow.

"Oh yes, it's true. It's your darkest secret."

"No!"

"Yes! You were a huge barrel of oil, and it's your greatest shame and darkest secret! And do you remember your nickname? I'm sure you do! You were called Oil Barrel! What a name, Oil Barrel!" Socky roared with cruel laughter.

"No! No! No!" Rudic Flow held his head with both hands. "Oil . . . Don't ever say that word to me again."

"Oil!" said Socky. Rudic Flow got up from his seat and went berserk, crashing about the room, and grabbing and throwing things. Everyone was shocked, but none did anything because none knew what to do.

"Ken, this is our chance," said Kate.

"What chance?" I asked.

"The chance to change things."

I got up from my seat and approached Rudic Flow, with Kate and Roger following behind. It was a gamble because Rudic Flow was a big man and he was rampaging like a bull. An opportunity appeared when for a brief moment the mad man had his back to me. I moved in quickly, but Rudic Flow made a sudden, sharp turn and the two of us came face to face. He snarled at me.

Then, for reasons unknown to me till this day, but perhaps it was instinct, I barked, "Oil!"

Rudic Flow held his head in his hands and gave a very long, painful roar. With a quick turn, he moved away and got behind me, but came face to face with Kate, which gave her a shock. Shivering before the mad man, Kate swallowed hard and managed to say in a soft, quivering voice, "Oil."

That so shocked Rudic Flow that he froze. Without warning, freezing air from the air-condition outlet directly above cascaded mercilessly onto him. He gazed straight ahead to infinity, open mouthed. For once, there was silence in the room; I stepped forward to check on him. Rudic Flow was white as a ghost. Then his lips moved. At first, there was no sound from him.

Then he mumbled, "Oil . . . oil . . ."

Socky stepped forward and, facing Rudic Flow, calmly said, "Oil."

That startled Rudic Flow, as if an electric current had passed through him. His lower arms started to move up and down mechanically, the rest of his body remaining still. After a few such movements, his arms became locked at the elbow at roughly right angle. Then the arms swung back and forth, like swings hanging from his shoulders. His eyes started to spin; his face was like a mask. He turned his head left and right mechanically a few times.

Then, in a strange, metallic voice, he said, "Oil . . . oil . . ."

Socky stepped forward to have a closer look. Then, as if trying to get away from Socky, Rudic Flow moved backward mechanically, break dance-style, but without any joy or life. Suddenly, as if someone had decided to continue with testing the sound system, music blasted out of hidden speakers. Like a machine, Rudic Flow went about in the room, his movements synchronized with the music.

Kate looked on in disbelief and said, "Oh no, the Robot Syndrome!"

Kong went up to Socky and screamed, "What have you done to him? We're finished. We're all finished! All our hopes are on him, but look at him now! How are we going to find Hidden Wagon? How are we to going find the WMD?"

"You can't depend on Rudic Flow anymore," I said.

"Then you find me Hidden Wagon; you find me the WMD!" Kong grabbed Socky by the shoulders with both hands and shook him hard.

Socky remained passive. The air-conditioner coughed out freezing air, which rolled down onto Kong, who by now was a man without hope, anguish written all over his face. Then, inexplicably, he froze and stared straight ahead to infinity, open mouthed. The next moment, his eyes started to spin. Then, to the shock of everyone, Kong started to move mechanically, like he was doing a break dance, but without any joy or life.

In a metallic voice, he said repeatedly, "WMD . . . WMD . . ."

"Oh no, not another robot," said Kate in shock.

"Look over there!" I said.

The three senior executive vice-presidents were also moving about mechanically, perfectly synchronized with the music, and saying in their own metallic voice, "WMD . . . WMD . . ."

"And there!" I said.

Lenny Loon, too, was doing a mean break dance to the music, but also joyless and saying in a metallic voice, "WMD . . . WMD . . ."

"Kate, do you have Dr Jade Choice's number?" I asked huriedly.

"Yes, I'm calling her now," said Kate, hands shaking and tapping furiously on the keyboard of her cellphone.

Socky stood laughing, while Kate, Roger and I tried unsuccessfully to round up the dancing freaks. One of the robot-men, it was not clear who or which, opened the door and all of them glided their way out of the room. A woman carrying some files came upon them. The sight so shocked her that she threw her files up into the air and ran off screaming. The three of us were in hot pursuit of the robot-men, but we really would not know what to do if we had caught one of them. After some minutes, the robot-men managed to go onto other floors.

"Oil . . . oil . . . ," said Rudic Flow.

"WMD . . . WMD . . . ," said Kong and the other robot-men.

Everywhere they went, people screamed and ran for their lives. Pandemonium erupted all over the Croctopus HQ building. In the confusion, the evacuation procedure was not activated and people abandoned the building in total disarray and gathered at the open area facing the building. A few minutes later, wails from multiple sirens converged onto the Croctopus grounds. Police cars and ambulances jammed the driveway, colored lights blazing on the vehicles' roofs. Policemen in riot gear, followed by medics, stormed the building. Then Dr Jade Choice appeared out of nowhere and, shielded by a cordon of grim-faced policemen, raced into the building. People stared open-mouthed as shards of glass rained down from broken windows every now and then. Shouts of "Over there!" and "Get that thing!" could be heard repeatedly.

After what seemed like a long time, order was restored. The robot-men, sedated, were wheeled out one by one on stretchers to waiting ambulances, which then sped off quickly with sirens wailing and lights flashing. Finally, Dr Jade Choice appeared to cheers and applause from the crowd. She slumped onto the steps, exhausted. Kate, Roger and I rushed to her.

"Dr Choice, are you all right?" I said.

She did not answer at first. Then she opened her eyes and said, "I'm quite all right, thank you; just get me out of here."

The next day, someone went to my department and pinned a sheet on the bulletin board, which immediately attracted the staff like iron filings to a magnet. The people jostled excitedly trying to read, with those behind shifting about or trying to stand on their toes. Being in front, I read the bulletin aloud for the benefit of those behind.

"The General is recovering in hospital from his illness. He wishes to thank management and staff for their heartfelt concern, as well as all the kind messages and baskets of flowers and fruits. As always, his spirit is with you.

"Management changes: Colonels Vento Voon, Sammy Sam and Sonny Song have been transferred to the Annual Ball Committee. New appointments to the posts vacated by them will be announced in due course.

"Important: The General hereby directs the management and staff to keep confidential yesterday's unfortunate incident at the HQ building in which the assistance of the police and health authorities was sought. No one shall discuss the incident with reporters or persons outside the company. Discussions on the incident among management and staff shall cease forthwith. Anyone who breaks this directive will face disciplinary action."

"Hey, why is the incident being hushed up?" said a woman.

"Yeah, why?" someone at the back of the crowd said.

"This is not fair," said a second woman. "My friends have been calling me all day to ask what had happened. You mean I've to keep quiet about the whole thing?"

"Everyone knows what had happened, so why hush things up?" said a man.

"Hey, the General is recovering in hospital, and the three former senior executive vice-presidents have been transferred to the Annual Ball Committee. So who's running the company at this moment?" said another woman.

"Hey, no one's running the company," said a second man. "It's party time!"

There was a burst of laughter and cheering. That seemed to be the signal for the small crowd to disperse and take things easy and have a good time for the rest of the day. The mood in Croctopus had never been so cheerful.

Chapter 22

The place seemed rather quiet for an international airport, as if no one had wanted to be there; I could even hear the splashing of water coming from a fountain a distance away. Other than Kate, Roger and I, no one else was there to send Socky off. "Thanks for coming; I appreciate this very much," said Socky. "If I've to leave without friends sending me off, I'd feel like a crook stealing off in the quiet of the night."

"We're sorry you've to leave this way and so suddenly," I said.

"They've finally packed me off for gross indiscipline and acting against the interests of the organization. Fortunately, it took them so long to get rid of me, so I had the opportunity to make some friends and learn about your country."

"We've all learned something," said Kate.

"Fancy leaving on the same day as Rudic Flow," said Socky. "It's fortunate that he left on a different flight; the plane's not big enough for both of us."

"He fled like a fugitive," said Roger.

We talked for a while more, and it was time for Socky to go. The three of us watched silently as Socky's back disappeared into the inner sanctum of the airport building. Then we took a slow walk to the car park.

"I think Socky has learned more about us than we have about him," I said.

"That's true," said Kate with a smile.

"We still know next to nothing about him," said Roger.

"How did it all come to this?" I asked, wondering whether the others had the same sentiments as mine. "I mean, the whole thing ended in disaster for everyone."

"Well, had some people cared more for the truth the whole exercise wouldn't have ended the way it did," said Kate. "Seems to me finding the truth could be difficult, even if we're staring at it. Why is it so difficult?"

"Finding the truth requires the most rigorous pursuit of the facts, and the honesty to face them," I said. Then as if I needed to get everything off my chest, I continued, "And honesty entails a commitment to the facts, all the facts, and go where the facts take us. And so getting to the truth involves a certain process. It's not like picking up a product from a shelf and using it. Rather, it's like refining oil—you put the crude through a process and discard the sludge and get what is refined. The purpose is to discard what is fictitious or unnecessary. And the process itself must be up to the task; that is, the process must be rigorous and honest; otherwise what we get at the end would not be the truth. As rigour and honesty are needed for this, it's not surprising that people often fail to get the process right and hence do not get to the truth. Rigour requires vigilance, and honesty requires courage. These are tough ingredients in any process. It's easier to just bump along and get something half baked."

When I arrived home, Mei and Min ran to me and insisted that I tell them a story. They said that as there would be no school the next day, they would sleep a little later, and a story would be nice. What story could I tell them? The kids must have thought that I could pull out a story as easily as taking out cookies from a jar. I really had no story; I had used up my stock. Well, tell them the latest big news in the country, I thought. Hey, it was the first opportunity to tell the real story, not the propaganda released to the news media. Of course, I would be telling it only to my kids and not to the whole world, but never mind; it would always be good to tell the truth, especially when falsehood was being circulated as the truth. And, surely, the story would be interesting even to little kids; I would only need to adapt it for them. So as Mei and Min sat themselves comfortably, looking at me in quiet anticipation, I began the story.

"Once upon a time, a band of adventurers set out to look for a fire taken from the sun. Many travelers from a far-away land had told them of the sun's fire. So the story must be true, the adventurers decided. Whoever holds the sun's fire in his hands would have unlimited power and become master of the world."

"Daddy, the sun's fire must be really hot," said Min.

"Yes, as hot and as limitless as the sun. It would go on burning by itself without end; there was no need to feed it wood or coal."

"Wow, that's really awesome," said Min.

"Daddy, did the adventurers get the sun's fire?" asked Mei.

"It was not easy for anyone to get it. The fire was kept in a special wagon, which could be moved about and hidden in the most unlikely places."

"Where was it hidden?" asked Mei.

"The keeper of the fire turned the wagon into little wagons, each with the sun's fire. He then hid a little wagon inside the mind of each adventurer."

"Wow! That was really sneaky," said Min.

"So, everywhere the adventurers looked, they would see a wagon with the sun's fire. They told everyone that they had seen the wagon with the sun's fire, but they could never get their hands on the wagons because those wagons were hidden in their minds. No matter where they searched, they could never find any wagon, although they would always see a wagon with the sun's fire. In the end, nobody believed them."

"Daddy, can a little wagon with the sun's fire really be hidden in a person's mind?" asked Mei.

"Well, not a real wagon. But if a person really wants to see a wagon with the sun's fire, then his mind would trick itself and he'd see a wagon with the sun's fire everywhere he turns to."

"Daddy, why would people want to see something that's not there?" asked Mei.

"Well, they desire it too much; what they desire becomes more important than the truth. As we could see in the story, it was easier for the adventurers to persuade themselves that what was not there was there, than to face the truth. The truth was unbearable to them."

"That's a strange way to behave," said Min. "Do people really act this way?"

"I'm afraid many people do; it's actually quite common."

"Daddy, surely after a while the adventurers would realize that there was nothing there because they could not touch the wagon or feel the fire," said Mei. "They could have told themselves and the others the truth."

"Well, maybe they were afraid to admit the truth to themselves and others."

"Why would the adventurers be afraid?" asked Min.

"Perhaps they lacked courage; the truth would end their hopes and dreams."

"Ha ha, what a bunch of chickens we have here," said Mei.

*

I managed to pack the last lot of things into my briefcase; the rest of my belongings I had already brought to my car. Kate, too, had only a briefcase to carry when she went over to my desk.

"How come we lost?" I asked. Sure, I had asked a somewhat similar question at the airport on the day we sent Socky off, but this time it was about us, Kate and me—we were even bigger losers than I had suspected at the airport.

"I don't know; there was no good reason to sack us over the 'unfortunate incident', when the interrogation became a rout for the interrogators; we actually did them a big favor by showing them that they were chasing shadows. But here we are, all packed and ready to leave this place forever."

"We're small fries, that's why. Still, I keep wondering whether we could have done anything differently from the start of this whole affair. Could we have prevented this thing from taking on a life of its own and going out of control, ending with the 'unfortunate incident'?" Actually, I knew the answer in my heart by then, but somehow I had to ask, as if Kate would tell me that we could not have done better.

"I'm not sure; maybe months or years later, when I could look at this from a more detached perspective, I'd know the answer," replied Kate. She was kind to me. Then after a pause, she continued, "Do you regret what you did during the showdown at the interrogation room?"

I smiled and replied, "No."

Kate and I bid everyone in the department farewell, and then went to other departments to do the same. As we passed by the boardroom, we went in to have a final look at the place where we had fought our battles. We did not speak, for there was nothing to say; we looked in silence.

My cellphone rang; it was Arm. "I call to say I've finally done it." There was a pause, as if she was waiting for me to respond, but I did not.

"I've filed the divorce papers; I couldn't take it anymore; getting yourself sacked was the last straw. I never knew you'd let me down this way. What did I do to deserve this? What did I marry you for? You didn't think of me; you didn't think of the family. You're not a man; you don't do your duty. I had to shoulder the family burden all by myself; you've done nothing for the family. Everything I do is for the family . . ."

I cut in and said calmly, "Even when you fart, it's for the family."

"How could you say such a thing to me? This is shocking, absolutely shocking . . ."

I put the cellphone on the table and walked around the room, stopping by the chair I usually occupied. Kate could hear the voice on the cellphone—not what was being said, of course, but just an angry voice ranting away. It was a while before it stopped.

"What happened?" Kate finally asked.

"Looks like I'm the biggest loser to emerge from this sorry affair. Not only have I been sacked from my job, I'm getting sacked from my family and both on the same day."

"You mean . . . She has finally done it?"

"Yes."

I'm sorry," said Kate, not knowing what else to say.

I returned the cellphone to my pocket and, as we opened the door to leave, I looked back and said, "Goodbye, Old Man; be good."

I thought I heard a sad but barely audible groan from the air-conditioner. We went about Croctopus headquarters to say our goodbye, accompanied by a vice-president—for the security of the company, just in case we were thinking of doing something nasty to vent any anger. Then we drove off from the company grounds for the last time. We arrived at a car park at about the same time as Roger. The equatorial sun was merciless and there was not a cloud in the sky; the heat was stifling and oppressive as usual. Strange to get kicked out of our jobs on what appeared to be a very normal day.

"Both of you okay?" asked Roger. "I'm leaving this weekend, so I thought we should get together." Roger took a newspaper from under his arm and turned the pages. There was a picture of Kong with a broad grin, flanked by a few unidentified people. "Hero honored," read Roger.

"Hero?" I said. "Who made him a hero?"

"Wow, they couldn't wait to give him a medal; such haste," said Kate. "The government must have been very relieved that the 'dangerous terrorist with a WMD' was finally kicked out."

Roger read further, "At a glittering ceremony attended by the upper crust of the country, the President pinned the Star of Orderland (Second Class) onto the hero whom everyone affectionately called 'General'."

"Who slipped in the affection part?" I asked.

"Not me," said Kate.

"Why only a second class medal?" asked Roger.

"Because the first class is reserved for ministers and visiting dignitaries," I said. "So a second class is about as high as an ordinary citizen can get."

"And both of you didn't even get boilerplate letters of commendation?" said Roger.

"Losers don't get anything," I said.

As we were walking across the car park, several cars came into it and took some lots a short distance away. Out came a group of men and women, boisterous and in good spirits. I soon realized that they were workers from Croctopus, probably out for lunch. They waved and called out to us.

"We salute the heroes of the 'unfortunate incident'!" shouted a man in a purple shirt to much cheering and laughter. He came to attention and gave a smart salute to us, to more cheers and applause.

"You were the only ones left standing after the 'unfortunate incident'," said a second man to more cheering and laughter.

"Are you here for lunch?" asked a woman, cupping her hands around her mouth to project her voice across the distance.

"Yes, we are," I shouted.

"No more 'unfortunate incidents', please," said the woman to much laughter.

A man jumped out from the group and did an improvised robot-man routine. Another man jumped out, and in slow motion put on what looked like insect-eyes dark glasses. He then proceeded to join the other fellow in robot-man dancing. The group roared with approval before disappearing into a restaurant.

A moment later, a car entered the car park and took up a lot some distance from us. Out came Kong, cellphone in hand, talking as if he was barking. He seemed very happy and gesticulated energetically, but he was too far away for us to make out what he was saying.

"Must be meeting people for a celebration," said Kate.

As the three of us took a slow walk to a row of shops and restaurants, Roger said, "You know what? In official circles you're the incompetent losers, but in the eyes of the ordinary workers in Croctopus, you're the real heroes."

"But to the rest of the country, we remain the incompetent losers," I said, still keeping an eye on Kong, who continued talking excitedly on his cellphone.

As if we understood one another's sentiments, our group walked at a deliberately slow pace to avoid catching up with Kong.

"Actually, I don't care anymore," said Kate. "People can say what they like, I really don't care."

Then, while we were still some distance away, Kong stood below the restaurant signage, still talking on his cellphone, unaware of our presence. Looking at Kong, framed by the signage and the entrance, something struck me, although I could not say what it was. It felt like an eureka moment, but I could not crystallize my thoughts and say what had seized me. Yet, it must have been quite a moment because to this day I could still picture the scene vividly in my mind. It was something apt, as if Kong had finally done something right. Yet, I could not comprehend the situation well enough to tell Kate and Roger my thoughts. I mean, Kong was just standing there talking on his cellphone. He was doing nothing out of the ordinary, yet it was a special moment. There was something striking about Kong standing there. Was it his pose? Nope. Was it the way he gesticulated? Not so; it was the usual way he expressed himself. So what was it that caused the scene to be stamped indelibly in my mind? I had no answer. As I walked slowly toward the row of shops and restaurants, I held my gaze at a scene that was inexplicably appropriate, a scene that spoke silently to me, to my heart.

Then Kong opened the door and disappeared into Number One Chicken.